FREEDOM
OF EXPRESSION
AND NEW
INFORMATION
TECHNOLOGIES

Collectif Series

The *Collectif* series brings together writing by various authors on a particular theme, or publishes the proceedings of colloquia.

Our goal is to offer more than just a random collection of articles by presenting texts that are unified and progressive thematically as well as accessible to a wide range of publics, while avoiding fragmentation of levels and interpretations.

As with our other series, we welcome your comments and suggestions. Do not hesitate to communicate with us.

Isabelle Quentin, Publisher
iquentin@sim.qc.ca
http://iqe.qc.ca

FREEDOM
OF EXPRESSION
AND NEW
INFORMATION
TECHNOLOGIES

Edited by Michèle Paré and Peter Desbarats
Preface by Federico Mayor

COLLECTIF

Canadian Cataloguing in Publication Data

Freedom of expression and new information technologies

(Collection Collectif)

Translation of: Liberté d'expression et nouvelles technologies

Includes bibliographical references

ISBN 2-922417-05-0

1. Information technology - Social aspects. 2. Freedom of speech. 3 Information superhighway - Sacila aspects. 4. Communication - Technological innovations - Social aspects.

T58.5.1.5213 1998 303.48'33 C98-941351-9

Legal deposit
Bibliothèque nationale du Québec, National Library of Canada
Printed in Canada

Revision: Sean McCutcheon
Layout: Trait d'union

© Isabelle Quentin Éditeur, 1998
http://iqe.qc.ca
ISBN 2-922417-05-0

ACKNOWLEDGMENTS

This book by a group of writers initiated by ORBICOM — the international network of UNESCO chairs in communications — has been made possible thanks to financial support from UNESCO as well as the meticulous work, skill, and expertise of a number of professionals, scholars, and information and communications practitioners, and by numerous international bodies specializing in the defense of human rights and freedom of information, in accordance with Article 19 of the Universal Declaration of Human Rights.

Our thanks go first to the authors who graciously accepted a tight deadline and a highly specialized theme. All these contributors have devoted years to reflecting on the effects and the uses of technology in the everyday practice of democracy.

We thank the translators who also worked to a very tight schedule: Jill Capri, Martine Demange, Jean-Pierre Fournier, Sylvain Fournier, Antoine Mondor, Pierre Nachou, Paul Paré, and Michel St-Germain.

Our gratitude also goes out to colleagues and associates in the Réseau ORBICOM who agreed to sit on the December 1997 editorial committee to outline an initial version of the theme. They are Claude-Yves Charron, Pierre Sormany, Pierre Trudel, Laurie Wiseberg, Peter Desbarats, and Michèle Paré.

PREFACE

Article I of the UNESCO Constitution, adopted in 1945, states that one of the Organization's chief missions is to promote the free flow of ideas by word and image. In the year when the world celebrates the fiftieth anniversary of the Universal Declaration of Human Rights, this mission is more than ever relevant, especially as the principle of the free flow of information finds its equivalent in Article 19 of that Declaration: "Everyone has the right to freedom of opinion and expression; this right includes freedom to hold opinions without interference and to seek, receive and impart information and ideas through any media and regardless of frontiers."

The new information and communication technologies now give us the means to fully enforce this right. Whether it be the satellite that beams down information from the sky on to television screens, or the Internet which turns each user into a publisher with a potentially unlimited public, the new technologies are transforming daily life in every domain; the citizen is now in a position to achieve personal sovereignty in the realm of information

This personal sovereignty is of vital importance for the development of democratic societies - particularly for the youngest among them. For only unrestricted communication, only free access to information can foster the emergence of a pluralistic democracy in which the voice of everyone can he heard.

For UNESCO, freedom of expression is the keystone in the edifice of human rights. It must therefore follow closely developments in the new information and communication technologies, which constitute a great opportunity for economic and social development and for democracy throughout the world At the same time, these technologies must benefit all humanity and must avoid creating a new rift between the "info-rich" and the "info-poor".

Furthermore, with the rapid expansion of the Internet, a great debate has been launched as regards the anomalies or excesses that such a development might entail. Thus, some people are demanding the introduction of devices to monitor the Internet, which seems to them a medium "fearing neither God nor man." With the proliferation of material that is pornographic or violent or that incites hatred, with the development of networks of pedophiles, terrorists, and extremists, and also with the risks that electronic trade represents for the protection of private data, for instance, people are indeed led to ask how much freedom the Internet should be allowed. This is just the question which is at the heart of this publication, a difficult question to which outline replies are provided by researchers worldwide, brought together through ORBICOM, the UNESCO network of chairs in communication.

Federico Mayor
Director General of UNESCO

FOREWORD

On the occasion of the 50th anniversary of the Universal Declaration of Human Rights, ORBICOM — the international network of UNESCO chairs in communications — with the support of UNESCO, the Canadian Commission for UNESCO, the Dutch Commission for UNESCO, the Comisión Colombiana de Cooperación con la UNESCO, and the Comisión nacional para la UNESCO-Uruguay, inaugurated this collective work on the theme of freedom of expression and the new information and communications technologies. The aim was to bring together diverse opinions on the interaction between these two realities.

The impact of technical progress and the transformation of private and public life in the past decades demand a new way of looking at our concept of freedom of expression and the challenges it poses to humankind of the year 2000.

The stakes are huge. Article 19 of the 1948 Universal Declaration of Human Rights established the outline for freedom of expression. Today, however, very few of the national signatory states recognize the universality of these rights in practice. The massive introduction of information technologies, principally in OECD countries, gives rise to as many hopes for openness and pluralism as fears of subversion and violence.

Some see this as a conclusive reinforcement of civil society that cannot be ignored, a tool for universal participation in public affairs as well as the emergence of a global and transnational citizenship. Others are concerned about the hazards of cultural homogenizing, about the effects of surveillance on private life, and the accelerated reduction of the state's role in managing social relations on national territories.

Between the principle of free access to and circulation of information, whatever its origin and destination, and that of the development and protection of cultures, languages, and markets for communications products, how will the contemporary interpretation of Article 19 of the Declaration be determined? This collective work explores many of the options and outlines some of the solutions that are beginning to emerge.

Thérèse Paquet-Sévigny
Secretary General, ORBICOM

BIOGRAPHICAL NOTES

Vytautas Butrimas, Deputy Minister of Communications and Information Technology, Republic of Lithuania, Vilnius, until the reorganization of that Ministry in June, 1998.

Louise Cadoux, Member, Conseil d'État, 1953-1992; since 1985 Vice President of the National Commission on Information Technology and Freedom in Paris.

Jean K. Chalaby, research associate, London School of Economics and, researcher in political science at the European Institute, London.
E-mail: j.chalaby@lse.ac.uk

Peter Desbarats, author and journalist; former dean, Graduate School of Journalism, University of Western Ontario, London, and senior consultant and associate research director, Royal Commission on Newspapers.
E-mail: desbarat@julian.uwo.ca

Christophe Duflos, responsible for new information and communications technologies, International Federation of Journalists, Brussels.
E-mail: ifj@pophost.eunet.be

Jane Duncan, coordinator of publications and education, Freedom of Expression Institute, Johannesburg.
E-mail: FXI@wn.apc.org

Lilian Edwards, senior lecturer in private law, University of Edinburgh.
Web site: www.law.ed.ac.uk/it&law.htm
E-mail: l.edwards@ed.ac.uk

Georges Ferné, French political scientist specializing in problems of science and technology policy, in the context of new information technology.
Web site: www.oecd.org

Mike Godwin, consulting attorney, Electronic Frontier Foundation, San Francisco.
E-mail: mnemonic@well.com

Anura Goonasekera, research director, Asian Media Information and Communications Centre (AMIC), Brisbane.
E-mail: amicline@singnet.com.sg

Andreas Harsono, Indonesian journalist, Jakarta correspondent for the Bangkok daily *Nation*; founding member, Alliance of Independent Journalists.
E-mail: harsono@nation.nationgroup.com

Hamdy Hassan, Head, Department of Mass Communications, Al alsun, International University, Cairo, and Head of Department of Communications, Al Ahram Regional Training Centre for Journalists.

Michael Hudson, principal advisor, Multimedia Victoria, Department of State Development, Melbourne; research associate, Media and Telecommunications Policy Group, Royal Institute of Technology at the time of writing.
Web site: www.mmv.vic.gov.au
E-mail: michael.hudson@mmv.vic.gov.au

Rainer Kuhlen, Professor, information science, University of Constance.
E-mail: kuhlen@inf-wiss.uni-konstanz.de

Fredric M. Litto, founder and scientific coordinator, School of the Future, University of São Paulo.
E-mail: info@futuro.usp.br

Jean-Paul Marthoz, European news director, Human Rights Watch, Brussels.
E-mail: jp.marthoz@skynet.be

Michèle Paré, journalist and chief researcher, Société Radio-Canada television, 1977-1997, Montreal.
E-mail: orbicom@er.uqam.ca

Alejandro Piscitelli, Professor, University of Buenos Aires; since 1995, co-editor of the electronic newspaper *Interlink Headline News*.
Web site: www.webcom/com/poetas/interlink

Alfonso Ruiz de Assín, Vice President, International Association of Radio Broadcasting (AIR) and European Radio Association (AER); secretary general, Spanish Association for Commercial Radio Broadcasting (AERC), Madrid.

Wayne Sharpe, Director General, Information Centre, Canadian Centre for the Protection of Journalists and of International Exchange for Freedom of Expression, Toronto.
E-mail: ccpj@ccpj.ca

Luis Suárez, President, Latin-American Federation of Journalists, Mexico.
Pierre Trudel, Professor, Centre for Research in Public Law, Faculty of Law, Université de Montréal.
E-mail: trudelp@droit.umontreal.ca

Chin Saik Yoon, editor and director, Southbond, a publishing firm in Penang, Malaysia.
E-mail: chin@south.pc.my

CONTENTS

NEW INFORMATION TECHNOLOGIES: IMPACT AND POTENTIAL

NEW MEDIA AND HUMAN RIGHTS

Jean-Paul Marthoz

Whether it is Bartolomé de las Casas castigating the massacre of American Indians in Santo Domingo in the sixteenth century, Albert Londres condemning the inhuman conditions of the Cayenne convicts in the *Petit Parisien,* or the Brazilian photographer Sebastiao Salgado capturing the wandering of refugees from war or famine in solemn black-and-white photographs, information, print, and images have been the preferred weapons of freedom fighters since the earliest times. Does technological change merely state in new terms this essential equation? From the use of the Internet by the Zapata rebels lurking in the forests of Chiapas to the "CNN effect," from the "paradiabolic" antennas mushrooming in totalitarian countries to the unobtrusive camcorder videotaping police brutality, from the proliferation of television offerings to the informational prairie fire lit by electronic mail, the new media, bolstered by technological innovation and economic liberalization, have caused a true revolution in the circulation of information.

Insofar as they herald a change in political practices, no organization involved in the struggle for democracy can escape their impact. Especially since these new technologies are at once the accelerator, the symbol, and the support of a still wider phenomenon, the advent of the cyberplanet,[1] which forces human rights advocacy groups to work continuously, like world news networks; to think about this "Home Earth"[2] vacillating between universality and tribalism, globalization and ghettoization; and ultimately to extend their mandates to other actors: multinational corporations, international financial institutions and, in the aftermath of weakening states, ethnic or Mafia groups.

INFORMATION AT THE CORE

Information is the main means of action of human-rights advocacy groups, which were among the first to grasp the advantages of the new information technologies and turn them against authoritarian regimes. These new media drill millions of holes through Great Walls. Parabolic antennas, cell phones, faxes, e-mail and the Internet leap over walls and break down censorship barriers. Paradoxically, for many years, even before the new technologies achieved their current prominence, the central, decisive role assigned to information within the human rights movement, and the attention paid by an important part of public opinion to international issues were in jeopardy. In a 1996 seminar sponsored by Index On Censorship at Oxford, participants noted "the apparent decrease of active response to reports on human rights."[3] Events in Bosnia and Rwanda a few years earlier showed the limits of information, and even pictures. Despite hundreds of hours of footage, public opinion and governments were not disturbed by ethnic cleansing and genocide. The century's first genocide, the massacre of the Armenians, occurred in the highlands of Anatolia, practically without witnesses; the century's latest atrocities were committed in front of the world's television cameras, in prime time, in a technological environment replete with cell phones, satellite antennas, and notebook computers.

1 Philip Wade and Didier Falcand, *Cyberplanète* (Paris: Éditions Autrement, 1998).

2 Edgar Morin and Ane-Brigitte Kern, *Terre-Patrie* (Paris: Le Seuil, 1993).

3 See "Human Rights Violations: Communicating the Information," a discussion paper from an International Workshop, Oxford, 1995, and related papers.

A NEW RELATIONSHIP WITH TIME AND SPACE

It is in the realm of internal and external communications that the new media have had the most impact, forcing many organizations to gradually flatten their structures, geographic spread, hierarchies, and work methods. E-mail and the Internet indeed make it possible to interconnect at little cost offices that used to be dependent on scratchy telephone lines and limping mail systems. Cell phones maintain contact with researchers in the field, videoconferencing enables all branch offices to take part in discussions hitherto restricted to the organization's headquarters staff.

The new technologies thus introduce a change in the relations with time and space, forcing organizations to disregard time zones and, like financial operators, react in real time to any event concerning them, anywhere on the globe. Thanks to modems, the exchange and solidarity network is increasingly compact and there is an impression of ever greater proximity. Electronic mail makes it possible to multiply contacts with non-government organizations, activists, and experts scattered throughout the world, while "links" put an organization's work into a more global context and build bridges with other groups and other campaigns. Beyond their practical use, the Internet, and especially the World Wide Web, are true anti-depressants for freedom fighters because they show a world in movement, teeming with initiatives, dissidence, and democratic resistance — a single world. While states would like to relativize the aspiration to freedom in the name of cultural criteria, the feeling of universality of the human rights struggle is, thanks to this World Wide Web, more and more palpable.

NEW FIELDS OF CAMPAIGN

The new media now give organizations devoid of a strong militant base the possibility to leave the exclusive field of research and denunciation and tackle that of mobilization. They allow this technically by virtue of their instantaneity: a simple click is required to relay the information collected by Human Rights

Watch on an attack against a journalist to the network of IFEX, the confederation of organizations for the defense of the freedom of expression, and to post it on thousands of computers throughout the world. From now on, there is but a nanosecond of interval between the alert and the reception of a message, between information and, hopefully, action.

They also allow expand it sociologically by enlisting in the organization's initiatives the world of net surfers, not only professionals —non-government organizations (NGOs), trade unions, political parties, churches, etc.— but the grass roots of the digital nation.

Will the interactive community be a hyperactive community, a field of new militancy, virtual only in method? Recent history has shown that 10,000 hands thumping away at the keyboards of computers linked to the network and flooding their targets with messages can make as much noise as 10,000 feet parading before the seat of a government or a big corporation.

FACTS BEHIND THE FACTS

More discreetly, far from the footlights, the Internet also plays a crucial role in increasing an organization's research capacity — a thorough and committed research, which recalls in many respects the work of this "journalism of indignation" to which we owe the finest pages of investigative journalism. For information to be at the heart of the promotion of human rights, it needs to meet criteria of absolute accuracy, independence, and pertinence. And impertinence: information, when it comes to human rights, is most often what authorities would like to hide from public view.

As I. F. Stone, the wise old man of American investigative journalism, used to say, "95 per cent of secrets are to be found in public documents." Documentary research, then, is part of the investigator's day-to-day work. With the introduction of search engines and the help of relay organizations like Human Rights Internet, the Network has greatly facilitated the perusal of data bases, and the location of documents, experts and witnesses.

The Internet has considerably widened the field of investigation, opening up many windows on hitherto invisible or inaccessible information sources.

NEW RELATIONSHIP WITH THE MEDIA

The new media force NGOs involved in the defense of human rights to study in all their complexity and all their dimensions the new media universe and its effects on the circulation of information and journalists' practices. They enable them to circumvent, to some extent, the priorities of journalists, these gatekeepers of the flow of information, whose choices do not necessarily concur with those of human rights organizations. The potential audience of the new media is reaching a critical mass: thus, the Association for Progressive Communications, which relays the information from many NGOs, has close to 30,000 subscribers worldwide, including thousands of opinion leaders and relay organizations.

The Internet, however, can hardly be seen as a way of evading the world of conventional media, their rules, and their influence. The large audiovisual and print media remain essential not only because they can, through the sheer weight of words and shock of pictures, sway public opinion and authorities, but they also validate the information, and build the credibility and influence of NGOs. The Internet, then, is a tool that serves at once to skirt the media and address them more efficiently. The World Wide Web is becoming more and more a source and resource of journalists, an increasingly connected, mobile profession, and one that is also increasingly overworked. Following the growth in the number of editorial rooms and the budget cuts affecting international information everywhere, nongovernment organizations are often called upon to take over for journalists. Whether it was the uncovering of the mass graves in eastern Congo-Zaire by Human Rights Watch in October 1997 or the investigation of child labor by trade union organizations, many international scoops of the past few years owe as much, if not more, to the investigative work of NGOs as to that of the media.

A similar phenomenon is observed in television. While the multiplication of television channels has fragmented audiences and sheltered them from messages, especially those about human rights, deemed boring or bothersome, it has opened up new opportunities for organizations because global, national, and community networks are in desperate need of content, analyses and commentaries.

The development of Web sites meets this desire to guarantee to the largest number, and especially to journalists, prompt and easy access to quality information. Today Human Rights Watch statements and press releases — several hundred a year — are automatically broadcast on the Internet, accompanied by numerous references and links enabling web site visitors to contact a researcher, join a campaign, find other sources of information, and retrieve photo or video documents. Soon all the organization's reports will be online, in many languages. Soon also, the site will become interactive and visitors will be able to click on an icon to take part in campaigns.

CYBERCENSORSHIP

The new information technologies have also opened up new fields of struggle for human rights organizations. It has become essential today to fight the censorship directed against the new media for, despite technical difficulties and the extraordinary ability of the Network and satellite antennas to dodge the sentry boxes of mind cops, authoritarian governments multiply roadblocks.

In its 1996 report, *Silencing the Net*, Human Rights Watch (HRW) published a long list of these "net inquisitors» who force servers to censor offensive sites. To better counter this international cybergagging, HRW joined the Global Internet Liberty Campaign (GILC), which advocates at once both the greatest freedom of expression on the Internet and the protection of the confidentiality of communications. A matter of principle, but also a practical need: The censorship of pictures or words in the name of such a vague concept as decency could prevent human rights organizations from transmitting on the Internet the testimonies of victims of the most atrocious violations. The coding of communications is necessary to ensure the safety of researchers and their information sources.

PROSPECTS

Human rights organizations, like many others, find it difficult to draw the contour of the new communication world, to anticipate its short- and long-term development and its effect on their work and their effectiveness. Organizations are torn between technological euphoria and doubt about a phenomenon that seems to go hand in hand with a massive concentration of power in the fields of telecommunications, the media, and the information and leisure industry — with inevitable consequences not only on the quality, daring and diversity of the democratic debate, but also on the notion of space and public interest, without which the human rights culture cannot really prosper.

Indeed, nothing guarantees that the democratic potential of the new technologies will not be marginalized by the nabobs of the new media, these Cybercitizen Kanes, some of whom have already shown their unwillingness to go against the interests of authoritarian governments. The development of the new media will not spare us the need to think long and hard about democracy in the media, at the local, national and world levels.

The new media do not radically change the balance of power. They can provide the Davids of the international civil society with occasional catapults. They can enable them to drop steel grit in systems believed to be all-powerful. But they should not create any illusion about the omnipotence of technology at the service of a cause. Those "opposite," whether neoNazi groups, religious extremists, ethnic purifiers or authoritarian states, can just as well appropriate these techniques and turn them against those who can only see their liberating virtues.

CYBERWORLD FRONTIERS

The word "cyberworld" is tempting, but it is deceptive by and large. The new information technologies do not remove access inequalities, which reflect the imbalances between — and within — the North and the South, nor the enormous dark spots on the world map whence no credible information reaches us. The Internet is no great help if one wants to find out what is happening in the planet's new *terrae incognitae*, where Mafiosi, paramilitary groups, guerrillas, private security forces, or the armies intimidate and deter information-gatherers. Beyond access to technology, there is the matter of access to information, which in turn raises basic questions about the right to know, the transparency of public and private authorities,[4] or violence against journalists.

WHAT TO DO?

Everything has changed, except ourselves. Everything has changed, except our way of thinking about and looking at the world.[5] The characteristics of the information conveyed by the new media — globality, instantaneity, abundance, uncertainty about the legitimacy of sources — call for appropriate attitudes, reflexes, and methodology. The use of global technologies does not mean that users instantly acquire a global mind.

Like governments, human rights organizations are pressed to react instantly to powerful images, to interpret outrageous events on the basis of fragmented information fed to them by media panicking at the thought of missing a show. This acceleration of information, this dramatization, play havoc with the mandates and methods of human rights organizations, threatening to make them hostage to the saturation-dearth information cycle dictated by the media and contributing, through this roller coaster, to confusion and, ultimately, indifference. Against the grain of this humanitarian shock we need to regain a sense of time, because this feeling of powerlessness that menaces us feeds on this fragmented, emotional, flitting knowledge of the world that the new media, and particularly television, give us in real time. We need to regain a sense of the slowness of history, to fight the culture of urgency and transience.

4 Jean-Paul Marthoz, *Le Droit de Savoir* (Paris: Unesco/IFJ, 1992).
5 Jean-Paul Marthoz, in *L'ONU dans tous ses États* (Brussels: Éditions du GRIP, 1995).

CONTRIBUTING TO THE QUALITY OF JOURNALISM

The new information technologies give human rights organizations an added responsibility toward journalism. When we see the journalists' motivations and methods, we could dream of an intense complicity between them and human rights advocates. "The only information," wrote Jean-Marie Colombani, publisher of *Le Monde*, "is the one that disturbs the dozing conscience and convenient consensus." Were not the finest pages of journalism written in the struggles for freedom? Why do we celebrate Guillermo Cano[6] or Gao Wu[7] if it is not because, amid the countless stenographers of dictatorships, these "freedom writers" managed to combine the noblest form of the trade with the bravest commitment to human dignity.

It would only be fair if human rights organizations, faced with the media invasion and the chaos of entertainment information, helped improve the quality of the democratic debate, and hence the quality of one of its main actors, journalism. Any other approach — the manipulation of emotions and facts — undermines the organizations' effectiveness in the long term by weakening their credibility and degrading the quality of the public debate, without which there cannot be any civic opinion. The new media change the tools of communication; they do not change its values nor its basic responsibilities. They demand on the contrary a greater respect for them.

CLOSING THOUGHTS

Finally, our reflection on the new media must extend to the role and the effectiveness of information as a weapon for the defense and promotion of human rights. At the end of a century marred by tragedy, the human rights movement perhaps does not need a supplement of information or new means of communication as much as a supplement of thought. The movement probably does not

---

6 Guillermo Cano, editor of the independent Columbian daily newspaper *El Espectado*, was assassinated by drug-lords in 1986. UNESCO'S prize for freedom of the press bears his name.

7 Gao Wu, a journalist, has been held in prison in China for several years. In 1997 she became the first laureate of the Guillermo Cano prize.

need new reports and new facts as much as an eloquent discourse showing to a passive or disenchanted public the interest that human rights represent for the integrity of individuals and the long-term stability and prosperity of societies and states. Because it is rooted in the deepest, most universal values, because it calls for responsibility and participation, the human rights movement is in a good position to help make sense of a world "bereft of purpose." "If technology is to make a political difference," says Benjamin Barber, "politics first has to change."[8]

8 Benjamin Barber, "The New Telecommunications Technology: Endless Frontier or the End of Democracy?" *Constellations, An International Journal of Critical and Democratic Theory*, vol. 4, no. 2 (October 1997).

SAFEGUARDING HUMANKIND AGAINST THE PURSUIT OF FALSE GODS: A SOCIOLOGICAL PERSPECTIVE ON THE HISTORY OF CENSORSHIP

Jean K. Chalaby

New media often get involved in struggles for new freedoms. Soon after the invention of the printing press revolutionized the dissemination of knowledge in the mid-fifteenth century, books and pamphlets became the principal means of propagation of religious reform. Published in defiance of papal and local authorities, books were the main medium through which the Protestant Reformation spread across Europe. Later, the nascent press became the medium most closely involved in the struggle for political rights. Newspapers became the mouthpieces of publicists calling for political reforms, more representative regimes, and the introduction of universal suffrage, the secret ballot, and fairer tax systems. Each political upheaval during this period was accompanied by an explosion in the number of newspapers. Historically, the press symbolizes the struggle for political freedom. Today's new media are in turn being used as vehicles for the advocacy and promotion of new rights. The book was instrumental in religious reform, the press was used by the advocates of democratic rights, and the Internet is now involved in the struggle for social freedoms.

Groups and individuals who use the Internet as a means of empowerment seek to promote rights which are related to the needs and preferences derived from their social and cultural identities. The liberties these people are fighting for are *micro-liberties* related to their lifestyles and to their membership in particular communities. Minority groups (based on gender, ethnicity, religious affiliation, sexual orientation, etc.) use the Internet to share information and resources and to coordinate their political lobbying. The Internet is the medium most closely associated with the struggle for these *freedoms of intimacy*.

Throughout history, the new communication capabilities of emerging media have represented a threat to those in positions of power. Political elites have always felt assailed by a seemingly limitless flow of discourse. When the new media actually help people to extend the frontiers of freedom, outright concern supersedes suspicion. Soon, authorities aim at controlling this new discourse. Procedures are put in place which seek to restrain this seamless flow of words and images and control the new dangers it represents.

So as new media enhance people's capabilities of expression, their development is often accompanied by new curbs on freedom of expression. Less than a century after the Gutenberg revolution, hundreds of authors were put on the indexes of banned books by local and religious authorities in Europe. As soon as books were published, a division was created between authorized and banned literature, between orthodox and "heretical" books.

In one respect, the development of digital technologies presents a somewhat similar situation. Contemporary political elites' attitude towards emerging media is comparable to that of their predecessors: to enact a stream of restrictive statutes and measures. However, we are also facing a new situation because the digital era has brought with it new means of curbing freedom of speech. For the first time, these means can be technological and integrated with the medium.

CENSORSHIP IN HISTORY: FROM BOOK-BURNING TO THE INTERNET-RATINGS SYSTEMS

Traditionally, there have been four principal means of restricting freedom of expression.

When legislation is enacted to curb press freedom, the means of coercion are legal. The most common legislative measures to restrict freedom of expression are censorship laws which make it illegal to write, publish, and disseminate literature which is considered to have a seditious character. Censorship laws can be traced back to the medieval codes of several European nations.[1] They prevailed in most European states until the end of the eighteenth century, after which their application became more problematical. Penalties and enforcement varied according to epochs and regimes. They included warnings, suspensions, interdictions, seizures, fines, imprisonment, excommunication, deportation, mutilation, and death. Precensorship measures were also commonly used — perusal by censors prior to publication, for example.

Progress toward more democratic legislative frameworks in regard to freedom of expression was slow and uneven. Article 11 of the French Declaration of Human Rights, enacted in 1789 but not applied for a century, was the first modern text of law to establish the principles of freedom of opinion and expression. Two years later, the US Bill of Rights promulgated similar rights. In international law, the turning point was the Second World War. After the trauma of this conflict, UNESCO was given in 1946 the mission of contributing to peace by advancing mutual knowledge and promoting the "free flow of ideas by word and image." In the same year, resolution 59(I), which promulgates freedom of expression as a fundamental right, was adopted by the General Assembly. Two years later, the rights to freedom of opinion and expression were enshrined in Article 19 of the Universal Declaration of Human Rights. When the Cold War ended, UNESCO renewed its efforts to promote freedom of expression and the worldwide dissemination of information. Several declarations were adopted by the General Conference, notably the Declaration of Windhoek in 1991 and the Declaration of Alma Ata the following year.[2]

1 D. Loades, *Politics, Censorship and the English Reformation* (Pinter, 1991).
2 See UNESCO, *Basic Texts in Communication, '89-'95* (1996).

Despite this, regulatory frameworks are still promulgated which are not in accord with standards of international law. Among nations currently engaged in the process of democratic transition, certain governments still propose legislation with the intent of using the law as a basis for control of the media. Examples include regulatory frameworks which use a vague or ambiguous wording to establish journalists' rights and protections, which give power to government to prosecute journalists on political grounds and which do not provide them with the right to refuse to disclose their sources of information. Some regulatory frameworks define the government's rights in matters of appointments at state broadcasting organizations. The ability of a government to make political appointments in state-run media organizations constitutes an important form of control over these organizations and a way to curtail their independence. The less democratic a system is, the more extensive is government control of media appointments.

A second type of censorship used widely in the past is administrative in character. This type includes such measures as the obligation to register, to obtain authorization for publication (licensing), and to deposit financial guarantees. The promulgation of such administrative procedures can be very constraining for the publicists and politicians of the opposition. These measures, which can be traced back to the sixteenth century in Europe, are still enacted in certain countries to impede the opposition press in ways that are indirect and less conspicuous than outright censorship. Thus, they allow governments to restrain freedom of expression without alerting public opinion. They encourage the authorities to take arbitrary decisions and apply a double standard — one for the governmental press, the other for dissident journalists. For example, newspapers from the opposition may encounter difficulties in registering or be subject to systematically biased judicial decisions.

A third means of coercion is violence: beating, kidnapping and arbitrary arrest, to cite three typical examples. When the rule of law is precarious and media personnel feel unprotected against arbitrary violence, that fear and sense of insecurity may lead to self-censorship.

Fourthly, means of coercion against the press can be economic. This efficient way of controlling the press has a long history. In 1712, in a move intended to silence a wave of fresh criticism in the press, the government of Queen Anne in England imposed four taxes on pamphlets and newspapers. These taxes, which became known as the "taxes on knowledge," were maintained by successive governments for 150 years. These taxes were clearly intended to put the press out of the financial reach of the majority. These taxes were finally repealed between 1855 and 1861. Similar duties were levied in France from the time of the Revolution to the Second Empire.

FILTERING AND BLOCKING

Some governments still resort to economic coercion against privately owned media organizations. A favourite technique is to take advantage of the economic fragility of some media outlets. Media organizations in desperate need of funds are less likely to reject financial backing that comes with strings attached. This strategy can even lead to governmental obstruction of the economic development of independent media. Restrictions on advertising revenue, or the refusal to privatize centralized and obsolete systems of printing and distribution, may be used. Arbitrary pricing decisions for printing and distribution services controlled by the state can make it difficult for independent media organizations to achieve financial independence.

Up to now, these legal, administrative, violent and economic means of coercion were the principal means of curbing freedom of expression. The advent of the digital era has brought a new way . For the first time, technology can be used as a means of censorship. This evolution may have a significant impact on public discourse because, for the first time, the instruments of control can be integrated with the medium.

Medium-integrated means of control are being developed in the form of rating and filtering software. These programs, which can potentially prevent users from accessing Internet content, involve a two-step process. The first is rating, which consists of classifying Web content according to categories such as violence, nudity, sex, and so forth. Although ratings systems use different types of categories and gradations, they are generally based on the same protocol, the Platform for Internet Content Selection (PICS).

Rating is followed by filtering. When the search engine of a Web browser is connected to blocking software, it filters content on the basis of the information

provided by the software's ratings system. If a site falls under one of the categories disallowed by the user or system manager, then it is blocked and access is
denied to the user.[3]

Legislators in several countries are currently attempting to pass legislation to
enforce the use of blocking software on computers accessible to the public. In
the United States, the Senate Commerce Committee unanimously passed a bill
in March 1998 which aims to require schools and libraries receiving public funds
to use filtering programs in accessing the Internet.[4]

Civil liberties groups are opposed to the use and development of such software
for several reasons. The first is the impracticality of rating and filtering the huge
amount of material available on the Internet. The seamless character of online
discourse also creates difficulties for rating systems. The most active rating
agency, the American RSACi, has rated less than 100,000 sites out of the millions
already in existence. Secondly, discourse on the Internet is too diverse to be classified according to a handful of categories. As rating categories are necessarily
vague and ambiguous, filtering software invariably blocks a large quantity of
information which is suitable for all users. A survey conducted in November 1997
by the Electronic Privacy Information Center showed that the search engine of
one of the most popular filtering softwares, Net Shepherd, set on the least restricting search option, "typically blocked access to 95-99 per cent of the material available on the Internet that might be of interest to young people."[5] It
blocked 99.8 percent of the documents retrieved by AltaVista for the key word
"American Red Cross."[6] This problem arises because filtering softwares operate
by key words and are unable to take into account contextual information. Thus,
they routinely classify as "obscene" safe-sex information or any form of nudity.
Civil liberties groups also warn of the danger of biased judgments in this process. Rating categories are laden with value judgments which are subjective in
character and differ between cultures and even between individuals. As a result,
ratings systems may affect the cultural diversity of cyberspace. Since the most
influential rating agencies are established in the United States, the filtering pro-

3 There exists a second category of blocking software, called stand-alone systems. They are not protocol-based,
but rather operate on the basis of a list of sites established by the system's vendor. See Computer Professionals for
Social Responsibility, "Filtering FAQ" at < http://quark.cpsr.org/~harryh/faq.htm >.

4 Internet Free Expression Alliance, "Internet School Filtering Act" at < http://www.ifea.net/news.htm >.

5 Electronic Privacy Information Center, "Faulty Filters: How Content Filters Block Access to Kid-Friendly Information on the Internet", p. 6, < http://www2.epic.org/reports/filter-report.htm >. See also The Censorware Project,
"Blacklisted by Cyber Patrol," < http://www.spectacle.org/cwp/intro.htm >.

6 See Electronic Privacy Information Center, *ibid.*, p. 6, for further information.

cedures will operate on the basis of North American moral values and assumptions. Organizations outside the United States contest the validity of these foreign value-laden categories, and claim that if they are to be implemented universally, it would further the global dominance of American moral values.[7]

Furthermore, it is claimed that rating schemes might homogenize the Internet. Only the most powerful publishers will have the resources to go through the self-rating procedures and to protect themselves against unfavorable ratings. As minority discourse disappears from the scene, powerful players will increase their visibility on the Internet.

Finally, filtering and blocking systems present the risk of widespread censorship. It appears that these softwares will enable governments to block entire domains on the Internet.[8]

Filtering and blocking software illustrates the application of technology to censorship, a phenomenon which is new in the history of censorship and restricted to the Internet. It constitutes the most powerful means of censorship ever invented. Its implementation and legal enforcement could inaugurate an era of widespread global censorship.

Furthermore, traditional means of censorship are still being deployed against online speech. In the United States, the federal government as well as several states enacted statutes to outlaw 'indecent' online speech over the last couple of years. All these laws, including the Federal Communications Decency Act, were successfully challenged in suits brought by civil liberties groups.[9]

In other parts of the globe, administrative and economic means of censorship are also curbing online free speech. In China, Internet accounts were made available in 1995 but priced so high that they were out of reach of the vast majority of Chinese. Charges for electronic messages are also prohibitive. Access to the Internet is further restricted by the obligation to register personal access accounts at the Postal Ministry.[10]

7 American Civil Liberties Union, "Fahrenheit 4512: Is Cyberspace Burning?" < http:www.aclu.org/issues/cyber/burning.htm >. See also Electronic Frontier Foundation, "Policy on Public Interest Principles for Online Filtration, Ratings and Labeling Systems", < http://www.eff.org/pub/Net'info/Tools/Ratings'filters/eff'filter.principle >; and Imaginons un Réseau Internet Solidaire, "Etiquetage et filtrage: possibilités, dangers, et perspectives," < http://girafe.ensba.fr/iris/rapport- ce/annexe6.htm >.

8 Global Internet Liberty Campaign, "Free Speech — Filtering and Ratings," < http://www.gilc.org/speech/ratings >.

9 Electronic Frontier Foundation, "Censorship — Internet Censorship Legislation and Regulation," < http://www.eff.org/pub/Censorship/Internet_censorship_bills >.

10 Electronic Privacy Information Center, "Silencing the Net: The Threat to Freedom of Expression Online," p. 10, < http://www.epic.org/free_speech/intl/hrw_report_5_96.htm >.

Other Asian countries combine legal, administrative and technological means of restricting the information that their citizens can access. The Singapore authorities enforce strict censorship laws that require Internet service providers to register with the Singapore Broadcasting Authority and promote the use of filtering softwares.[11]

Thus, at the same time as digital technologies expand individuals' communicating capabilities, they provide more sophisticated means of restricting freedom of expression. This creates an ambivalent relationship between new technologies and freedom of expression.

BOOK-BURNING

This overview of the means of censorship can be concluded with an observation on the changing nature of censorship through the ages. Among the most potent symbols of censorship are the book-burning scenes of the Inquisition. In Spain and Italy, seized books which had been prohibited by the authorities were burned in public spaces.

These rituals were laden deliberately with symbolism. The fire symbolized the power of the Holy Spirit, and the action of burning, the purification of erroneous knowledge. On the other hand, at least in Italy, the enforcement of penalties against authors and booksellers who had infringed censorship laws was erratic and inconsistent. Long periods of calm were interrupted by sudden waves of repression. Coercion was highly visible, but in actual fact not terribly efficient.

The current trend in censorship reverses this pattern. Censorship methods are becoming increasingly efficient and decreasingly visible. The first step in this direction was the emergence of economic means of censorship, such as stamp duties on pamphlets and newspapers, early in the eighteenth century. Now Internet filtering software can take censorship even further away from demonstrative justice. It is not flames that now destroy information but invisible and anonymous digital codes. Filtering systems block information before users even know it exists. Political authorities who enforce the use of these softwares intend to control the flow of discourse and information on the Internet in the most effi-

11 *Ibid.*, pp. 11–12.

cient and least intrusive way. Digital technologies allow them to set up instruments of censorship that are almost invisible, permanent and global.

Freedom of speech on the Internet will not be tested in the arena of traditional politics. The fact that all political persuasions are able to express themselves on the Internet (albeit with very unequal resources)[12] is not in dispute. The test will be made in the realm of the formation of new social identities. Just as the Inquisition targeted religious minorities, restrictions on the Internet will mainly affect new minority groups. The crucial question will be whether or not these groups will be able to use the Internet to define and assert their emerging collective identities. Their ability and freedom to do so is relevant to everyone. In much the same way as the rights gained by Protestant reformers benefited other religious communities, the micro-liberties these emerging minorities are fighting for will be seen by future generations to have transcended their local preferences and interests.

12 M. Margolis, D. Resnick, and C. Tu, "Campaigning on the Internet: Parties and Candidates on the World Wide Web in the 1996 Primary Season," *The Harvard International Journal of Press/Politics*, vol. 2, no. 4 (1997), pp. 59–78.

FREEDOM OF EXPRESSION AND THE VIRTUAL COMMUNITY

Mike Godwin

Your first experience of free speech in cyberspace may not seem like speaking at all. Or much like writing either, for that matter. You enter a command at a computer console with your keyboard or pointer and after a short pause, you may hear a dialtone and a rapid series of tones coming from your modem. One or two rings later and the modem on the other end responds with a high-pitched squeal. Your modem answers back with a similar squeal. The login message prompts you for your name and password, and soon you're connected.

But connected to what? It may be a hobbyist's computer bulletin-board, a university's mainframe computer, a commercial information service or a home page on the World Wide Web. No matter what you're connected to, you've just become another explorer, perhaps even a settler, of the newest frontier for the exercise of the freedom of expression guaranteed by Article 19 of the Universal

Declaration of Human Rights. But Article 19 is not the only provision of the Declaration applicable to this new sphere of human activity. Increasingly, we have begun to recognize that Articles 27 and 29, which relate to each person's rights and duties in relation to his or her community, apply in cyberspace as well. And from this recognition of the existence of both freedom of expression and of community in cyberspace, we may draw at least two preliminary conclusions

The first is that our interests in freedom of expression and in these new virtual communities are not, in fact, competing interests. They complement and reinforce each other because the strength of communities depends upon their toleration of and support for freedom of expression.

The second conclusion is that coming to terms with the immense expressive power of the Net, and with the legal and social issues that it generates, will be one of the central challenges of our generation. And it won't be just the politicians, lawyers, activists and technicians who take up the challenge. It will be every one of us who explores this new frontier, which is in one sense a medium and in another sense a territory.

GEOGRAPHY OF THE NET

Mapping this territory, usually referred to as "cyberspace" or "the Net," requires a discussion of the technologies on which it is based.

Perhaps the earliest model of the virtual community is the computer bulletin-board system (BBS). The operator of a BBS typically dedicates a computer and one or more phone lines at his or her home or business for the use of a virtual community of users. Each user, using his or her own computer and modem, calls up the BBS and leaves public messages that can be read by all other users. Each user also can send private mail that can be read by another individual user while remaining inaccessible to all others. For their users, BBSs become digital forums resembling public houses, salons and Hyde Park corners.

A step up from the BBS in complexity is the conferencing system or information service. Functionally similar to BBSs, only much larger, these systems are typically based on a single computer or set of computers located in a particular geographic area. They differ from BBSs primarily in their capacity: they have the capability of serving dozens, even hundreds of users simultaneously. America Online (AOL) and the WELL (Whole Earth 'Lectronic Link) are two of the better-known examples of such conferencing systems. Each is home to a lively set of communities of users located all across the United States (but including "citizens" from other parts of the world). AOL and the WELL were at one time reachable primarily through proprietary computer networks that enabled users to dial in without racking up immense long-distance charges. Nowadays, these systems are all reachable through the Internet, as discussed below

Still higher in the scale of complexity is the distributed network, which is not located in a particular geographic area but is maintained and supported on a large number of computers located all over the country or the world. The best-known example of a distributed network is the Internet, which connects thousands of computers at universities, government agencies and commercial and noncommercial organizations around the world. The Internet is a key conduit for "Usenet," a distributed worldwide conferencing system whose "newsgroups" (discussion forums) touch on just about every topic imaginable. The Internet is also the foundation for the World Wide Web, a relatively recent form of graphically-oriented publication on the Net that has grown dramatically over the last three or four years.

Together, this range of increasingly interconnected computer forums constitutes the Net. Its public and private conferencing systems (from Usenet to America Online to the WELL), its new modes of publication (such as the World Wide Web), and even its simplest electronic-mail services have enabled hundreds of virtual communities of like-minded individuals to spring up. The immediacy of Net communications has already led to their supplanting scientific journals as the major communicators of scientific discovery and research.

NETIZENS AND VIRTUAL COMMUNITIES

It might seem paradoxical that conferencing systems like the WELL and America Online support stable "virtual communities" while also supporting individual freedom of expression — even highly provocative or disturbing expression. In truth, freedom of expression for individuals is the key element in creating stability and connectedness for communities. It is so important that I've explored the interdependence of these two elements in a book.[1] If one had to summarize that interdependence in a single sentence, it might read as follows: "Only a strong tolerance for provocative and even unruly expression on the part of its citizens will provide a community with the kind of intellectual and spiritual robustness and diversity necessary to adapt to the challenges of the future."

Not everyone has been able to accept that what we call "virtual community" in reality amounts to a community at all. The first wave of widespread optimism about the potential of cyberspace was soon followed an equally powerful wave of skepticism and fear. We have since been told people don't really communicate well on computer networks, that something about using computers makes people act badly toward one another, and that what some people call "virtual communities" are little more than consensual hallucinations — fantasy lands without any real meaning. And we have been given the impression that cyberspace is essentially uncivilized, a community of sociopaths, child pornographers, criminal conspirators, and terrorists. But while the Net unquestionably raises new issues for law enforcement, much of what people are told about cyberspace by their governments or by the traditional press is wrong and unnecessarily frightening. The reality of the Net mirrors the reality of our physical communities in that its citizens or netizens, for the most part, are well-meaning, benevolent, cooperative, and aware of our common interest in maintaining a civilized society.

For some people, the concept of virtual community is troubling, since "virtual" is often used to connote the opposite of "actual" or "tangible." As a result, many people think that a "virtual community" can't be as real as, say, a community that grows out of a neighborhood or village. As a lawyer, however, I've never had much trouble with the concept that virtual communities are both real and intangible. The same can be said about the Universal Declaration of Human Rights itself. What we call "Article 19," for example, is not something that depends on words on a piece of paper or parchment. Burn every copy of Article 19 and it will still exist in the minds and hearts of countless citizens, many of whom have memorized the words of its text. Lawyers, diplomats, and government officials also routinely learn that those words represent, in turn, virtual entities such as

1 Mike Godwin, *Cyber Rights: Defending Free Speech in the Digital Age* (Times Books, 1998). See also < http://www.panix.com/"mnemonic >

fundamental principles, plus some rules of interpretation. These rules arise when the language, history, and principles of the Declaration interact with the material world. The world of these abstract or "virtual" entities and the concrete, tangible material world of cases and controversies are constantly shaping each other.

THE THREE PROPOSITIONS

Nevertheless, a lot of people including many of our leaders see the Net as marginal, illusory or unreal, and lawless and immoral. In response to this, if we intend to preserve freedom of expression on the Net, we have to frame three counter-arguments or propositions for the guidance of governments:

▨ That our interest in, and love of, the Net, freedom of speech online, and virtual communities represent mainstream human concerns.

▨ That what we experience online, although primarily mediated by language, is as real as anything else we experience.

▨ That most of us can be trusted to use responsibly the freedom and expressive power the Net gives us.

I believe that virtual communities have the potential to restore to the world's citizens a stable sense of community. Ask anyone who has been a member of a virtual community, and they will tell you that what happens there is more than an exchange of electronic impulses. It may be a virtual communal barn-raising of the sort I personally experienced when, after my library was damaged in a moving-van fire, my "neighbors" on the WELL sent me hundreds of volumes to replace the ones I'd lost. It may also be the comfort from others that a man can experience when he's up late at night caring for a child suffering from leukemia, and he logs onto the WELL and pours out his anguish and fears. People really do learn to care for each other and even fall in love over the Net, just as they do in geographic communities. And that virtual connectedness is a real sign of hope in a world that's increasingly anxious about the fragmentation of public life, the polarization of interest groups and the alienation of urban existence.

THE NATURE AND PURPOSE OF VIRTUAL COMMUNITIES

One of the most common tragedies of urban life is our sense of having lost "community," that feeling of being part of a larger whole with neighbors we can talk to, and who will help in difficult times. Is it any surprise that the notion of "virtual community" has such resonance these days? Many of us sense that community is what we've been missing all this time. This is why we identify it so quickly and treasure it so deeply when we find it in the online world.

Increasingly we hear stories about ordinary people (as distinct from dedicated computer hobbyists) who use online communications as an integral part of what can only be called communal activities. Citizens' groups rely on electronic forums to organize events, develop policies and conduct meetings. Lonely individuals find new ways to connect with the rest of humanity. There are millions of individuals around the world who have already begun the hard work of settling these online communities, investing tens of hours in learning arcane computer operating-system commands and telecommunication tricks, and then spending hundreds of hours online. These people are our trailblazers and our guides as we discover what kinds of online communities succeed and what kinds of laws and institutions are needed to encourage and preserve the successful ones. As journalists, communications theorists and policy makers begin to recognize more and more the significance of events on the electronic frontier, the experiences of these early pioneers will point the way to the new social forms of the 21st century.

Through his writings in a number of publications as well as through his 1993 book *The Virtual Community*[2] Howard Rheingold has become closely identified with the concept of virtual communities. He defines them as "social aggregations that emerge from the Net when enough people carry on ... public discussions long enough, with sufficient human feeling, to form webs of personal relationships in cyberspace." He still is the best-known popularizer of the concept and one of the most gifted at persuading people that a virtual community is just as real as any other kind.

2 Howard Rheingold, *The Virtual Community* (Addison-Wesley, 1993).

EXPLORING THE VIRTUAL CITY IN CYBERSPACE

If Howard Rheingold is the best-known popularizer of the notion of virtual communities, the earliest and most influential theorists about them are Starr Roxanne Hiltz and Murray Turoff, two social scientist who pioneered the study of what academics have come to call "computer-mediated communication." Their 1978 book "The Network Nation"[3] was the first attempt to undertake a comprehensive exploration of the design, functions and consequences of online communication.

Their book turned out to be prophetic. There is hardly an aspect of anyone's experience in the online world that is not foreshadowed in it to some extent. Because Hiltz and Turoff began by attempting to find out what makes online conferencing systems work, they often focused on the question of what kind of design decisions are required if the system is to work efficiently. Eventually they discovered that one of the key tools for improving system design is the fostering of community, and that this in turn is connected to free speech. This has been a significant discovery — that the most successful online communities seem to be the ones that tolerate the greatest freedom of expression.

Of course we all know that freedom is never limitless. Every society, even an online society, has norms and taboos that simultaneously protect and define its culture. In many virtual communities, for example, it is considered exceedingly bad-mannered to publish publicly the content of someone's private mail, especially when the person e-mailed you with the expectation that the communication was private.

The WELL, the virtual community I know best, has adopted this principle but it is also generally accepted that there may be times when it is okay to violate it, as when someone is being harassed in e-mail. (Public re-postings of such private mail are extremely effective at getting the sender to stop.) Another taboo is the re-posting or re-publishing of someone's WELL postings in some other venue, either print or another online forum, without the originator's permission. Cross that line on the WELL, and you'll be shocked at the sudden, steep (but usually

---

3 Roxanne Hiltz and Murray Turoff, *The Network Nation; Human Communication via Computer* (MIT Press, revised edition, 1993).

temporary) downturn in your social fortunes, as many journalists who were WELL members have already discovered. These journalists couldn't understand what was wrong with quoting people who had written something in a public forum like the WELL. (I have no categorical answer to this, except to say that I pay a lot of attention to the rule myself if only because the WELL is the place I live when I'm online, and I'm willing to sacrifice a little freedom to stay a part of it.) But even if there are some taboos — and the existence of social norms, including somewhat arbitrary ones, may be essential to the definition of a community — the primary principle that keeps the WELL strong and growing is the exercise of freedom of speech, not its denial. Talking to other people, both singly and in groups, and sharing what matters to you, is the attraction that keeps users coming back. This sense of being connected to others is created and mediated by freedom of expression.

If you talk to a friend who's not yet online, and you start to wax poetic about the pleasures and rewards of your online community, your friend may think you're living in a fantasy. After all, as your friend knows, such communities in the everyday world are rare. But one of the proofs of the existence of these virtual communities, that they are not fantasies but real, is that it's so hard to find good ones. It's easy enough to get an e-mail address, or to find an online service where you can discuss a television show or government health-care proposals or human sexuality, but it's far more difficult to find true communities of people where you feel a sense of belonging. The root of this problem lies in the fact that few people are planning virtual communities.

There still isn't enough discussion about how one builds such communities. Rheingold's book focused on one of the chief benefits of online conferencing systems — that they can restore a sense of community to a society that is feeling alienated and disempowered. But he didn't address what may turn out to be the most pressing problem: How will the explosively growing cyberspace population find its way into such communities? How can such communities be designed and constructed?

Most demographers agree that the movement of the general public to the Net is accelerating. Yet of the many people who have taken steps toward integrating cyberspace into their daily lives, only a fraction have found a place in a virtual community. For many, freedom of speech on the Net means little more than access to electronic mail. Some individuals simply acquire an e-mail address for its social value, just as many Americans in the post-war world saw value in own-ing a house. But in cyberspace, increasingly, the dream is not just "owning a house." It is living in the right neighborhood. One of the reasons why the WELL, with only about 10,000 registered users, is such a well-known address in cyberspace is that the perception of community is so strong.[4] This "virtual com-munity" perception derives directly from the WELL's commitment to individual freedom as a requirement of community-building.

A community built around the principles of freedom of speech and individual autonomy, however, has to be planned. WELL's pervasive sense that it is a com-munity freely constructed, shaped and reshaped by its users has to be the result of planning. As Hiltz and Turoff's research showed nearly two decades ago, that kind of planning has to foster free communication which in turn feeds back into the design of the community. I believe this "planning for freedom" is why the WELL is regarded as one of the "great good places" of cyberspace. True, the WELL has yet to come to terms with how it wants to handle growth, but it does enough things right that I'm comfortable using it as a model for understanding the rules for planning virtual communities around free-speech principles.

Working from this model, I've come up with a set of principles that provide a starting point for building these communities. After I published an earlier ver-sion of these rules in Wired, I was frequently asked for permission to republish them elsewhere online, and I've changed them a bit since the first version, so you can find these rules in a number of places on the Net. Here is the updated and Improved version.

NINE PRINCIPLES FOR MAKING VIRTUAL COMMUNITIES WORK

1. Use Software That Promotes Good Discussions

In the days before the WELL invested in the development of a Web-based inter-face for the system, WELL users made a habit of complaining about PicoSpan, the system's text-based conferencing software. PicoSpan may seem like a dino-

4 The WELL is based in Sausalito, California, in the San Franciso Bay area.

saur in today's world of GUIs (graphic user interfaces) but in fact it remains rather advanced in comparison to the slicker interfaces you can find on other systems. PicoSpan still does several things right, often by using what software designers call constrained choices. For example, one can't start a new topic merely by responding to an old posting, so discussions and topics tend not to fragment the way they do on Usenet and CompuServe. And you can't respond to individual postings unless you either read everything that's been posted previously in the topic, or else make a deliberate decision to skip those earlier postings. This tends to reduce the amount of redundancy and to make threads of discussion more coherent.

2. Don't Impose a Length Limitation on Postings

Some systems limit the length of postings to 25 lines. This doesn't matter much if what you're interested in is banter and short tidbits, but it puts a crimp in discussions of history or politics or literature. Individuals should be able to post essays as well as one-liners.

3. Frontload Your System With Talkative, Diverse People

The WELL made a strategic decision early on to give free accounts to individuals and hosts who could be counted on to make interesting and provocative comments. One of the things that made the WELL work was not that there were likeminded people but that there were different-minded ones — users who inspired conversations and controversy by the strength and heterodoxy of their views.

4. Let the Users Resolve Their Own Disputes

On the whole, WELL management has taken a hands-off position when it comes to users' personal disputes on the WELL. Experienced users don't turn to management to complain; they choose instead to hash out their differences in public. The WELL has imposed few rules on public discourse and as a result, the user population has developed or adopted its own norms that are enforced largely by social pressures.

5. Provide Institutional Memory

Some of the WELL's conferences have postings dating back to the mid-1980s. New users can come online and read about things that happened on the WELL early in its development, giving them a sense of the community's history.

6. Promote Continuity By Keeping Old Postings Available

What makes the WELL feel like a community is what makes any place feel like a community — you see the same "faces," know the same personalities and have ongoing relationships. At the same time, new users are made to feel welcome. Not everybody is a Welcome Wagon type, but it's important to have at least of few of that type on your system.

7. Be Host to One or More Interest Groups

The WELL is the cyberspace home of Deadheads — Grateful Dead fans who regularly congregate on the WELL to share information and converse about their favorite band. Their participation provides important cash flow to keep the community operating, and it also provides diversity, as Deadheads go "over the wall" to converse on non-Grateful Dead forums. If you can be a host to stable but enthusiastic interest group, it can provide the backbone of your system, financially and otherwise.

8. Respect Children

Like many systems, the WELL provides links to the "KidLink" networks for 10- to 15-year-olds but, more importantly, it has a tradition of treating young people with respect, on the assumption that what they say is as worth reading as anyone else's contribution.

9. Commit the System to Maintaining Public Spaces for Public Communication and Public Events

What makes a sense of community is shared experience and that means experiences shared by some large percentage of the membership. The common assumption that communities define themselves by excluding others with divergent views is, I think, a distortion of what really happens. Vital communities, virtual or otherwise, are those that give potential members something to share with veteran members from the moment they first log on. That's why lively public discussion spaces remain important, and why basing those public spaces on the principle of free speech is absolutely necessary.

These rules, although incomplete, amount to a blueprint for successful cyberspace communities, and the systems I know that have a truly "communal" feel (the WELL, ECHO in New York City, several MOOs and BBSs, and a few pockets of Usenet) abide by most of these rules. All of these places manifest what I take to be one of the best indicators of a healthy virtual community — they have remained stable over time.

If all that cyberspace gives you is an e-mail address — a place to hang your virtual hat and chat about your hobbies — you've been cheated. What most of us will want in the future, I think, is a place where we're known and accepted on the basis of what Martin Luther King Jr. called "the content of our character." But without planning, without a deliberate architectural vision about shaping virtual communities — and most of all, without true freedom of speech — the incoming hordes of cyberspace inhabitants will be continue to be alienated and isolated — in effect, "virtually homeless."

RADICAL PLURALISM

Both the technology and the culture of virtual communities encourage individuals to speak out more frequently and to become involved in the public life of their communities. They are also likely to engage in what I call "radical pluralism." This is the kind of public participation that will characterize political life in the next century, and we're seeing the first wave of it in the 1990s.

Radical pluralism is what happens when you put the power of a mass medium — computer communications — into the hands of individual citizens who could never have dreamed of attaining creative access to mass media such as TV or newspapers. Everyone becomes a "content producer" as well as a consumer, and the balance of media and political power shifts fundamentally.

Will radical pluralism be comfortable? Hardly. Sometimes traditional mass media and political establishments will wish for the rest of us simply to shut up. But I have a message for those folks: "Fasten your seat belts — we've spotted turbulence ahead."

DIRECT DEMOCRACY: THE ROLE OF ELECTRONIC COMMUNICATION FORUMS FOR A NEW PUBLIC IN THE INFORMATION SOCIETY

Rainer Kuhlen

Direct democracy is a form of political organization in which direct participation of the citizens in political decision-making is dominant, or at least occasionally practiced, in contrast to indirect or representative forms of democracy, in which political (legislative and executive) practice is delegated to special people (delegates, representatives) who have been elected by those with the right to vote. Direct democracy as a form of self-governing democracy is more common on the municipal or regional level. On higher political levels, such as that of states, where more complex tasks need to be carried out, forms of indirect, representational democracy are dominant. The direct election of the president of a state, anchored in the constitutions of many states, is one striking counter-example to the otherwise representational dominance.

In addition to the direct election of delegates, one distinguishes as principles of direct democracy between initiative, referendum, and recall. An initiative is a procedure by which a prescribed number of voters can enforce a binding poll on new or existing laws. The legislative referendum, also determined on the basis of a specified percentage of voters, petitions to approve or to reject a bill that has passed through parliament. The recall enforces the right of the people to petition for the holding of a vote on the removal of a public official. All these classical forms of direct democracy are obviously more effective and also safer if they are organized in an electronic environment. The argument that not everyone has access to these systems or is willing to use techniques such as electronic polls is not really convincing. People would still have the right to go to the polls personally, but electronic elections would be a perfect substitute for the postal vote. The explosive force of electronic polls lies in the potential of immediate feedback, with the consequence that voting patterns are susceptible to being influenced by the intermediate results.

If the concept of direct democracy is taken literally, not only the criterion of participation needs to be fulfilled but also the criterion of co-presence. Co-presence in time and space is, of course, only possible when a very limited number of people is involved. In theory and practice co-presence is not demanded as an exclusive condition for direct democracy. As we will see, this is also true for the modern means of direct democracy. Although synchronous communication (with limited multipresence) is of growing importance, for instance in chat boards and teleconferencing environments, asynchronous and, of course, dislocated communication is dominant in modern electronic communication devices such as e-mail or electronic forums. The latter are considered in the following as an appropriate means of direct democracy in the electronic information society. Direct democracy in contemporary societies is not considered by most political scientists and politicians as a real alternative to the existing political system of indirect democracy, where it is mainly political parties and political institutions which have the mandate to formulate and to carry out official politics, which are made public by the mass media. The greater rationality and efficiency achieved by delegating political tasks to professionals and competent specialists are considered the main advantages of indirect democracy.

The media are also part of indirect democracy. Journalists and their employers, the media companies, co-decide which topics are policy-relevant and they clearly contribute to the construction of public opinion. In addition to the media, many (professional) interest groups from all areas of society are involved in establishing public and societal consensus and compromise, through which opposing interests can be reconciled. These interest groups work in different arenas and do not have a common platform of publicity. Therefore there is only a limited exchange of positions between them. This is one of the potentials of electronic communication forums, in which people with different organizational backgrounds can communicate with each other.

To conclude this section on direct democracy: Indirect, representative forms of democracy are still dominant, but there is a tendency in many states to strengthen forms of direct democracy, permitting active citizen participation not only in the direct election of representatives such as mayors of cities or even presidents of states, but also in legislative and executive processes such as initiatives and referendums. Therefore there is no mutual exclusion between direct and indirect forms of democracy. In the current climate of openness to experimentation with new forms of direct democracy, electronic communication forums are likely to spread and to be find use, not only in the realms of science and economy but also as tools in the general political arena.

INFORMATION, COMMUNICATION, MEDIA, AND DEMOCRACY

In general, the interrelation between democracy and information is quite obvious. What is true for professional politicians — viz., that only information-based decisions are rational and will be accepted by the people, in contrast to decisions made on a charismatic or non-transparent basis — is also true for the people of a state: Only well-informed citizens will act consciously and responsibly as members of a democratic state, although the right to vote is not bound to a certain degree of active information behavior. To care about being well-informed is not a legal but a moral obligation in modern societies. Modern societies can be judged according to the degree to which they provide everyone with access to the information resources which are in principle available. Therefore the right of (free) access to available information resources has been explicitly anchored in many modern constitutions. Free access does not necessarily mean cost-free access to all resources, but it does mean access to those resources through which a basic information supply *(informationelle Grundversorgung)* can be achieved. The long-lasting debate about whether information can be considered a public or a private good is therefore also a debate about political participation and the chances of direct democracy. With the spread of electronic communication services the right to access information can be extended to the right to communicate, that means to have reading and writing rights and have access to electronic communication forums as platforms for the exchange of individual statements and positions. Not only information competence but also communication competence in all (professional, political, and private) environments is needed in the information society, which, given its democratic basis, will be a communication society.

ELECTRONIC COMMUNICATION FORUMS

The main disadvantage of mass media such as newspapers, journals, or traditional TV is considered to be absence of feedback and interaction. Letters to the editor and phone-ins are only very limited means of creating a media public in which the public itself or its individual members can actively participate. The limitations on feedback and interaction are mainly created by the technological restrictions on producing and distributing information in the media. Today with the advent of modern information and communication technologies and the growing usage of Internet services, these limitations are beginning to disappear and will likely be overcome in the near future. It is foreseeable that in a few years almost everyone will be able not only to read information — i.e., to access information — but also will have the right to write information in the open Internet. This combination of reading and writing information will create a new form of public and will inevitably modify the existing forms of mass media. Consequently, there will be a change in the forms of representative democracy, which was, and still is, mainly based on information and on better access to the media in order to distribute the information which is considered to be politically relevant or correct. These information and media privileges will gradually disappear. This does not mean that the now-existing forms of creating a public and public opinion will disappear. But what will disappear is the existing media monopoly. It may be that large parts of the population will continue to practice a passive (receptive) information behavior rather than an active (reading and writing) one, but the alternative is available and more and more active citizens will take advantage of it.

Usenet newsgroups, e-mail services, list servers, bulletin boards and chat boards were the early communication platforms on the Internet. Today, with the dominance of Web technology, more and more web-based communication forums with user-friendly, graphical and hypertext-based interfaces are being created which are attractive to a broader public, in principle to everyone. It was the early communication tools available only to a minority of net users, primarily in academic environments, which created the early Internet image of a basic-democratic communication form and where the concept of the *netizen* — some one who considers himself a member of the global information society rather than belonging to a single state — was created. Jon Katz, one of the leading columnists in HotWired, *Wired*'s online network, coined the terms *netizen* and *digital nation* and speaks rather optimistically about the way the Net will change our democratic attitude:

"It may very well become a central forum for informed and civil civic debate, a medium in which individuals are reconnected to one another and the democratic process they share. It is also a vehicle for transmitting rational thought and truth instead of the paralyzing dogmas that have so disfigured our political process."

Today, with the take-over of the Net by commerce and the general public, the majority of Internet users take a more pragmatic view of the potential of network communication. Only very few still believe that the medium will cause a radical change in our political system. But, as already mentioned, it is likely that the distributive monopoly of mass media for the creation of public opinion will gradually be transformed into a form of interactive and self-initiated media. And this, at least in the long run, may have consequences for the political system as a whole. The transformation of the media will be characterized by the following:

▨ The media professionals will no longer have a monopoly on public opinion; they will no longer be the main content producers in the media world.

▨ The production role of the media may change into a monitoring role, namely to organize, stimulate, and summarize the forums' discussions.

▓ Information will no longer be distributed unilaterally but will be interactively produced and used.

▓ Mass communication products will gradually be replaced by individually-tailored newspapers and individualized TV programs.

▓ Media products will develop into open products. They will thus be real-time products which are not stable but are open to the permanent process of commenting, adding new contributions, and linking to other resources.

Electronic communication forums are likely to be an appropriate platform for these new open media products. Mass media as the dominant means of distribution of the past (and still of the present) will gradually be replaced by interactive, flexible and open media products, produced, displayed, and used through electronic communication forums. Information will mainly be based on communication. Electronic communication forums — rather than the mass media — can be considered the appropriate means in the information society to create a public. As value-added effects of electronic communication forums the following deserve mention:

▓ They allow exchange of information between people who are not likely to meet in real life. Electronic communication forums bring people together with different background, different professional experience and different life styles. The forum statement only is what counts, not the reputation.

▓ They are designed for interaction. Each statement is subject to comment, each position is subject to modification.

▓ They are organized according to hypertext principles, allow flexible navigation in heterogeneous information material, and can thus develop into a platform of knowledge with respect to the topic of the forum. Statements and comments in a forum can thus rely on a growing web of information, unlimited in size and in principle open to all knowledge available on the information markets.

▓ In a Web-based technical environment, they are normally organized in an asynchronous mode (although synchronous chat techniques or teleconferencing facilities are being used more and more for forum purposes as well). Asynchronous communication allows quasi real-time reactions to the forums' statements, but also allows delayed reactions after a period of information gathering or, simply, thinking.

▓ Compared with the high costs for real conferences with participants from all over the world, they are a cheap technology, once the technical equipment is available.

▪ Particularly when they are data-base supported, they allow flexible adaptation to different user's needs or expectations such as dialogue behavior, and to different pre-established parameters such as access and editing rights.

As mentioned above: what newspapers and television were for the development of democratic behavior and attitudes, namely creators of public opinion, will become the role of non-distributive but interactive communication forums. The main question with respect to the potential of forums to build a new form of public is whether this will be one general public or an ensemble of many isolated atomized "publics". Typically the same accusation has been made with respect to hypertext value-added services in the Internet in general: the accusation of atomizing and decontextualizing knowledge. It is true that electronic forums in general assemble only a very small number of people, small with respect to active participation in individual forums and small with respect to the number of the total population. But the hypertextification of knowledge is a prerequisite for the new contextualisation of knowledge in open hypertexts as they develop in the global network of Web sites. Therefore, a similar development in open electronic communication forums can be expected. So far forums do not take advantage of the open environment they inhabit. They act for themselves and take only very limited notice of the activities of other forums. The different forums which have been established as the federal election in Germany approaches do not interact with each other. A first step towards open communication forums has been taken by the information science department of the University of Constance. We have established a metaforum which permits discussion of election topics directly, but also provides information about other publicly available election forums and allows direct access to them. The real potential of electronic communication forums for creating new forms of public and for creating relevant forms of direct democracy undoubtedly lies in the development of forums as open interrelated forums.

We do not want to overemphasize the influence of information and communication on political decision-making processes. It is well known that exchange of information is not the only requirement for establishing a consensus or a majority, but it is a very important prerequisite. Therefore communication forums cannot be considered a new wonder drug in the pursuit of democracy but they can be a very helpful device, if controlled carefully and used methodologically.

ELECTRONIC COMMUNICATION FORUMS IN THE CONTEXT OF THE 1998 FEDERAL ELECTION IN GERMANY

There are many ways electronic communication forums can be used in politics, and a broad variety of providers organize the platforms for them. It is not the case that completely new players thereby dominate the political arena. Of course there are new institutions and new initiatives with the know-how to establish electronic forums: e.g., civil-rights movements, alternative groups, non-governmental organizations (NGO), private organizations, electronic market providers, and single individuals. But the old players — the political institutions, the parties and, of course, the traditional media — are becoming more and more involved in electronic forums, too. Almost every political institution, every party, and every major media organization (newspaper, radio, and TV) in countries like Germany have their own Web site, and they often organize forums to permit target group participation or as an efficient and low-cost marketing tool to attract visitors to the site. We give a few example of institutions in Germany which provide political information and often a discussion platform for the public:

■ The Chancellor's office *(Bundeskanzleramt)*

■ Federal Office for the protection of the constitution *(Bundesamt für den Verfassungsschutz)*

Many political services and interest groups also offer Web information and forums, such as:

■ Politik-news.com

■ Intrasat Deutschland

■ Greenpeace

■ Research institutes such as the Institute for Applied Knowledge Processing (FAW), Ulm

Political parties with special-purpose forums include:

■ Rot- grüne Online-Wählerinitiative (to support a coalition between the Green party and the Social-democratic party)

■ A city initiative from a sub-city of Berlin — Rudow Im Netz

■ Spiegel Online — special forum for the election

▓ Wahlen De, a forum of private enterprises (SystemDesign and HSL Information & Kommunikation)

These forums are mainly organized according to the thread paradigm known from the early usenet newsgroups. Once a new topic is raised, the comments and comments on the comments build a thread of discussion. Experience shows that it is very difficult to keep track of complex threads. Therefore intensive embedding is rather unusual. It is still a challenge for forum design and monitoring to stimulate and to adequately display real interaction between people's statements. It seems absolutely necessary that there be a moderator or a topic chair (or however such a communication jockey should be called) who gives some guidance to the discussion. The "lost in space" syndrome, well known in the hypertext world, easily repeats itself as the "lost in forum's space" syndrome. Orientation problems, in particular if one cannot follow the discussion continuously, still need to be solved. Therefore more powerful visualization techniques are needed for the representation of a complex and highly interrelated discussion. These must go beyond the linear representation of embedded threads. Experiments with 3D virtual-reality forums are needed.

In order to live up to the aim of being a means for the construction of a rational public opinion communication forums need to establish rich knowledge bases about the topics of the forum. These bases can be constructed by the forum's monitoring team and/or can be built up gradually by the forum's participants themselves. The hypertext methodology underlying the Web forum's architecture allows intensive linking to the forum's external resources and expertise. In addition, the participants of the forum need to be provided with powerful search and navigation tools in order to productively access the forum's knowledge bases and the external link information.

THE RELEVANCE OF ELECTRONIC COMMUNICATION FORUMS FOR DIRECT DEMOCRACY

At the time of writing this article (June 1998), the federal election is still to come (September 1998) and the communication forums established especially for this major event have not yet entered the hot pre-election phase. Therefore we can only provide a preliminary assessment of the possible consequences. In particular we cannot evaluate the influence of this new public on the result of the election.

Active, reading and writing Internet usage is still the privilege of a minority and a special demographic part of the population (well educated, above-average income, approximately 30 years old, and predominantly male). Therefore any direct influence on the election may be very limited or it may be considerably biased due to the skewed representativity of the forums' participants. An example for this bias is provided in the election forum of Wahlen.De, which includes a poll on prospective voting. According to the electronic votes on June 23rd of 1998 (still three months before the real election) only 4.58% are in favour of the CDU (which is at the moment the main government party), whereas 23.6% are for the Green party. Both these figures are highly unrealistic. This demonstrates quite clearly the demographic bias in the electronic medium.

What is more important at the moment, however, is that we are beginning to experiment with new forms of creating a public and public opinion. This may not lead to a "new" media democracy, comparable to the "old" TV democracy, but it may lead to a new kind of direct democracy. This new form of direct democracy will not replace the indirect representative forms of democracy but it may create a value-added effect, namely broader public awareness and participative responsibility for the whole society. As media theoreticians following McLuhan have pointed out, the medium not only influences the message but also the structure of the whole system of which it is a part. The medium, in this case the electronic communication forums, in particular when organized according to open system principles which allow forums to be interrelated, is the environment in which the whole system may gradually change.

TELECOMPUTER ART: DEMOCRATIZING THE CREATOR/SPECTATOR FRONTIER

Alejandro Piscitelli

World communication networks transmitting data, voice, and picture have existed for almost three decades. But they have become a new means of popular artistic expression only with the advent of Web sites five years ago.

Beyond their technical and economic significance,[1] these innovations allow interaction in the creative processes of communication, cooperation, democracy, and transparency in the human relations network.

---

1 M. Meeker and C. DePuy, *Morgan Stanley. The Internet Report* (New York: Harper Business, 1996).

THE ESTHETIC GLOBALIZATION OF CONSCIENCE

More than 20 years ago, Roy Ascott tried to make the new vision of the latest technologies converge with a practice of communications where transparency, symmetry between information producers and consumers, and the socialization of the means of expression would take over from classical art[2].

Artists like David Rokeby, Giovanna Colacevic and Robert Adrian have been attempting for a while to convert the forms of presence, outline a new space-time phenomenology, and create a new technical/organic mix. Among the highlights of this type of research was a Copernican change, which has diverted us from the quandary of the artist and his work to the more interesting subject of the conditions of its acceptance and the indivisibility of art production and consumption. These initiatives could have been restricted to an esthetic avant-garde with a propensity for the use of technology. But with the globalization of communications, they herald a new popular esthetic language.

In the early 1970s, Douglas Davis's televised performances via satellite, interactive sessions between cities like New York and San Francisco, the teledances of Galloway and Rabinowitz, and the first teletransmissions of Nam June Paik and Josef Beuys in Kassel's Documenta VI, paved the way for what is today a daily occurrence. In the early 1980s, artists like Robert Adrian X, who linked 16 cities for 24 hours across three continents with his "World in 24 Hours," portended the concern of the esthetic universe for the potential of telecomputing and the need to return art (and technology) to the ordinary people. The main notions featured in these works, and those of other members of the Graz or Ascott workshops, were the dissolution of the creative movement in the collective of the ordinary people, and the need to go beyond national, local, disciplinary, and ideological borders toward a globalization of conscience. These pioneers' intention was to promote worldwide creative networks, based on the intuitions of Wiener and cybernetics, but relying on the spectacular progress of communication networks, to carry out transnational esthetic projects.

---

2 Maria Grazia Mattei, "Arte telematica," in *Oltre il villaggio globale* (Milan: Ente autonomo, La Triennale di Milano, 1995).

THE TRANSFORMATION HYPOTHESIS

The computer epitomizes and surpasses the inventions of the human senses like language, writing, printing, and audiovisuals.[3] Such mode of creation changes our method of perception because new forms generate new mental states. As offspring of McLuhan,[4] we should not be surprised by this, especially since we never stop noticing the correlation between cognitive styles, the different hemispheric functions, and the construction of divided worlds.[5] We have also seen significant effects in the field of visualization.[6] Complex structures, phenomena and processes, which hitherto could only be imagined through an endless manual process, are now built with the digital image. Thus, a new type of interaction becomes possible between the senses and abstract intelligence.[7]

Digital imaging techniques induce a new way of looking. Unlike traditional representations, the digital image is essentially dynamic. Its horizon is the "utopian window" through which the entire universe can be seen in every imaginable scale and representational mode. A universe in which the spectator/actor can, upon oral commands, cause droughts, double the earth's population, make supernovas explode, or travel as far into the past or the future as his imagination will allow. In this universe, the distinction between the spectator and creator of images has finally disappeared.[8] How do digitalization and modularity affect our understanding of the link between art and society? Is telecomputer art obscure because it is unable to anticipate what is coming? And if classical art is also passé, are we witnessing the death of art? Would telecomputer art be the manner in which classical art renews itself and continues to give meaning to the computerized civilization?

3 Robert K. Logan, *The Fifth Language. Learning and Living in the Computer Age* (Toronto: Stoddard, 1995).

4 Marshall McLuhan, *Understanding McLuhan in the Electric World Change Is The Only Stable Factor* (Voyager, 1995, CD-ROM).

5 Paul Levinson, *The Soft Edge. A Natural History of the Information Revolution* (London: Routledge and Keegan Paul, 1997). The results of the use of computers for the creation of new visual worlds are well documented in H. Robin, *The Scientific Image From Cave To Computer* (New York: Harry N. Abrams, 1992). For a general study of the effect of digital technique on art, see L. Jacobson, *Cyberarts. Exploring Art and Technology* (San Francisco: Miller Freeman, 1992).

6 R. S. Wolff and Larry Yaeger, *Visualization of Natural Phenomena* (Santa Clara: Springer Verlag, 1993); Richard Saul Wurman, *Information Architects* (Hong Kong: Palace Press, 1996).

7 The most promising developments in this field are obviously those which involve an improvement of the interface, until the user merges (through verbal or even telepathic controls) with the machine. One of the most advanced sites of such research is MIT's Media Lab.

8 Howard Rheingold, *Realidad Virtual* (Barcelona: Gedisa, 1993); Ramón Gubern, *Del bisonte a la realidad virtual* (Barcelona: Anagrama, 1997).

For 25 years, digital technology has helped push back the frontiers of esthetic expression through the increase of processing speed and storage capacity, user-friendly interfaces, high-definition graphics, stereophonic sound, laser color printers, high-level programming languages, and an impressive array of peripherals useful to artists, like graphic pencils, scanners, and synthesizers.

As Cynthia Goodman, curator of the *Digital Dreams* exhibition, says: "For 20 years, computers have endowed some art works with visual effects of an unprecedented complexity. The whole relationship between spectators and art has been deeply transformed by the development of sophisticated interactive computer systems dominating art works that can truly be different for each viewer at every instant. The art *experience* is no longer visual. Seeing is part of the event."[9]

ART FOR WHOM?

Contrary to classic art, interactive art demythologizes form for the sake of the public who becomes a participant. The role of the artist is no longer to encode unidirectional messages, but to define a context open to experimentation. What is sought is not the author's or the participant's expression, nor the channel to communicate clear, distinct messages. Neither is it a pictorial space limited to geniuses as in the classical age.

These new trends are well represented on the Web, but the site of Brazilian Eduardo Kac is a case in point.[10] He has managed a new form of communication with his installation *Platypus on the Moon*, a project of telepresence between Chicago (USA) and Graz (Austria). By pressing the buttons of a touch-tone telephone, participants in Graz can control in real time the vision and movement of a platypus robot in Chicago and make it turn in any direction. By releasing the buttons, they send from one continent to the other a picture showing what the platypus sees. The public thus builds a work of art to its liking and its ability.

---

9 Carol Goodman, *Digital Visions, Computer and Art* (New York: H. N. Abrams, 1987).
10 See his site at < www.ekac.org >.

What matters is not so much the technological miracle of such systems — the incredible feeling they give of being somewhere else, or their practical military or commercial benefits — as the challenging of unidirectional communication specific to art (painting, sculpture) and the media (television, radio).

Kac — and he is not alone — believes the merger of art and technology is achieved in such experiments, resulting in the art of telepresence.[11] For Kac, the art of telepresence is disproving the social principle of organization, which says that what is closer to us is more important, real, or concrete than what is far, and that it is difficult to gain access to sidereal space. Hence, one of Kac's most recent productions, his *Life on Mars* essay, written on July 4, 1997, as the Pathfinder probe was landing on Mars, and published the next day on the World Wide Web. "I am trying here to bring out the cultural meaning of *telepresence* as experienced simultaneously by millions of people both on television and on the Web," Kac wrote. "The pictures may seem crude to high- definition video fans, but it should be recalled that they traveled 112.5 million miles in 10 minutes before being displayed on our screens. Our collective telepresence on the surface of Mars has given us a new image of the universe and ourselves. The feeling of telepresence was so strong that NASA technicians cried out with joy, *'We are there!'*" Since Pathfinder took seven months to reach Mars, the near instant transmission and reception of the pictures gave physics a very distinct proximity.

The other distinctive features of this experiment were the nature of the man-machine interface (the remote control of the long-range Sojourner space ship); the remote control of the robot; the instantaneity of the pictures; the live television broadcast; and the impact of the event on the collective conscience.

For an artist like Kac to try to present this event as an esthetic blessing shows that, beyond the technological paraphernalia, intelligence lies in the eye of the observing artist.

11 Alejandro Piscitelli, *Ciberculturas. En la era de las máquinas inteligentes* (Buenos Aires: Paidós, 1995).

THE ADVENT OF DIGITAL EXPRESSION

The eye of an era is the spirit of the era. Tell me how you see, and I will tell you what you think! Perceptual changes are multiplied by the conditioning to which we are subjected by our technological horizon and the transformation of the means of representation in keeping with our perceptual history.[12]

In the modern era, three major innovations (perspective, the camera, and cinema) have multiplied our viewpoints of the worlds we share. But human processes and interactions are never linear. We move simultaneously toward the past and the future. It is an organic progression, similar to the growth of a tree. A tree does not grow from the bottom up. It expands from the center, concentrically. Cut a section and you will see the concentric circles. Technological integration is achieved the same way in the artist's studio.

French painter Henri Matisse was well aware of it. Our senses have a development age which is not that of our immediate environment, but of the period of our birth. We were born with the sensitivity of our time and the civilizing phase counts more than what any apprenticeship may bring us.[13]

The current civilizing phase is characterized by the increasing presence of telecomputing as a means of linking information and esthetic research. The core of esthetic work in computing lies in the new aspects of picture processing, simulation, control, reinvention of reality, and interaction with our fantasies and those of others. The computer is a metatool incorporating its own program. Electronic tools have an occult aspect more complex than that of the painting brush, the printing press, or the camera. To think (electronically) is to have *everything*. [14]

12 In the past ten years, many studies have been published on the cultural roots of perceptual change. The majority of authors attach too much importance to the speed and acceleration of images, neglecting, curiously and unfairly, the role of sound and silence in the make-up of modern subjectivity.

13 We are from the generation that is no longer 20 years old. As time passes, and frustrations and nostalgia increase, our roots in the illusions and emotions of that golden decade go deeper. Perhaps, as so many adaptational psychology or sociology theories would have it, we reach maturity when we manage to neutralize this bewitchment. For others, including me, it is a sign of vitality never to break completely with childhood aspirations. Though we may accuse the computer of distorting the limits of our ability to create virtual worlds of unlimited freedom, the fact is that, in this sense, the computer updates our juvenile urges to rebel against the status quo. Although the machine and networks will more than likely be usurped, as were the counter-culture projects of the 1960s, the fact remains that they make a lot of noise and alter the status quo in a way that is worth exploring.

14 The computer introduces us to high-speed visual thought. If the relation between the artist and the computer can just as well be synergetic as parasitic, given their mutual dependence, the artist retains his right of veto at all times. McLuhan's theory that the medium is the message is being modified by the distinct manifestations of collective, interactive art. The recent advent of tridimensional surfing on the Internet also makes it possible to observe forms of esthetic experience yet unimaginable only a short time ago.

The digitalization of thought makes it possible to use telecomputing for the creation of music and the combination of sounds, text, movement, animation and pictures, opening unprecedented prospects for the esthetic experience. The computer facilitates the merger of artistic forms because a unique substrate contains all the information. The multiple perspectives of digital information go well beyond the metaphor of the photo bank. They are more like a personified model of Joyce's *stream of consciousness* where we constantly doubt that what we choose is significant at any critical instant. Telecomputing works curiously like the human memory in that we struggle to relive a version of the past to provide a context and an historic perspective for the messages received from total experience.[15] Digital expression allows the building, through this intelligent prosthesis, of *inside out* rather than *outside in* images, generating functions without images, contrary to classicism which represented what, hypothetically, preceded the observer's perception.[16]

Whoever has used a digital graphics or animation program, while conscious that the artist *is* always the user/programmer, knows that the individual realities of these interactions are but interpretations of the mind. Art is a true illusion, not an objective reality.[17]

Digital culture takes to its height what Vertov already suspected in 1923 when he claimed: "I am an eye, I, the machine, show them a world that I alone can see. I free myself once and for all of human stillness. I am in perpetual motion. I coordinate all points of the universe. My path leads to the creation of a fresh perception of the world."

Like Brassaï, the photographer, who believed that photography could free painting from all literature, anecdote and even themes, electronic collages, intelligent environments and esthetic initiation software once again defy our cognitive peace

15 This possibility is not necessarily borne out in the world of actions. One of the interesting corollaries of current research in neuronal networks is not so much their effectiveness, because it will still take decades, if not generations, for these programs to imitate human faculties, as the challenging of behavior models generated by social and human sciences.

16 This road taken by digital art finds an interesting echo in the parenthesizing of objectivity in constructivist epistemology. For a general introduction to the theme and a fascinating reconstruction of the pictorial universe and the cultural conditions that make some eyes see the world more or less realistically or idealistically, see Alejandro Piscitelli, *(Des-)haciendo Ciencia. Creencias, cultura y conocimiento* (Buenos Aires: Ediciones del Riel, 1997). Nevertheless, recent works cast doubt, once again, on the relativization of the categories of perception and insist on the existence of constant cross-historical perspectives which would not require any apprenticeship to build reality because they are innate.

17 A rich merchant who had commissioned Picasso to make a portrait of his wife complained to the artist after comparing a photo of his wife with the cubist representation he made of it. "Don't you see that it doesn't look at all like the picture," he said, outraged. Picasso retorted: "Don't you find the picture looks even less like her since it is much smaller than my painting?"

and end up destroying the little that is left of the classic ideals of pure art, above conflicts and uncluttered by technical or mercantile overtones.

NETWORKS AND THE RECONSTRUCTION OF SOCIOCULTURAL IDENTITIES

For more than 20 years, networks have provided scientists with an experimental medium for new forms of textual cooperation, and artists with an extraordinary means of probing the frontiers of communication. Today ordinary people have appropriated them, seeking to extend their limits of expression.

If the early examples of popular art (visual as well as musical or performance) remain poor and sporadic, following what happened with digital publishing, there is a lot to expect from these new tools that are multimedia, the World Wide Web and hybrid CD-ROMs for elevating the intelligence of ordinary people.[18]

When a largerlarger data capacity is offered on the Internet,[19] artists will direct their efforts on interactivity in a virtual environment, long-distance cooperation, participatory democracy, relations between the information society, democratic politics and installations. By paving the way so that what they do exceptionally is converted into a daily exercise of imagination, they have broken with cognitive inertia, they have cooperated decisively to push back the frontiers of imagination, and above all they have shown that it is possible to knit together this ambiguous discontinuity that until recently separated art from technology and the people.

Nobody guarantees that the Internet will be more esthetic nor that people like us, mere wordsmiths, will learn to develop our poor visualizing skills. But either of these possibilities will have to come about, or preferably both, if we are not to regress, and that would be unthinkable.

18 The abstracts made by Daniel Donnelly, which combine the flexibility of the paper with the access power of CD-ROMs referring directly to Web sites, provide an extraordinary example. Daniel Donnelly, *In Your Face. The Best of Interactive Interface Design* (Cincinnati: North Light Books, 1996); Daniel Donnelly, *Cutting-Edge Web Design* (Cincinnati: Rockport Publishers, 1998).

19 We are very skeptical of access in Latin America. But we don't want to overdo imitations and would rather insist on the possibilities offered by these metamedia. For a highly critical study of the possible reappropriation of knowledge technologies in Latin America, see Raul Trejo, *La nueva alfombra magica. Usos y mitos de Internet. La red de redes* (Madrid: Fundesco, 1996); and Alejandro Piscitelli, *¿Hay vida despues de la televisión? El platonismo en la era de Internet* (Buenos Aires: Paidos, 1998).

Participate, communicate, incorporate experiences. Such is the direction in which we encourage artists to reread and use the computer metamedia.

Today there are machines that play chess at the level of Grand Masters and win, as we saw recently with Kasparov, whose subsequent depression was well publicized. Perhaps one day a machine will rival our admiration for the works of Leonardo da Vinci. What is of interest is not so much who will win this pseudo-competition, but how our potential will expand through the effective use of these contraptions. In the realm of freedom, there is room for everybody, including cyborgs. Overcoming the resistance and interests of the world of traditional art has not been easy. Even today, although a majority of artists have adopted the new medium, there remain some for whom any flirtation with technical reproducibility contaminates an artist's work and, by eliminating the original aura, ends up denying it the status of art.

There is a long way to go before these still-too-spectacular technoworks come out of studios and museums to invade the street, public spaces, and especially the world of education. We are fighting for this moment to arrive soon and to benefit the greatest number.

THE INTERNATIONAL FEDERATION OF JOURNALISTS AND THE DIGITAL REVOLUTION: INTERESTS AND RESPONSIBILITIES

Christophe Dufflos

The New Information Technologies (NITs) do not fail to instigate an increasing number of questions as they force themselves daily on an ever-larger public of users, professional and otherwise.

The lightning progress of telematic networks, among which Internet remains the most publicized, signals the victory of a convergence promising a great future: the union of telecommunication operators, computer constructors, software editors, and developers of educational, informative or leisure programs. This progress makes entire series of activities, which formerly were separate, converge, and gives multimedia products — products containing texts, sounds, and images — more and more sophistication.

The technological ground-swell we are witnessing is a challenge to the professional and political responsibilities of the International Federation of Journalists (IFJ),[1] which must answer professionals' queries about the interpretation to be given to the technical developments affecting the working conditions of journalists.

In fact, questions arise as soon as the issue of new technologies and new media is raised. What is the responsibility of a world-wide professional organization in analyzing the present-day digital revolution and in implementing professional, educational, social, collective, and of course, technological solutions beneficial not only to the IFJ members, but also to the majority of people? How is the IFJ expected to react to the state of technological delerium affecting post-industrial societies? Which approach should this federation adopt in areas of the world afflicted with technological backwardness? How could and should the IFJ intervene in a debate with such huge political and social implications?

CHALLENGES BY NEW INFORMATION TECHNOLOGIES TO THE INTERNATIONAL FEDERATION OF JOURNALISTS

Challenges facing the IFJ are formulated in different terms according to various perspectives. Schematically, a distinction should be made between two different lines of approach: one, strictly technical, emphasizes advice and solutions to problems relating to computer software, hardware, and networks: the other, more general, takes into account some of the professional (including ethical), social, economic, and commercial consequences induced by the digital revolution.

---

1 Created in 1926 and started afresh in 1952 in its present shape, the International Federation of Journalists (IFJ) is journalists' largest world organization (it represents more than 420 000 journalists, among which 200 000 are represented within the European Federation of Journalists). The IFJ main office is in Brussels. The Federation has offices in Asia, Africa, and Latin America. The IFJ is recognized by the United Nations, the European Council, the European Union, and the European Organisation for Security and Cooperation.

The Technological Watch

The rapidly changing character of information and communication technologies requires that the IFJ follow-up any hardware or software innovation and evaluate its impact on the profession.[2]

It is indeed the responsibility of the IFJ, being an organization representing a profession, to provide the best information to its affiliated members. By refraining from such a technological watch, the entire organization could run the risk of being penalized. Therefore, the analysis of technological developments remains a firm obligation for the IFJ to its members. The IFJ has many other commitments that cause it to fear more general consequences of present technological changes.[3]

What Is a Journalist?

The rapid growth of the new electronic media raises the crucial problem of the professional legitimacy of journalists. Indeed, as an article published in the newspaper *Le Monde* (9 November, 1997) put it:

"The emergence of new means of communication available to all citizens is a threat to the traditional journalistic monopoly on information. Some are delighted in the name of diversity and plurality, which are badly flouted by the present media system. Others are worried by this situation, stressing the irreplaceability of journalists whose task is the selection and checking of news. Is a collaboration between journalists and non-journalists possible in order to get better information?"

This commentary finally calls for an answer to the following questions: What describes the specificity of journalistic work? What contributes to the identity of the journalist?

2 For instance, the problem of World Wide Web browsers takes all the attention of the IFJ. Indeed, newcomers regularly join the two big players in the browser market — Netscape (with Communicator) and Microsoft (with Internet Explorer). A recent example, among many others, is the HTML-text editor Web Construction Kit, sold on the Web as shareware. Another example is the navigator Opera 3.1, developed by a Norwegian society, Opera Software. The arrival of such challengers is synonymous with fairer competition, a matter that satisfies our organization. Similarly, public domain software products interest the IFJ, as it intends to encourage alternatives to commercial solutions characterized by their monopolistic trends.

3 We refer our readers to the articles of a Seminar held in Lille (France) in December 1997 dedicated to electronic journalism. Some of these seminar articles can be consulted on the Lille Journalism College Web site.

Newspapers Without Journalists

If we refer to the three following information Web sites: *BBC Online Channel,* *Drudge Report,* and *Kanda News Network,*[4] it appears that only the first site actually meets the overall requirements of journalistic professionalism. In fact, the BBC online editorial staff is made up of experienced and certified journalists whose method of processing information is in complete accord with traditional journalistic requirements.

This does not mean that the two other Web sites are regarded as lesser quality products. The *Drudge Report* (whose importance has just been emphasized in the Lewinsky scandal involving President Clinton) and the *Kanda News Network* (which sees itself as being the smallest digital TV station in the world), both have some of the characteristics of the new journalism whose distinctive feature is the high velocity of information processing and dissemination.

The *Drudge Report* and the *Kanda News Network* are the symbols of a system where, theoretically, any person in possession of computer hardware and relevant software knowledge can assume the title of journalist. Thus, there is a real danger of the proliferation of newspapers without journalists.

It has been said that the Web displays the best and the worst as to quality of information intended for the public. Undeniably true! The wild overflowing of electronic bulletins, online information magazines, and e-fanzines in which information delivered to readers is not systematically weighed and validated by professional journalists has to be carefully watched.

It is the responsibility of the IFJ to see that professional ethics requirements are evenly implemented across all types of media, whether they are traditional, new, or prospective. For that reason, the IFJ supports the definition and the adoption of an online good-behavior code. Any person wishing to become an information provider on the Internet should abide by it, in order to reduce the danger of manipulation or misinformation.

4 BBC Online Channel: < http://www.bbc.co.uk/inform/index.html >; Drudge Report: < http://www.drudgereport .com >; Kanda News Network < http://www.knn.com >.

Web Journalism and Internet Script

Web journalism, which is certainly a new form of journalism, shares with the World Wide Web its main characteristics, namely immediacy and interactivity, making more real every day the global village of Marshall McLuhan.[5]

Yet, the definition of electronic journalism still remains very confused. What does this definition encompass? Several elements must be accounted for. The added value of the online information, if compared to the written press, resides at first in its immediacy. The possibility of downloading data stored in a documentary database (files, archives, etc.) constitutes a second advantage exclusive to online services. Finally, the interactivity of new media eliminates, in a certain way, the invisible barrier separating readers from editing staff in traditional newspapers. Online editors had to invent a writing style suitable to their new medium. Consequently, a new "editing engineering", intended for electronic media, gradually evolved.[6] The digital newsroom is also defining its own rules. That is why the IFJ regard the modernization of the teaching techniques of journalism as a major challenge in coming years.

We do not wish to demonstrate in any case the existence of an impervious boundary between Web and traditional journalism! Examples abound of newspapers that knew how to cleverly bridge the gap between their paper edition and its digital partner.[7] Moreover, the Internet provides samples of these products, partly identical and complementary to those presented in the traditional media.

Our intention is to see that professional and ethical demands, which are today a must for affirmed and recognized journalists, will be applied tomorrow to the persons who will provide information to the Internet-users community.

---

5 Another Web feature that facilitates the establishment of this global village is the relatively low operating cost of an Internet site, whether this site is devoted to information, education, or leisure. This argument will have to be qualified when an online real edition (in the journalistic meaning of the word, i.e., including an editors' room) shall, continuously and in real time, make information available to the world network.

6 Maybe it is here that lies ultimately the specificity of the online journalist. The online editor would be defined, by not only his technical and software knowledge, but by his ability to take up this Internet style.

7 The French newspaper *Libération*, from this standpoint, offers the example of a successful synthesis between the paper edition and its digital version < http://www.liberation.fr > which is more than a mere reflection of the paper. Refer specifically to the "Cahiers Multimedia" of *Libération*, a section which exploits with discernment the potential of both print and electronic media < http://www.liberation.fr/multi/index.html >.

Media Concentration

Our Federation cannot overlook the economic and commercial aspects of the new media. Indeed, the narrowing gap between the worlds of information and commerce must neither be detrimental to the quality of journalism nor threatening to the status of journalists.

The IFJ must be aware from the beginning of developments in new electronic media, as is the case in the USA and Canada, which could result in ever-increasing employment of ill-paid, contract manpower, comprised mainly of free-lance workers and journalists.

Two other major problems must be dealt with by the IFJ: the creation of jobs linked to the development of new technologies in media, and the unsettled question of the intellectual copyright of journalists.[8]

TECHNOLOGICAL MUTATIONS AND POLITICAL IMPLICATIONS

Throughout its history the IFJ has evolved a whole body of texts whose content is directly or indirectly related to the effects of technological changes. The exponential growth of the Web since the opening of the nineties has required a re-thinking of the role played by the new technologies of information, within the journalists' community and in the society as a whole. A reading of the different texts generated by these analyses enables us to determine what courses of action the IFJ should undertake.

Access and Plurality

In a document entitled "The Information Society; Access and Plurality," the IFJ underlines that it is not convinced by the exclusively liberal approach taken, for instance, inside the European Union and the USA. This approach states that if the market is unregulated, benefits of the information society will automatically follow. Actually, within both these areas, the influence of powerful communication and information holdings is growing (mainly through lobbying and effec-

8 Both themes shall be elucidated, in the third part of this article, by examples of actions initiated by the IFJ within the scope of certain of its projects.

tive public relations) and has a tendency to disregard the interests of the great majority of citizens.

For that reason, the IFJ insists that journalists, who are the information experts, have a direct interest in the social and political dimensions of the digital revolution.

Redrawing Public Space

For the IFJ, the Web must induce a new definition of public space. In societies where this significant information mutation is taking place, everything must be done, with respect to the redesigning of this *res publica*, to strengthen the social and civic fabric.

Web sites of political institutions (international, national, or even regional), public administrations and associations should aim at the same objective.

By securing real democratic access to the NITs, the Internet will not remain the exclusive property of a cast of privileged users using it for their own information, leisure, and business purposes.

Electronic business will most certainly be of primary importance for the future development of the Web. However, commerce should never be given preference over the necessities of democracy and the respect of culture.

NITs are a unique opportunity for the world. To grasp it requires looking upon the online citizen first as an actor perfectly aware of civic obligations and, only after, as a cyberspace consumer.[9] Commerce should never annihilate the political potential of the Internet. The equality that exists between online citizens should encourage freedom of expression and its consequence, political plurality.

New Technologies and Job Creation

Another essential concern of the IFJ is the manner in which the NITs should create jobs. It is advisable, indeed, within the information society, to maximize the capacity for job creation. At first glance, however, we see that while the NITs lead to the creation of more jobs, notably in multimedia, they also massively wipe out more traditional professional functions.[10] From this standpoint, a quick comparison between the industrial revolution of the last century and the modern day

9 The term "cyberspace" was created in 1984 by William Gibson in his book *Neuromancer.*

10 The introduction of personal computers to editing rooms at the beginning of the eighties had already resulted in the cancellation of numerous intermediary posts.

digital revolution yields many lessons. Technological upheavals in the mid-nineteenth century necessitated, especially in the field of heavy industries, an unskilled but always increasingly numerous labor force. Contrary to this, the digital revolution, the result of science and technology, offers fewer opportunities and offers them to professionals with more sophisticated competence and expertise.

Surely, in the short-term, there will be a need for telecommunication cable layers to finish creating appropriate infrastructures for information highways. There will also remain job opportunities, during a limited time, for encoders to capture data to feed data banks.

But globally, what will be the balance between created and redundant jobs? Shall new jobs created by the NITs add to the uncertainty of employees and increase the number of outsiders' jobs (mainly free-lance journalists)? Nobody today can answer these questions with certainty.

The challenge confronting the IFJ consists in doing whatever is necessary so that political leaders, through their employment policies, will encourage the creation of permanent and equitably remunerated positions.[11] The technological revolution must not be used as an excuse for creating second and third class jobs.

Cultural Identities, the Sofia Declaration, and the Internet Charter

Respect for national, regional, and even local culture, is another forceful idea that the IFJ tries to defend daily. Defending national identity means protecting self-expression in the language of choice. The IFJ actively endorses the Sofia Declaration of the December 13, 1997 which it helped to prepare on the invitation of UNESCO. Finally, on the basis of all these strong positions and declarations of principle, the IFJ strongly recommends the publishing of an Internet Charter. Such a charter would fix general principles to delimit network objectives and moral obligations that would restrain users.

---

11 The Rights to Intellectual Property (RIP) focuses all the attention of the IFJ. In respect to authors intellectual property, the Federation has closely followed the action brought against Central Station by the General Association of Belgium Professional Journalists. Central Station was a project developed by Belgian publishers for online broadcast of about thirty publications. Employers refused to conclude an agreement to remunerate the journalists for the service they had provided. The European Federation of Journalists has supported Belgian journalists in this important battle to safeguard their copyrights. Belgian courts decided that the publishers had behaved illegally by creating such a network without obtaining beforehand the journalists' permission to reutilize their material. Nevertheless, editors preferred to give up the project rather than negotiate a deal with journalists. The EFJ deeply regrets that refusal.

PLANNING THE DIRECT RESPONSE: TOOLS DEVELOPED BY THE IFJ

Early on, the IFJ made the best possible use of its analysis of the issues at stake in the digital revolution. Within the limits of its responsibilities, it has developed a full set of actions encouraging its members to adopt and use the NITs in an optimal fashion.

So that the new technologies are not passively used by individuals, but wisely controlled by those involved with them, the IFJ and other professional organizations sharing identical analyses and objectives have agreed upon adopting a common strategy, partly based on the initiative of the International Committee of Entertainment and Media Unions (ICEMU).[12]

Declaration of Principle

The ICEMU initiated a *Declaration of Principle* adopted in Geneva on June 8, 1995, a document devoted to the information society. This document, which is a reference text as regards new technologies and union policy, indicates the main axis guiding the activities of the six international members of this committee.

Deriving assurance from this Declaration of Principle, the IFJ initiated and/or is a partner in some of the projects whose purpose is to prepare its members to accept present and future technological challenges.

JET PILOT, a project financed by the European Commission, intends to define a training structure particular to journalists working within the information society. Electronic journalism requires this new editing engineering. But the information society requires also that a European dimension be discerned in the continent's media if this new model of society is to be an example of a humanist society in which political, economical, social, and cultural components are not governed by market laws alone. By suggesting solutions in harmony with this new set of problems,[13] JET PILOT elaborates teachings beneficial to all journal-

---

12 ICEMU was created in 1991. It is composed of six international unions:
Communications International (CI), < http://www.ptti.ch >; Media and Entertainment International (MEI), < http://mei-its.org >; International Federation of Journalists (IFJ) < http://www.ifj.org >; International Graphical Federation (IGF); International Federation of Musicians (FIM); and International Federation of Actors (FIA).

13 It is a plural set of problems where training in new crafts, editorial innovation, and profession ethical requirements have — amongst other things — a capital importance.

ists working for the advent of a European information society. The IFJ is the organization in charge of the project coordination.

MUSENET is a feasibility study made by unions of the media sector with the support of educational and research organizations, and with financing by the European Commission. MUSENET aims at evaluating the needs of European media unions in the fields of information and training to ensure that they are adequate for the development of the information society.

Besides informing the unions and workers of the media sector on questions related to the information society, MUSENET services and applications take particular care in putting forward the utilization of new information and communication tools. The Centre of Activity of the European Commission Information Society (ISAC) supports the MUSENET project.

NITs and Developing Countries

The IFJ insists on participating in projects devoted to assisting journalists' associations in operating areas plagued by acute technological backwardness. While European journalists have more or less succeeded in managing the rapid changes generated by the NITs, African reporters continue to encounter two major hindrances to media development: censorship, and lack of resources. Even if access to the Internet develops slowly in Africa, some of the countries of the continent already have imposed very strict rules about what should be said online. At the same time, it appeared clearly that it was virtually impossible to block information coming from abroad from appearing on local networks. African organizations for the defense of freedom of expression have used the NITs to make sure that all dissident voices can be heard. Therefore, the IFJ was one of the founding members of the International Freedom of Expression Exchange (IFEX), an electronic network linking journalists' associations and groups defending freedom of expression all over the world. However, computers connected to the "network of networks", remain the privilege of a privileged minority. During a conference in Brussels,[14] the South-African vice-president Thabo Mbeki noted that more than half of all Africans have never made a telephone call in their lifetime.

14 G7 Conference on *Information Highways*, February 1995.

Most African media, whether public or private, cannot afford to start online editing. In order to meet this requirement, the IFJ was heavily involved in the establishment of Press Centers in Africa to enable journalists to get access to modern communication tools (computers connected to the Internet) as well as documentation .These Press Centers are accessible to all journalists, and in some countries they became nerve centers of the local media landscape. This system expanded as centers opened in Ghana, Tanzania, Burkina Faso, Togo, Mali, Burundi, Namibia, and Liberia. The IFJ is now trying to establish an electronic network linking these Press Centers to journalists' organizations outside of Africa. In this way, and through conferences, seminars and partnerships, the IFJ expects to remain a vigilant and lucid participant in the technological transition affecting the profession it represents. This transition, borne by the digital wave, is inevitable. Our Federation shall optimize its effects.

Monitoring the Concentration of the Media

One last field of operations in which the IFJ is expected to have its say, through the ICEMU, concerns a project entitled *Global Media Monitoring*. This project is set within the context of converging telecommunication and audiovisual technologies. This convergence is generating a new and broad global market, and presenting the union movement with new kinds of problems. Indeed, millions of workers, efficiently organized up to now in traditional sectors, now see themselves obliged to adapt to new employers, new styles of work and new threats to their conditions of work and regulations. This partnership with ICEMU could be considered a response of the union movement to an increasingly acute problem. In its pilot phase, this project is concerned with an international communication group, Bertelsmann. If the pilot phase is successful, a research office will be opened in the USA to focus exclusively on this type of monitoring.

CONCLUSION

Jean-Claude Guédon from the Université de Montréal noted, at the Lille seminar, the transitional character of the present publishing chain and its progression towards "direct creation in digital". This problematic, central to the profession, draws the attention of the IFJ and triggers its three responsibilities as an International General Secretariat:

▨ An informative responsibility — the analysis of technological mutations and their effects for the IFJ affiliates .

▨ An educational responsibility — the training of journalists on the skillful utilization of NITs, as well as the updating of the teaching of journalism techniques.

▨ A forecasting responsibility — studying future technologies and evaluating their utilization.

In the prospective restructuring of crafts devoted to the processing of information, the chief concern of the IFJ remains its contribution to the development of a professional space protecting the independence of publishing in all media.

The IFJ is equally aware of its more global responsibility, which is to enable the largest number of people to access the NITs under the best conditions. This position derives from its political responsibility as a civic organization.

The IFJ shall remain alert and vigilant as to appropriation, developments, access, and new utilization of the NITs. The Federation shall be careful not to give in to technological euphoria. In reality, NITs are only tools in the service of man; they should never be regarded as an end in themselves.

USES AND ABUSES OF NEW TECHNOLOGY: SOME LEGISLATIVE APPROACHES

ELECTRONIC NETWORKS AND HUMAN RIGHTS

Georges Ferné

"Our generation," says Donald J. Johnston, Secretary-General of the Organisation for Economic Cooperation and Development (OECD), "stands on the very cusp of the greatest technological revolution that mankind has ever faced. Some compare this age of electronic communication with the arrival of the Gutenberg press, or with the industrial revolution. Yet this revolution when it has run its course may have a greater impact on the planet than anything that has preceded. The applications of electronic transmissions are just beginning to be felt... and the breadth and depth of what lies ahead is only beginning to be fathomed. How and where we are educated, where and how we work and live, our health care systems, our shops, our commerce, our reading, our leisure... no part of human enterprise will be spared. Even our notions of sovereignty and governance could be profoundly affected."[1]

1 Donald J. Johnston, in *Electronic Commerce: Opportunities and Challenges for Government* (Paris: OECD, 1997).

The impact of information technology (IT) will be so extensive that it is no wonder many concerns have arisen about how to protect human rights and freedoms. New global networks like the Internet have also raised a number of questions about consumer protection, the safeguarding of privacy and human dignity, and the prevention of economic, social, and cultural exclusivity. These networks owe their rapid development to their capability for meeting the specific and general needs of a myriad of users. The convergence of these needs and developments has created an economic marketplace that opens up vast commercial perspectives. However, this marketplace is hard to regulate on a national basis since it also creates many possibilities for evading regulations by selecting platforms in countries with more lenient regulations, and by taking advantage of anonymity to mask illegal transactions. In providing a global framework for storing, processing, and transmitting information, these new networks create a wealth of possibilities which we still have difficulty imagining or quantifying.

A few examples are enough to illustrate this. To protect IT users, the identity and geographic location of players doing business or exchanging information over a network needs to be verified; the degree of trust of all players depends on it, as does the determination of which laws and regulations apply in the event of a dispute.

The protection of privacy is also endangered because the new technologies do not guarantee the confidentiality of transmissions on insecure networks, allowing access to a broad range of information about each and every Netsurfer. Networks also facilitate the routing of data on a global scale; information about business partners, clients, and contacts may be instantly and invisibly relayed to a country where the customary protection of privacy rules do not apply.

Furthermore, the anonymity of transactions and of data transmission facilitate illegal traffic and the dissemination of propaganda infringing on human dignity (about pedophilia, prostitution, or racial hatred, for instance). Lastly, as the new electronic environment becomes an indispensable arena for culture and trade, an inability to access networks will exclude certain elements within society or even certain countries by raising barriers that will be hard for them to overcome. Although such problems are not new and have been resolved to a certain extent by the creation of national regulations, the global dimension of the new networks presents an unprecedented challenge. No country by itself can claim to control the use of these networks in its territory without risking isolation from the emerg-

ing electronic marketplace and consequently condemning itself to exclusion from
the ensuing economic and employment growth.

NEW PARTNERS

Governments cannot afford to ignore these developments. The responsibility
they have to maintain order makes it imperative for them to insist on the right
to control information transmitted on networks in order to curb the development of electronic money-laundering systems and illicit traffic. However, many
individuals and business organizations have contested the necessity for such
control, claiming it endangers the right to privacy.

In addition, governments would like to define the conditions governing civil and
criminal liability online. The simplest solution would be to make access providers liable for content. Service providers, however, have argued against both the
injustice and the ineffectiveness of this measure; it is not easy to monitor content, particularly since a network permits surfers to visit sites around the globe.
Radically differing approaches often claim to be based on the same principle,
i.e., economic liberalism. From this perspective, the new economic environment
is expanding so dramatically that any untimely intervention by government could
be seen as endangering the future. It cannot be denied that problems exist, but
the public sector can be expected to come up with solutions to solve them. In
some cases these will be technical, such as the adoption of filters to enable parents and teachers to prevent minors from accessing certain sites. In other cases,
new practices will be introduced; for example, an access provider might require
notices to be posted indicating the nature of controversial sites. Lastly, some
solutions will be institutional, involving the creation of new intermediary business services to protect the identity of players and provide information about
them only with their consent.

How can we simultaneously limit the freedom of private players and the scope
of government intervention? The issue becomes even more complicated when
we consider that any government intervention in a field undergoing such rapid
technological change is, by definition, extremely problematic. Governments are
poorly equipped to define mechanisms of intervention that are both technologi-

cally neutral and effective, and which can provide the desired results without impacting adversely on whatever developments will emerge in future.

As long as one innovation follows another so swiftly, the situation is too unstable to permit anyone to determine exactly what safeguards are needed. But once a level of technological maturity characterized by less rapid and less widespread change has been reached, it may be too late to intervene because some situations have become irreversible. For instance, it is now already clear that an online economy enables certain players to carve out impregnable positions. We now all realize how difficult it is to revise processes for allocating addresses on the Internet, processes which were designed when the Net was still in its infancy. Tomorrow, the same may be said about processes for validating identity or centralizing personal data.

At the same time, the private sector does not always clearly perceive the extent of the dangers it must safeguard itself against. That states most often serve as guarantors of the identity of citizens and organizations is no accident of history. Only society as a whole can in fact be responsible for protecting itself against the risk of error or fraud in situations where the stakes are crucial; for example, in the case of terrorist acts. It is hard to imagine a private, profit-oriented organization agreeing to assume responsibility for risks of this magnitude.

The future of electronic-communications regulation will thus depend exclusively neither on private nor on public players but will require new forms of partnership between the two sectors.

In many cases, government organizations have had very little experience in working with the private sector. Furthermore, many players (associations, manufacturers, and distributors of staple consumer goods) have rarely felt the need to develop partnerships with government. But such partnerships will prove indispensable, and should be systematically encouraged and sustained.

The task is even more complicated because the main issues to be resolved call for international solutions, given the nature of emerging transborder networks. This is a huge challenge for international organizations and businesses of all sizes, which will have to be able to defend their interests, as well as for citizens, who will doubtless need new modes of representation. It will not always be easy to develop new forms of cooperation that strike a balance between involving a broad array of players and making effective decisions.

THE RIGHTS OF ELECTRONIC CITIZENS

Decision-making modes themselves will also undergo sweeping changes. Already, in the context of many national and international negotiations, groups of users and electronic communications providers have brought about tremendous change. Online discussions complement or replace meetings as a faster and cheaper way to develop policies. Technical agencies use electronic discussions to develop standards in a multitude of domains. In all countries, a growing number of government topics under consideration are submitted to Netsurfers, while politicians and institutions are opening their servers to comments and questions from the public.

The future of this electronic citizenship raises a number of questions. Specifically, how can we avoid the development of a cyberocracy, a society in which only a computerized elite and the most electronically literate pressure groups have the means to influence day-to-day decisions, thus limiting the scope of major democratic debates? How can we prevent more militant groups (who are often involved in not entirely legitimate ventures) from exerting excessive influence?

One of the major issues at stake is that access to and use of networks must be available to all classes of citizens. Economic, social, cultural or even linguistic differences between groups and countries could lead to considerable divisions. The existence of industrial and commercial interest groups so powerful that they can control the nature and the activities of users could also constitute a threat to democracy. Along with the need for national dialogues on the conditions of citizenship, there is a need to develop new global rules for developing and accessing networks.

Giving citizens access to networks promises to substantially extend the exercise of real citizenship, on both a national and a global scale. But translating the promise into reality by overcoming inherent inequalities and preventing misuse of the new technologies is no mean feat.

The concept of electronic democracy is thus the issue at stake. It is obvious that the emerging technologies offer democracy a new space for fostering greater citizen participation. However, to achieve this goal will require a huge effort on the part of our institutions to adjust and to visualize imaginative solutions.

FREEDOM OF EXPRESSION AND LAW

Pierre Trudel

Freedom of expression and other human rights are components of human freedoms and dignity. All are essential to the existence of freedom and dignity. They are even inherent in the existence of a society ruled by law. But freedom of the press and other rights are stated rhetorically as if there were never any situations where it becomes necessary to determine their scope. As these principles are the equivalent of rules, they inevitably have a general character strengthened by the formality of their proclamation. Therefore, the effectiveness of freedom of expression is dependent on mechanisms that determine its limits in relation to the other values and rights. To describe the dimension of the freedom of expression proclaimed in the Universal Declaration of Rights, we have to see how the concept is defined in contemporary international law.

The evolution of freedom of expression has paralleled the development of the media and techniques for the production, storage, and distribution of information. A stable historical trend is apparent in the development and expansion of the scope of freedom of expression: there is a relationship between the advent of new information production, distribution, and conservation techniques, and the measure of freedom extended to citizens.

At each stage of development of communication techniques, states created mechanisms to control the media. Thus, the invention of the printing press coincides with the *imprimatur* and the grant of printing monopolies. With cinema came censorship. Radio was in every country of the world subject to a license to use the air waves to broadcast programs. The current debate on state regulations and the regulation of other sources in cyberspace reflects this constant, recurring tension between the potential of the media and the limits to freedom of expression.

THE MAIN COMPONENTS OF FREEDOM OF EXPRESSION

In its current state, freedom of the press means the right to print, criticize, and report. This is mitigated when media use resources said to be public, like Hertzian waves.

The Right to Print

Freedom of expression is often thought to have coincided with the abolition of printing licenses. Thus, in England, the first printing press dates back to 1476, but it was only in 1694 that licenses were abolished. The right to print and publish was then recognized, but printers and publishers remained accountable for seditious and other illegal publications.

So, the right to print without a license was recognized some two hundred years after the introduction of the technique of printing. Cinematography followed the same pattern. In many countries, the right to present films was subject to authorization. Even today, throughout the world, the right to broadcast radio and television programs is subject to licensing by the state. In some countries, people are required to file a statement, even seek government authorization, to connect to the Internet.

The Right to Criticize

The recognition of the right to criticize did not coincide with the right to print. In many countries, strict legislation limited the right to criticize government. Thus, in eighteenth-century England, and even in the United States before the First Amendment was adopted, laws on seditious publications made it unthinkable for the press to blame government.

Criticizing the operations of the state or government was deemed illicit. Worse still, the accuracy of the criticism was not admissible as a defense. Quite the opposite, it was felt that the bigger the truth, the bigger the offense. Serious limits to the right to criticize persist in the laws of many countries. They are often based on an exaggerated concept of the right to reputation and privacy.

The Right to Report

The right to report is the least protected of the three, yet it is essential to the exercize of the other two. Of what use is the right to print or criticize if one can't get the facts or the news? So, it is agreed that for the press to exercise freedom, more than a mere proclamation of this freedom is required. A combination of immunities and the right to access places and events is needed.

This is why many journalists' associations measure freedom of the press by the immunity rules protecting those who report the statements of elected officials relevant to public debates. Journalists' demands to protect information sources are consistent with these rules.

THE RECOGNITION OF THE FREEDOM OF EXPRESSION

The main notions pertaining to freedom of the press developed and spread in the cultural universe of late nineteenth-century Europe. At the time, the rest of the world, with the exception of the United States, pretty well kept out of changes occurring in Europe, where the press was enjoying considerable development coinciding with the conquest of freedom. Technical advances made the production and distribution of newspapers cheaper. Economic development helped finance press activity, while the higher level of education of the population increased readership.

The greater press freedom helped create conditions for expanding the scope of freedom of expression. The abolition of censorship was accompanied by mechanisms articulating conflicting rights and values. From that point on, the limits to freedom of the press theoretically had to be based on the defense of other values, ranging from reasons of state to basic individual rights (like the right to reputation and privacy).

Nearly every constitution recognizes freedom of the press. The practice has now spread enough to conclude the existence of a true legal principle recognized by all states. In addition, freedom of the press is explicitly recognized in many international texts that have acquired manifest authority.

In practical exchanges between states, the principle of freedom of information was not asserted until after the Second World War. At its first session, the United Nations' General Assembly stated that "freedom of information is a fundamental human right, and the touchstone of all freedoms the United Nations vow to defend."[1] In 1948, the Universal Declaration of Human Rights incorporated in Article 19 the following text adopted by the United Nations' Conference on Freedom of Information:

"Everyone has the right to freedom of opinion and expression: this right includes freedom to hold opinions without interference and to seek, receive and impart information and ideas through any media and regardless of frontiers."

However, when we look at the practical terms of the exercise of this freedom, deep differences appear. Even though many international texts indicate massive support for the principle, the enforcement of the corollaries of freedom of expression remains embryonic at the international level.

Discussions held at the United Nations since the Conference on Freedom of Information in Geneva in 1948 bear witness to this situation. The final act of the conference on April 22, 1948, was the drafting of conventions on the international gathering and transmission of information, the international right of reply, and freedom of information. To this day, only the Convention on the International Right of Reply has been enacted. The adoption of the other two would have required consensus on the practical content of freedom of information. The documents of the 1948 Conference, which first drew the attention of the international community to information problems, remain a source of inspiration and

1 Resolution 59(1), December 14, 1946.

serve as a basis for the work that the United Nations laboriously carries on.[2] According to Roger Pinto, this clearly shows that "there is an international consensus on the principle of the freedom of information and opinion."[3] Agreement is far more difficult to achieve on some of the concrete implications of the principle.

In 1960, the Social and Economic Council adopted a draft statement on "freedom of information, a basic human right." The draft included an explanation of what freedom of information really involves.[4] While reaffirming the inalienable character of the right to freely seek the truth, or seek, receive, and impart information, the draft imposes obligations on governments and sets limits to the exercise of freedom of expression. These presuppose that governments cannot merely assert the principle without bothering to enforce it. Article 3 states that information must be at the service of the public and, therefore, precludes the idea that governments or public or private organizations can exercise control to prevent the existence of a diversity of sources of information or deprive individuals from freely accessing these sources. Finally, the obligation imposed on whoever imparts information to see in good faith to the accuracy of the facts reported, and to respect the dignity of others, completes this attempt to flesh out the principle of freedom of information.

Since 1960, this draft statement has been studied by the Third Commission (social issues) of the General Assembly. Although no clear objections have been formulated, this study has failed to bring about an official declaration. The draft convention on freedom of information had the same fate; its preamble and Articles 1 to 4 were only adopted in 1961. These include a declaration of principles, excluding state control of information inspired by discrimination based on race, sex, or religion, and a list of limits to the freedom of expression.[5] Since then, member states have not found the time to further the project.

However, the debate has been altered somewhat with the enactment of the International Pact on Civil and Political Rights and the Final Act of the Helsinki

2 About this conference, see "La conférence des Nations Unies sur la liberté d'information," *Revue générale de droit international*, no 52 (1948), pp. 518-565.

3 Roger Pinto, "La liberté d'information et d'opinion et le droit international," *Journal du droit international*, no. 108 (1981), p. 479; Pierre Trudel, "Réflexion pour une approche critique de la notion de droit à l'information en droit international," *Cahiers de droit*, no. 23 (1982), pp. 847- 871; Karim Benyekhlef, "Liberté d'information et droits concurrents : la difficile recherche d'un critère d'équilibration," *Revue générale de droit*, no. 26 (1995), pp. 265-306.

4 R. Pinto, *op. cit.*, p. 481.

5 The text of the draft is excerpted from R. Pinto, *op. cit.*, pp. 481-482.

Conference. It should also be noted that many international conventions lay down the principle of freedom of information in various sectors. Thus, the UNESCO Charter states that the Organization will:

"Collaborate in the work of advancing the mutual knowledge and understanding of peoples, through all means of mass communication and to that end recommend such international agreements as may be necessary to promote the free flow of ideas by word and image."[6]

No doubt, the Convention on the International Right of Reply is, in the current state of the law, the best form of recognition of the right to information as it aims to "make effective the right of people to be informed completely and loyally."[7]

The Convention on the Elimination of All Forms of Racial Discrimination also sanctions the right to freedom of expression, just like the International Pact, which formulates it in greater detail than the Universal Declaration of Human Rights. Article 19 states that:

▓ Nobody can be harassed for his opinions.

▓ Any person has the right to freedom of expression; this right includes the freedom to seek, receive, and impart information and ideas of any kind, regardless of frontiers, in oral, written, printed or art form, or by any other means of his choice.

▓ The exercise of the freedoms listed in paragraph 2 of the present article imposes special duties and responsibilities. It may therefore be subject to certain restrictions which, however, must be expressly set down by law and which are essential to a) the respect of the rights or reputations of others; and b) the safeguard of national security, public order, health or morals.

On the other hand, the Final Act of the Conference on Security and Cooperation in Europe (Helsinki, 1975) is the basic document cited by those who claim the freedom of information.[8] The Final Act does not impose true obligations.[9] Yet,

---

6 R. Pinto, *op. cit.*, p. 483. See also Stephen Marks, "UNESCO and Human Rights: The Implementation of Rights Relating to Education, Science, Culture, and Communication," *International Law Journal* (Texas), vol. 35, no. 13 (1977), p. 52.

7 Canada is not a signatory to this convention. See UNO, *Collection of Treaties*, vol. 435 (1962), pp. 193-203.

8 The provision relevant to our topic reads as follows: "2. Information. Member States set as their objective to facilitate the freer and wider spreading of information of any nature, encourage cooperation in the field of information and the exchange of information with other countries, and to improve the conditions in which journalists of a member State practice their profession in another member State and express their intention to help improve the distribution, on their territory, of newspaper and printed publications, periodical or non-periodical from other member States."

9 See on this issue Jean-François Prévost, "Observations sur la nature juridique de l'acte final de la conférence sur la sécurité et la coopération en Europe," *A.F.D.I.*, vol. 21 (1975), p. 129.

according to Jean- François Prévost, it expresses the unprecedented consensus of 35 states on problems of great importance for international peace and security.[10] Among these, of course, is the information that is the object of what can be qualified as unprecedented commitments by the signatory states,.

The Final Act comprises clear statements of intentions, including three sets of measures. The first has to do with improving the distribution of information, access to information, and the exchange of information.[11] To promote cooperation in the area of information, member states agree on measures of encouragement. They agree to promote greater cooperation between media and news agencies, facilitate travels and stays of foreign journalists on their territory, facilitate contacts with information sources and the temporary import of technical equipment, and guarantee the full transmission of the results of their professional activity. The signatories to the Final Act reaffirm that journalists cannot be expelled for the legitimate exercise of their professional activity.

The Final Act also includes measures that would likely improve the movement of information between states. Thus:

"Member states, eager to improve conditions in which journalists exercise their profession on each other's territory, intend to: look favorably upon, and process within reasonable and appropriate time limits, visa applications submitted by journalists; and grant permanently accredited journalists from member states, under arrangements, multiple-entry and exit visas for specific periods."

The debate on the new international information order has had the merit of pointing out the limits of the principle of the free flow of information. For Roger Pinto, "this new order first involves remedying technological and professional inequalities suffered by the Third World, and this through the assistance of industrial countries and international organizations."[12]

This debate began during the study of a draft statement on the contribution of the press in "strengthening peace and international understanding, promoting human rights, and fighting racism, apartheid, and incitement to war." The initial draft mentioned the use of information media in the struggle against racism and other evils, which suggests that media work is confined to narrow goals. Not

10 J.-F. Prévost, *op. cit.*, p. 130.

11 The excerpts from the Final Act of the Conference on Security and Cooperation in Europe are drawn from the *International Commission for the Study of Communication Problems - Communication: Excerpts from International Instruments* (document no. 22), pp. 20ff.

12 R. Pinto, *op. cit.*, p. 485.

surprisingly, the draft met with keen resistance from Western media and governments, although the version finally adopted no longer spoke of media "use," but "contribution." The statement especially appealed to the moral and professional responsibility of the media and formally reasserted the principle of freedom of information. Nonetheless, many Western media felt such a statement would serve to legitimize state control of the media and restrict the activity of the media that were still free. One of the main instigators of this concept, Mustapha Masmoudi, said that "far from threatening freedom of the press [the idea] tends rather to expand this freedom by multiplying information sources and thus offering a much broader range of choices."[13]

The International Commission for the Study of Communication Problems, chaired by Sean McBride, also showed the difficulty of actualizing the principle of freedom of information and the right to information in the international order.[14] While we can deplore that the report is only a summary of current thoughts and ideas on world communication problems, it has at least the merit of presenting attempts to go beyond the ambiguous concepts of freedom of information and the right to information.

Unanimous support for the principle of freedom of information and the right to information is a little suspicious. It is aided by the ambiguity of the notions. The countries subscribing to it in fact have widely divergent views of what freedom of information and the right to information are or should be.

This generates deeper consequences. The maintenance and protection of freedom of information have become an "international obligation" or, at the very least, a value over which the unfavorable perception of the international community can be embarrassing for a state.

Such recognition, though timid, is the foundation of this "international regulation." While we cannot contemplate an international tribunal setting and enforcing rules on a sovereign state for now, the development of international customs and principles stating the inviolability of freedom of information, makes it an international standard.[15]

---

13 Cited by R. Pinto, *op. cit.*, p. 488. See also M. Masmoudi, *The New World Information Order*, document no. 31 of the International Commission for the Study of Communication Problems.

14 The Commission was launched following the Nairobi Conference in 1976. It was chaired by Sean McBride, winner of the Nobel Peace Prize and founder of Amnesty International.

15 This is now the prevailing opinion about the Universal Declaration. See Réal Forest, "La Charte internationale des droits de l'homme de l'ONU," in Michel Lebel, Francis Rigaldies, and José Woehrling, *Droit international public-Notes et documents*, (Montréal: Éditions Thémis, 2nd edition, 1980), p. 805ff.

In such a context, the resulting problems of actualization cannot be dismissed. The absence of constraining mechanisms makes it impossible to conceive of freedom of information in international law as anything more than the affirmation of a need for a balanced flow of information. While it is possible to achieve this ideal flow of information in domestic law through constraining regulating mechanisms, the principle of state sovereignty leaves only the weight of custom and the rhetorical force of principles as means to attain this goal.

THE REALITY OF THE GUARANTEES OF FREEDOM OF EXPRESSION

There is no consensus on the definition of freedom of the press, since every state has its own interpretation of freedom of expression. Of course, this situation affects the reality of international guarantees of freedom of the press. Therefore, it is appropriate to look at the processes which determine the limits of freedom of the press and the rights competing with it.

The State of the Law

As we are reminded by Jacques-Yvan Morin, "[...] neither individual rights and freedoms nor the democratization of societies are possible if the political power is not subject to rules, that is, if the state is not legitimate."[16] While acknowledging there is more than one way of building a legitimate state, there is no point in talking about the effectiveness of freedom of expression in a context where a legitimate state does not exist, since the real content of freedom of the press lies in judicial or regulating processes, i.e., limits set to it. The ultimate guarantee of this freedom is the assurance that the process determining its limits is open and transparent. The concrete meaning of rights and freedoms is not a matter of definition, but primarily a matter of process harmonizing the different values which sometimes come into conflict in every society.

---

16 Jacques-Yvan Morin, "L'État de droit : émergence d'un principe du droit international," *Recueil des cours, Académie de droit international*, no. 254 (1995), p. 447.

Factors Determining the Limits

The rights in question in the movement of information are all linked. When one or more contradictions need to be resolved between fundamental rights like freedom of expression, the nature and limits of each right and freedom need to be identified, and then the limits of these rights need to be structured and harmonized.

For instance, there is certain information which, in given circumstances, is included in the protected area of privacy. This is delimited by the requirements of the exercise of other rights and freedoms, such as freedom of expression. From these requirements are derived the limits to the right of privacy. But it then becomes necessary to see how courts go about determining the respective limits of the various interacting rights.

It is difficult to clearly separate private and public life, but it is possible if we recognize their obviously relative character. By considering structuring factors between privacy and the other values they must protect, courts manage to identify this limit. Most of the time, the scope of a right or freedom is defined by the limits proceeding from the imperatives of another right or freedom claimed against it. For instance, to determine the limit of media freedom to divulge information about the private lives of persons occupying public functions, we need to identify the nature of the rights in question, the hierarchical relation between them and factors to be taken into account to set the respective limits of the rights.

Depending on the country, this process is carried out by the legislator or a judge. They often refer to vague standards or notions, like public interest, the right of the public to be informed, or the "requirements of public information." These notions play an essential role in determining the concrete scope of the rights relating to information since they contribute to structuring the limits of such rights. This is why they are called structuring factors.

The Public Interest

The notion of public interest[17] is one of the main structuring factors of the reciprocal limits of rights and freedoms. It is a principle expressed or inferred by laws. In any case, it is an issue that nearly always takes on a plurality of meanings.

17 On this issue, see: Emmanuel Derieux and Pierre Trudel, *L'intérêt public, principe du droit de la communication* (Paris: Éditions Victoire, 1996).

A Principle Expressed

Public interest is sometimes defined in principle by the legislator as he proceeds to delimit conflicting rights and values. It is then used to argue that limits to rights are justified by the need to harmonize the interests of individuals with the public interest, which is a founding principle of rights and obligations defined in the texts.

Communication legislation is often presented as policing legislation. It determines the framework of freedoms by setting a priori limits justified by the need to harmonize the interests of individuals with the public interest.

Thus, public interest, understood as the preservation of the conditions for the existence of a democratic debate and pluralism, is at once a motive for the intervention of the law and, sometimes, a limit to conceivable interventions. This process of delimitation has different levels of achievement. Sometimes, the demarcation is effected very precisely. In other cases, it is provisional, seems inconsistent, and in every case perfectible. Whatever it is, public interest is postulated because it justifies and legitimizes the legislator's choices, which the interpreter endeavors to take into account in the review process. The determination of the public interest does not proceed from an exegesis of the text, but supposedly from the legislator's wisdom.

Then, there can arise a difficulty resulting from the gap between what is said to correspond to the public interest in the law, and the various perceptions of this interest which may coexist, or even oppose themselves in civil society. Communication law offers many examples of this, like the controversies arising from the regulation of advertising. In short, it is easier to assume that the legislator is acting in the public interest when there is a consensus on the issue or the solution. In other situations, the legislative decision is a subject of controversies revolving around what should be considered in the public interest.

An Issue

The notion of public interest forces the interpreter to weigh opposing interests, decide between values and issues, and set concrete limits to the various conflicting fundamental rights. The notion of public interest takes on the appearance not of a right likely to produce by itself prerogatives, but a legal tool, a frame of reference, to help resolve a contradiction proceeding from the conflicting affirmation of a right to impart information and a right to prevent such information from being imparted. Such rights, linked to the pluralism of information or the transparency of the judicial process, can only be defined concretely in their relation to other rights and freedoms. Standards and notions demand that the interpreter inquire as to what is acceptable in the community where the decision is to be enforced. This leads to the recognition that the notion of public interest has a plurality of meanings and that these meanings are established within the framework of multiple processes, ranging from judicial and professional forums to the more diffuse processes of common sense and ethical considerations.

The Plurality of Meanings

The notion of public interest may have a plurality of meanings, which can all claim some legitimacy. This is why it becomes the center of issues opposing various interest groups in civil society.

Seldom do the definitions of this notion win unanimous support. Where such unanimity exists, it often becomes easier to spell out a priori and in detail the different rights and obligations of the actors, as well as their respective limits. Without unanimity, a rule is stated, leaving the interpreter to ponder the public interest. This involves resorting to a standard that will guide decision-makers in their arbitration. The meaning of the notion of public interest will then be determined as concrete situations arise.

THE DETERMINATION OF THE MEANING

The proclamation of conflicting freedoms (freedom of expression, privacy) occurs within a judicial system. Outside this system, freedoms, like rules, have no compelling meaning. This is why the determination of the practical meaning of public interest is an issue. This issue opposes the various pressure groups, which have an interest in seeing one meaning prevail over another.

While the notion of public interest finds a readily-compelling meaning in the judicial system, other systems contribute in defining rules and rights. The significance of the notion results from the combined action of a plurality of normative systems within the social environment. It proceeds from the coexistence of provisional and permanent arbitration in pluralist societies.

We can talk of heavy systems, such as the political system, political and judicial institutions, moral standards, customs.[18] In these settings, there is a commonality of interpretation, from which stems the meaning of rights and freedoms. This commonality generates reference points enabling us to resolve contradictions. Legal knowledge here appears to be decisive.

The meaning of the notion of public interest is also defined in diffuse systems: morality, ideology, common or commonly-admitted beliefs, more or less widespread representations and fantasies in civil society. In short, the common sense of the time, the morality found in the social body as a whole.

No source of law, not even legislation, can act definitively on the emergence of concepts or approaches spontaneously combined, confronted and recombined. The refinement of reasoning, concepts, and perceptions, which make up the norm of what the public has a right or a legitimate interest to know, goes through the maintenance of an alert society in which various concepts and systems can be in opposition.[19]

The arguments leading to the articulation of the fundamental rights and values related to communication activities draw from both dense and diffuse systems. They appear in deontology, and are settled in law through court decisions or in doctrinal analyses. These systems contribute, by their synergy, in determining the meaning of rights and freedoms. To ensure that the meaning given to the notion of public interest reflects at all times the underlying values of the rights and freedoms in question, it is important to maintain a balance between the different sites of research and determination of the meaning of notions such as privacy and freedom of the press.

18 Philippe Jestaz, *Le droit* (Paris: Dalloz, 2nd edition), p. 25ff.

19 Christian Atias, *Savoir des juges et savoir des juristes. Mes premiers regards sur la culture juridique québécoise* (Montréal: Centre de recherche en droit privé et comparé du Québec, 1990), p. 110.

THE COROLLARIES OF FREEDOM OF EXPRESSION

Once proclaimed, freedom of expression has normative and practical consequences that appear in the operations of the media. Among the main corollaries proceeding from freedom of the press is the right to publish, but also the responsibility of the one who exercises this editorial freedom, that is, who determines what is published. Finally, freedom of expression would hardly be significant without the right to receive the information imparted.

Freedom to Publish or Editorial Freedom

Editorial freedom is the form taken by freedom of expression when applied to the media as an entity.[20] It has long been recognized that governments do not have the power to interfere in media operations. The principle of editorial freedom reserves to the broadcaster, apart from any other authority, the right to decide the content of broadcasts.

Editorial freedom presupposes in principle the autonomy of decisions relating to the choice, treatment, and publication of information. As a corollary, there is a responsibility: the holders of editorial freedom have to account to a third party for the information broadcast apart from any other person.

Editorial Responsibility

The publisher publishes information. Publishing means imparting information to third parties, knowing that this information will be read, seen or heard. Since the publication is made voluntarily, it presupposes a knowledge of the content of the information imparted.

The decision to publish belongs to the publisher. He has the power to publish, but it is not an obligation. In the world of press and publishing, it is customary to hold that the director of a publication is in a position to ensure the accuracy of the information published by his enterprise.[21] From this power proceeds the responsibility for imparting harmful information.

---

20 Susan D. Charkes, "Editorial Discretion of State Public Broadcasting Licensees," *Columbia Law Review*, no 82 (1982), pp. 1161 and 1172.

21 Pierre Trudel and France Abran, *Droit de la radio et de la télévision* (Montreal: Éditions Thémis, 1991), pp. 292ff.

Public Organizations and Editorial Freedom

Democratic tradition, cultural traits, and political morals count for a lot in the degree of importance attached to the autonomy of the audiovisual public service in relation to political authorities. Nevertheless, the audiovisual public service can only truly play its role if it has a real measure of independence from political authorities. It cannot be submitted to a hierarchical authority of political leaders. These only exercise a restricted administrative supervision.

The analysis of the status of public radio and television has to take into account the importance of editorial freedom.[22] We can't analyze the status of a public corporation dedicated to the mandate assigned to it without taking into account the primacy and consequences of editorial freedom. Public broadcasting organizations are not government broadcasters, but public broadcasters — the difference is important. The analysis of their status must take into account the requirements of freedom of expression and the need for appropriate mechanisms to ensure the sound management of the public funds put at their disposal.

The characteristics of the national systems regulating television result from the particular features of the various countries and the imperatives or constraints flowing from their history and their political, economic, and geographic environment. It is therefore essential, in any reflection on the status of public radio and television, to take these into account and to act according to their dynamics and political traditions. We must, in particular, get away from approaches based on applying solutions that worked in another country. In this respect, there are few ready-made solutions: it is a world requiring tailor-made approaches. On the other hand, problems experienced in other contexts can usefully be considered in the light of solutions and experiences lived in other contexts. However, this is not an excuse to justify denying the principles of editorial freedom.

The Right to Receive Information

The right to receive information is considered inherent in freedom of expression. Thus, the International Pact on Civil and Political Rights states that the right to freedom of expression "includes the freedom to research, receive and spread information and ideas of any kind." Thus, there is in the notion of the free flow of

22 Pierre Trudel and France Abran. "La compatibilité des mécanismes de détermination du financement public de la Société Radio-Canada avec la liberté éditoriale," *Revue juridique Thémis*, no. 31 (1997), pp. 149-201, *Pour un financement de la radiotélévision compatible avec la liberté d'expression, Décision du Tribunal constitutionnel allemand du 22 février 1994 et commentaires* (Montreal: World Council of Radio and Television, 1996).

information the recognition of some right to receive information. But if this right to receive is already included in the freedom of expression, what is the purpose of designating as right to information a basic freedom whose ins and outs are already well established?

The right to information is also a fundamental right. For some, it is a sort of extension or synonym of freedom of the press or freedom of expression. We can then wonder if this designation of right to information adds anything to the edifice of fundamental rights.

The inclusion of the notion of the right to information in the debate proceeds from a criticism of the liberal concept of freedom of the press and coincides with the emergence of a more social notion of information. After the Second World War, criticisms of the liberal concept of freedom of the press multiplied. It was argued that freedom of expression, as understood in liberal philosophy, appeared as an official freedom ignoring situations of inequalities. A more social notion of information was put forward, based on its role in the flow of information within civil society, while the objectives of information in relation to the receiving public were stressed.

It was enough for many media to claim the right of the public to information, rather than freedom of the press. Should we see in this a search for renewed legitimacy, in the face of criticisms formulated against the press and its excesses in most Western societies, or an attempt to base media freedom on a purpose more respectful of readers and viewers?

The notion of the right to information is at once a value-right or a slogan, because it has considerable evocative strength. This evocative strength is perhaps not foreign to the fact that the right to information appears as the basis of standards used to interpret legal rules applied in litigious contexts. But, in certain situations, the right to information appears as a due right, carrying obligations for the possessor of the right or for the state. Sometimes, like in the Spanish constitution, it appears in the form of a container right, including other rights and freedoms.[23]

But most often, it is a well-delimited right with clear obligations in precise situations. Such demands are then expressed in specific texts and do not result from the proclamation of the general principle of the right to information. It is often

---

23 Carlos Soria and Emmanuel Derieux, "Le droit à l'information dans la constitution espagnole," *Revue de droit public* (1985), pp. 1205-1238.

through a doctrinal effort of systematization and search for consistency that we see a set of rules grouped under the term of "right to information." This expression sometimes specifies powers pertaining to already known legal notions, like freedom of expression and access to documents held by public organizations. Thus, access to one's personal file is assimilated to the right to information, but it is often because of the recognition of the right to privacy that this power is recognized to the possessor of the right as a corollary to a right of control of the information concerning him.

Likewise, it is to enforce freedom of expression that the right of access to public documents has been recognized in certain countries. The right of obligations sometimes recognizes that one of the parties possesses, toward his cocontractor, a right to demand certain information, like the information that must be divulged to a patient in a contractual or legal relationship on medical care. There again, this due right to certain information does not result so much from the proclamation of the right to information as from the obligations peculiar to certain legal relations.

Most often, the right to information does not in itself generate any obligation for the administration or individuals: it is an objective to attain, for which interest groups mobilize.[24] Its practical enforcement may require the development of a more precise legal framework, such as laws on access to documents held by public organizations and on the protection of personal information which determine the content of fundamental principles governing the management of documents held by public administrations. These texts determine clear obligations regarding information which this right may justify, but they produce their own legal effects, and not because of the existence of the principle of the right to information.

This right to information also points out the interest of considering the right of the public to information as a factor determining the limits of the freedom to inform or not inform in certain circumstances. The jurist's basic work is to identify the respective limits of rights and freedoms. Resolving the contradictions between fundamental rights is not an easy task. The common experience of Western countries teaches us that we must always resign ourselves to entrusting to the courts the thankless function of arbitrating between conflicting values and

---

24 Pierre Trudel, Jacques Boucher, René Piotte, and Jean-Maurice Brisson, *Le droit à l'information* (Montréal: P.U.M., 1981).

rights in the flow of information. Through their decisions, courts develop the principles governing situations where fundamental rights conflict. To set these respective and reciprocal limits of the rights and freedoms related to information, courts resort to structuring factors, of which the right to information is an essential part.[25]

Authors such as Pierre Kaiser have shown that the right to privacy finds its limits in what he calls the requirements of public information.[26] In many countries, an analysis of court decisions shows that the right of the public to information is one of the norms used by courts to determine, in a situation of conflict, the specific limits of freedom of expression and the rights that limit its exercise, such as the right to privacy and reputation. The right of the public to information, understood as referent to the interest of the public in being informed, seems to have served as a structuring factor of the limits to the freedom of expression.

Called upon to determine the limits of freedom of expression and other rights, such as the right to honor, reputation or privacy, courts invoke what seems to them to go in the direction of the public interest. The public interest in being informed then becomes a reference notion helping to determine, in the legal context, whether the behavior in question goes beyond what allows each of the rights cited in support of the claims of parties.[27] Thus, the rights of a person to his reputation and his privacy find their limits in the interest recognized to the public to be informed of certain aspects of his personality to judge, for instance, whether there are good reasons to maintain their confidence in him in the case of a person in public life.

The harmonization of fundamental rights and freedoms is one of the main tasks of the legal system. It is on the basis of norms, vague notions, or tests that the divergent interests involved in the circulation of information are assessed.

---

25 Pierre Trudel, Jacques Boucher, René Piotte, and Jean-Maurice Brisson, *op. cit.*, pp. 217ff.

26 Pierre Kaiser, *La protection de la vie privée* (Paris: Économica, 1984), p. 133.

27 See in general, Pierre Trudel and France Abran, *Droit du public à l'information et vie privée : deux droits irréconciliables?* (Montreal: Éditions Thémis, 1992), p. 208; Pierre Trudel, "Liberté d'information et droit du public à l'information," in Alain Prujiner and Florian Sauvageau, *Qu'est- ce que la liberté de la presse?* (Montreal: Boréal,), pp. 174–180; Pierre Trudel, *Droit de l'information et de la communication, Notes et documents* (Montreal: Éditions Thémis, 1984), pp. 13ff.

PRIVACY: OUR FUTURE UNDER CLOSE SURVEILLANCE

Louise Cadoux

Unlike the familiar mainframe computer, industriously processing information in a central unit out of sight of the user, the new information and communication technologies permeate every aspect of our day-to-day lives — increasingly intelligent, highly integrated, yet still invisible.

Digital technology is *the* major breakthrough of recent years. Poaching on what were formerly the private preserve of mainframe computers, it has taken over in the realms of sound, voice, still, and animated images. As information technology, telecommunications, and audio-visual systems converge in the same infrastructure, everything will be relayed over networks, everything will be digitized, everything presented and manipulated like a computer file.

However, for all that, traditional information technology is still alive and well. Mainframe computers are still widely used, and traditional systems will continue to coexist alongside the new technologies.

The dramatic increase in the use of new technologies in business, government organizations and departments, and communities of all kinds will undoubtedly lead to a reduction of repetitive tasks, fuel creativity, promote communication, and bring progress to our everyday lives. In fact, most human activity will substantially benefit from these technologies. What's more, they promise to be the greatest source of future employment. Nonetheless, everyone should be aware that they also pose serious threats to our fundamental right to freedom and privacy. And what are these threats?

INFORMATION BANKS

Information and communication technologies are able to produce and store a vast quantity of personal information. Two years ago, an MIT research team estimated that the volume of data created by the new technologies on a global scale doubles every 20 months. Considering the number of times we come into contact with computers daily, these findings should come as no surprise. Are we digitally «captured» 500, 600 times? Figures like these are often trotted out without being supported by any source of reference, but they attest to the omnipresence of computers in Western society.

But is it all that incredible that such a wealth of information is now on file? When you think about it, the coordinates of our telephone conversations are saved for a certain period of time, whether it be for legal inquiries, official wiretap purposes, or for dealing with potential complaints about billing. With the new digital television services, it is possible to know at precisely what time on which day we consulted which newspaper, watched which program, or ordered which product from a virtual shopping mall. The new technologies allow for the stockpiling of evidence.

On the basis of data thus retrieved, service providers and marketers will be able to draw up an individual profile of each customer, his or her habits, lifestyle, interests, etc. Electronic commerce will squeeze the most out of these millions of pieces of information.

The mobile telephone industry will make it possible to track and record our movements. Each and every day, all kinds of sensing devices are being developed to feed information directly into a computer that can perform a multitude of functions, from establishing a diagnosis through medical imaging to electronic route guidance systems in the field of intelligent transport. The future will be dominated by digital cameras, microphones, the Global Positioning System, roadside screening devices, and sensors which will enable drivers to monitor their heart rate, or even determine their susceptibility to fatigue or sleep.

Because the practice of medicine has been largely computerized, social security agencies can now collect a wealth of extremely sensitive data about patients. This also applies to all the socially disadvantaged or vulnerable populations who might be required to fill in forms asking probing questions in order to access legally available social benefits.

Any activity or domain that's based on targeting specific sectors of the public will benefit from this huge pool of personal data — consumer profiles, predictive medicine, discrimination models in the workplace, risk-oriented segmentation in the consumer credit and insurance sectors, detection of potential swindlers or other offenders, and more. All these activities are greatly enhanced by such a stockpile of personal data.

INVISIBLE FINGERPRINTS

Another striking feature of the new technologies is their invisibility. Data is usually captured without the knowledge, and hence without the permission, of the individuals involved. With ever-expanding storage capacities and the breakthrough of mobile networks and mobile information technology, this practice has become increasingly widespread. Even the right to anonymity so fiercely defended by guardians of the right to privacy does not prevent people from being identified.

Each time you use a credit or debit card at an automated banking machine or a highway toll-booth, you unwittingly leave a «fingerprint.» In France, authorities recently tracked down a driver who had used a credit card to pay for gas, thus confirming that his financial transactions had been recorded. Furthermore, contrary to recommendations made by authorities in charge of protecting personal information, hidden or unmarked surveillance cameras are often set up in public places for security reasons.

Consider also that an IP (Internet protocol) address on the Internet and a "log files" disclose, more than anything else, a Netsurfer's interests. There is no longer any need to use an Internet access or content provider to discover surfers' names. It is enough to obtain their IP address in order to bombard them with advertising or other unwanted messages.

Again, unknown to surfers, at least to those who haven't the faintest idea how the system works, the Net allows «cookies» to be stored on their hard disks to monitor their browsing. The information amassed in this way can be fed into files to measure how frequently sites are visited, analogous to the way Nielsen and Audimat data is used to measure television viewing. And how many people are aware that any search conducted on the Internet can be traced?

THE PERSONAL INFORMATION MARKET

It no longer seems to shock anyone that the world is becoming a veritable personal information market. Personal data has now become a commodity. Such information can be exchanged for perks, freebies, rebates, bonus points, rewards, etc. And while it is true that these kinds of incentives have indeed been offered in the past, they were offered in a less disturbing guise. Traditionally, businesses sought to promote customer loyalty by issuing cards, coupons and so on. All that consumers had to present to benefit from these advantages was a card; no personal information was required.

Society now recognizes the following four means of paying for a service or a product:

The consumer pays the full fixed price.

The service is partially or fully subsidized by the government, providing users with access at a reasonable price (as is the case for television in some countries).

Advertising contributes to cutting the cost of the service. In the print and audio- visual media, for example, subsidies thus reduce the costs incurred to make the service or product available to consumers, but in neither case were consumers given the opportunity to negotiate the price. However, a different arrangement could be envisioned. Telephone companies, for instance, might grant rebates to those subscribers who would agree to tolerate advertising messages on their line before being connected.

▨ The provision of personal data has become a fourth method of payment. And the expected gains from this acquisition of information has led to a unique relationship between buyer and seller: in exchange for the data, the buyer is entitled to a discount on the price of the service or product.

This information is gathered in a variety of ways, depending on the circumstances. The most effective means is to match individual names with transactions performed on communications networks (telephone calls, Net searches, etc.). This method of collecting data is painless for consumers, arousing no suspicion in their minds because it is covert and after the fact. However, because only a limited amount of information can be collected in this fashion, a new tactic was developed. Under this new method of payment, Internet users will only be permitted to access network services it they answer a «demographic» questionnaire that provides an intimately detailed profile of the interests and financial means of Netsurfers and their families. These surveys ask for details about their consumer habits, the age and first names of their family members, their marital status, level of education, etc. It should also be remembered that many government departments in the U.S. are making their files available to the public, thus adding to the pool of obtainable personal information. In both the United States and in Europe the press regularly denounces these practices, warning of their potential danger.

Trading personal information is a very lucrative activity, and identified as such by the New York Stock Exchange. Many personal data bases are available on the market, despite the ill-fated Lotus experience several years ago.[1]

Obviously, we cannot accept the principle of the market value of personal information without examining at least two issues. First of all, what are the moral implications of trading personal information for gain? We should not forget that it is prohibited to treat the human body as a marketable commodity. Secondly, if we are willing to allow the selling of such information, how can we use market mechanisms to determine the price? In any event, we should remain alert to the fact that greed and the usefulness alone of the data are effective incentives to amass and retain as much information as possible.

---

1 A CD-ROM produced by Lotus Ltd., containing data on the life styles of 20 million American households — including data on their cars and magazine subscriptions — had to be pulled from the market under pressure from consumers.

INTELLIGENT SOFTWARE

Another characteristic feature of the new technologies is the ever-expanding intelligence of software. From the very beginning, decision-makers have envisioned interconnecting data bases, preferably using a number common to all files. In 1978, after France drafted stringent legislation monitoring IT practices and freedoms, the use of a national ID number became subject to strict regulations. Methods have subsequently been fine-tuned. Typologies of populations have been established to be used as a frame of reference for future data enhancement. Information technology (IT) experts now claim that a unique number is no longer needed for tracing purposes, that simply matching literal information such as an individual's name, first name, date and place of birth will lead straight to the person in question. They have discovered that a person's address is probably *the* most indicative information. In all Western countries, administrators and politicians have dreamed of being able to merge taxation and personal information into a single data base.

Identifying populations at risk medically or socially, pinpointing individuals suspected of fraud or deviant behavior, differentiating people with fixed domiciles from the homeless and good from bad, loyal from disloyal, customers in order to target a stable clientele... all of these processes depend on tracking down the pertinent indices.

Two new software programs are now available to help users uncover these clues: Datawarehouse, and Datamining. Datawarehouse is based on a large volume of information collected and stored in data depositories. Datamining helps users discover hitherto unsuspected relationships between various pieces of information. Both programs use the varied resources of tried and true methods such as detailed statistics, data analysis, neuron networks, decision trees, and so on. Not a week goes by that a consultant or a software publisher doesn't organize an information session or offer hands-on experience on Datamining. This program has come under the scrutiny of a number of authorities concerned about protecting personal data in the Netherlands, Canada, and France.

Shape-recognition software has been developed that uses images captured by video-surveillance cameras to detect supermarket shoppers whose behavior indicates that they might be planning to shoplift. Similar use is made of pictures taken by roadside cameras to isolate individuals whose driving could endanger public safety. Online shoppers can take advantage of intelligent agents, programs that shop for them in a JAVA environment. For example, these agents can choose a suit in the desired size and colour, put together a vacation package, monitor stock exchange prices, buy or sell shares on their behalf, or even record appointments in their diaries. They can act as users' personal managers, meeting other intelligent agents from various companies and negotiating the best deals. Obviously, unless consumers supply substantial information about personal tastes, requirements and needs, these agents won't be able to perform effectively. But their use raises a number of questions. How long will information be retained, and what use will be made of it? Will one agent simply be able to relay it to another? In other words, how will customers be able to exercise control over this sensitive personal information?

There will be no limit to the expansion of information technology in the years to come. Processors will be more and more powerful and have greater storage capacity; sensors will be increasingly sophisticated, and communication ever more instantaneous. And software, not people, will be the major beneficiary of these advances, for better or for worse.

THE PERILS OF INFORMATION TECHNOLOGY

Lastly, the implications of how global networks and virtual objects operate merit a closer look. Not so long ago, one of the best ways to safeguard privacy from the encroachment of information technology was the physical, or even geographical, separation of applications and files, each with its own data dictionary. But then SGDBs and their multiprocess data tables arrived, closely followed by the creation of networks. As corporate networks and the Internet developed, the globe virtually shrank and national borders no longer sufficed to insulate and protect information. Networks had made it possible to centralize and to disseminate, almost simultaneously. Not only could more and more data be retrieved, collected and centralized, it could also be extensively disseminated and re-disseminated. The increasingly widespread adoption of identical standards and formats and the ensuing potential for interconnection have rendered our sense of security illusory. Files can now be re-centralized virtually at the flick of a wrist. In addition, interactive contexts and real time have taken the world by storm. In today's digital age, very few processes are performed in non-real time.

Mechanisms such as decentralizing processes and isolating files to protect personal data and freedom have become obsolete. The perils inherent in IT now need to be addressed by ethical, legal and technical solutions.

ETHICS, LAWS, AND TECHNIQUES

Ethical solutions first require individual reflection before they can be submitted to the collective in order to reach a consensus and devise regulations for monitoring the invisible economy. This approach could encourage decision-makers and information technologists to give some serious thought to the future. In a world ruled by economic competition and the race for productivity, we cannot seriously expect decision-makers to voluntarily limit the use of any resource such as this that can help hone their competitive edge. Information technologists are in the best position to anticipate the dangers and find solutions. However, those tied to the corporate hierarchy cannot sound the alarm. Only IT experts, researchers, academics, and a few other professionals outside the corporate structure, and whom cultural tradition still allows to listen to their own consciences, are able to firmly draw the moral line. Yet while the ethical approach is invaluable in raising the level of awareness of certain dangers and prompting citizens to serious reflection, it isn't enough.

Some 40 states have chosen to address the issue by legal means. Of the various recommendations and initiatives put forward by international organizations, the Council of Europe's Convention 108 (January 28, 1981) deserves special mention as the first international document to take a stand on human rights and IT. The Convention requires each member state to "take the necessary measures in its domestic law to give effect to the basic principles for data protection..." Supplementing Convention 108, the European directive of October 24, 1995, requires each state in the European Community to establish an independent authority to monitor the implementation of rules to protect information.

With these two documents, the European states have enacted legislation to ensure the protection of privacy with regard to information technology and established monitoring mechanisms. Québec, New Zealand, and Hong Kong have followed their lead in the public and private sectors, while other Canadian and Australian provinces have adopted limited legislative provisions in the public sector. European countries that have applied for membership in the European Community have begun drafting similar legislation and regulations.

The European Community has taken a number of steps to promote these principles in international negotiations with third countries. The widespread implications of the Internet have convinced the European states that since national laws cannot apply beyond national borders, they need to be supplemented by an international agreement on the protection of privacy.

Since none of the authorities mandated to protect the public believe that legislation alone is adequate to effectively shield the individual from any negative impact of information technology, it is imperative that technical solutions also be developed. Confirming the old maxim that science finds within itself the resources it needs to counter the adverse effects of its progress, efforts have been deployed in the following three directions.

The first, and most radical, is to ensure confidentiality through data encryption. If the information is illegible, no one will want to access it, never mind retain it. Therefore sensitive data, such as patients' medical files, should be encrypted. In addition, if personal information is transmitted to countries where the protection of individual rights is inadequate, data encryption will safeguard it from prying eyes.

Another solution is to make data anonymous, which was the option France chose when it introduced Minitel. Canadian, and Dutch colleagues have recommended PETS (Privacy Enhancing Technologies), which are based on the principle that many applications only really require the individual's identity on two occasions (once to access the system, and once to make payment). All other transactions could be performed using pseudo-identities. Thus, as many pseudo-identities can be generated as needed by means of a smart card which allows them to remain constantly under the individual's control. This need for anonymity is so strong that the market has responded by offering Internet users a variety of "anonymizers" to choose from.

Another more recent option is the electronic filter, although it is more complicated to implement. Researchers have been working on this solution since the
Internet first became accessible to the general public. With this option, software
filters can be installed on a user's workstation when groups of users have indi-
cated preferences. The same technology is used for "watchdog" devices designed
to prevent minors from accessing sites containing violence, Nazi propaganda,
pornography, and other unsuitable messages. However, there is a significant
time-lapse between the moment a user decides to apply a filter and the actual
filtering process because it takes time to analyze needs, develop programs, and
determine update and maintenance conditions.

Thus protection against the misuse of silicon technology can be achieved by combining a variety of options. All that remains is for us to be determined to do so,
and to demand the same commitment from our political decision-makers.

REGULATION OF FREEDOM OF EXPRESSION ON THE INTERNET: THE ROLES OF LAW AND OF THE STATE

Lilian Edwards

As we near the end of the millennium there can be few who now doubt that the Internet and its related communications technologies are fundamentally changing the way we communicate, research, publish, and express ourselves. Its strength as a medium of communication lies in its versatility, global accessibility, and cheapness of access.

The Internet can be perceived as a range of zones or environments for communication. Perhaps the most important Internet zone is the World Wide Web, where information of all kinds — text, pictures, sound, digital information or multimedia performance — can be displayed; read, searched or interacted with by browsers; and downloaded or printed out for permanent reference or use. What is certainly true is that any one of the millions of Web home pages which now exist can reach an audience of millions of people in virtually every country in the globe. This has enormous implications for freedom of expression, and for the regulation of information and content by states. In the past global media or publishing organizations have been expensive to run, few in number, located in costly physical facilities, advised by professional lawyers and, in general, heavily regulated. By contrast, using the facilities of the Web, every person can effectively become a global publisher at a cost which can be minimal both for the provider and receiver of the information.

The questions raised are numerous.[1] It is important to realize that there are few neutral speakers or statements in the area of the Internet and freedom of speech. The debate is polarized between cyberlibertarians, who tend to view any attempt by the state (or other agencies) to regulate Internet content as potential or overt censorship; and those who might be called "cyberpaternalists," who take the view that the new medium offers special and extensive risks. This second group would state that to protect the interests of parties such as children, women, minority races, and religious groups, as well as the general moral character of society, and to secure the successful and continued growth and economic exploitation of the Internet, a certain degree of regulation is justified. As we shall see, this attitude has been adopted to a greater or lesser extent by many Western governments, and is a significant concern to the European Union in its ongoing attempts to create a vibrant and competitive single market in Europe.

LEGAL REGULATION: OVERVIEW

Legal regulation of freedom of expression and communication can take two main forms: civil, and criminal. Civil law involves the bringing of a civil action by one private party (or a state organ acting in a private capacity) against another party of the same status. Criminal law almost invariably involves the state acting in its public capacity to proscribe and prosecute certain acts.

---

1 For a recent general critique of how free speech is regulated and restricted globally on the Internet, see V. Mayer-Schoenberger and T. E. Foster, "A Regulatory Web: Free Speech and the Global Information Infrastructure" in Kahin and Nesson, eds., *Borders in Cyberspace* (MIT Press, 1997). Up-to-date information on the whole area of cyberspace and freedom of expression can best be gathered from Web sites: in the UK Cyber-Rights and Cyber-Liberties, run by Yaman Akdeniz, is the most comprehensive source < http://www.leeds.ac.uk/law/pgs/ yaman/yaman.htm >; in the USA, numerous good sites exist including the Electronic Frontier Foundation and its associated Blue Ribbon Online Free Speech campaign < http://www.eff.org/blueribbon.html >; the Campaign for Internet Freedom < http://www.netfreedom.org >; and the First Amendment Cyber Tribune < http://w3.trib.com/ FACT/ >.

The principle civil control on free speech on the Internet is the law of defamation or libel. Other civil law controls which are relevant include the law of privacy and confidence, laws of intellectual property rights including copyright and design, and data-protection rules relating to transmission of personal information (which are well entrenched in Europe but still embryonic in the USA). Historically, the earliest litigation on the Internet arose in the area of defamation, and as a result much of the academic debate on freedom of expression online and Internet Service Provider (ISP) liability has been constructed around defamation. For these reasons we will focus on defamation as our principal civil-law area of interest.

Criminal law controls on the Internet content take several forms. Perhaps the most prominent image of the Internet in the average person's perception is as a repository of pornography; the Internet has been described as "the biggest dirty-book shop in history" and as an "Internet Babylon."[2] State control by means of criminal sanctions of obscene and pornographic text and pictures is therefore an area of major concern for would-be users and exploiters of the Internet. Rules of criminal law applicable to Internet content also exist to prevent the making of antireligious statements (the law of blasphemy), the making of racist or inflammatory statements (incitement to racial hatred or "hate-speech" rules), and the making of politically subversive or seditious statements. In the US for example, considerable moral panic has been created over the availability of bomb-making recipes on the Web. Rules of this kind tend to vary a great deal from country to country depending on social, ethical, legal, and religious history.[3] The fact that standards as to what material is criminally offensive vary so much from jurisdiction to jurisdiction complicates even more the issue of control of Internet content, given the fact that content is freely distributed across physical national boundaries.

Finally, if restrictions are to be placed on freedom of expression on the Internet, who is to pay the penalty if these restrictions are breached? To obtain a connection to the Internet requires the service of an Internet Service Provider (ISP). This may be a commercial operator such as CompuServe, America On Line, or Microsoft Network, or a noncommercial host such as a university or library. In all these cases the ISP's role is to relay the words of original content providers to

2 Anne Wells Branscomb, "Internet Babylon? Does the Carnegie Mellon Study of Pornography on the Information Superhighway Reveal a Threat to the Stability of Society?" *Georgetown Law Journal*, vol. 83 (1995), p. 1935.

3 See *R. v. Bow St. Magistrates ex parte Choudhury* [1991] 1 All ER 306 (the "Satanic Verses" case).

those who wish to read or access that content. The ISP may find that in this role as a carrier, publisher, or distributor of Internet content, it may be held liable in respect of content which runs afoul of the law (such as a defamatory statement or pornographic picture) rather than, or as well as, the original content provider. ISP liability in relation to content is a major current issue in the area of freedom of expression since ISPs act effectively as the gatekeepers of the Internet. If they are placed in a position where they can be sued or prosecuted in respect of speech originated by others but distributed via the ISP, then their natural response will be to limit their risk by refusing to carry that material. Cyberlibertarians might characterize this as undemocratic censorship. It is useful to consider if it is better or more efficient for the state to censor those who originate content; those who read or access it; or those who participate in publishing and distributing it. We will briefly consider the issue of ISP liability in relation to civil and criminal liability before considering some options for future legal control of content on the Internet.

CIVIL LEGAL CONTROL: THE LAW OF DEFAMATION AND THE INTERNET

Defamation is a civil wrong which occurs when a verbal or written statement is published which constitutes an injurious attack on a person's character, honor and reputation.[4] Defamation was one of the first hot topics to develop as the new discipline of Internet law emerged. Defamation lawsuits effectively illustrate the struggle on the Internet between the cyberlibertarian view of the world, and the cyberpaternalist view, because they place in direct conflict the principle of unfettered freedom of speech, and the right of other interests, notably protection of reputation, to derogate from it.

There are at least three other major reasons why defamation on the Internet is of particular interest:

▒ It is not an accident but directly related to the predominant norms of Internet culture that libelous comments are far more likely to be made on the Internet than in other media or in "real life."

---

4 In English and US law there is a division into libel (written statement) and slander (spoken statement): no such conceptual division is made in Scots law.

■ Internet defamation cases show, graphically, the difficulties caused by the transjurisdictional nature of the Internet alluded to earlier.

■ Until recently the Internet was the first area in which serious attempts were made to grapple with the issue of the potential liability of ISPs for Internet content.

Why Is the Internet a Defamation-Prone Zone?

Internet users may make libelous comments via e-mail, on electronic mailing lists, via newsgroups, or by publishing them on or to Web sites. Each "zone" of the Internet has its own difficulties in relation to libel. As anyone who has used e-mail will know, it is remarkably quick and easy to use. Comments can be typed in haste and sent at the click of a mouse. Compared to conventional written correspondence, where there is typically time to draft the statement, print or type it out, re-read, re-draft, and then *think* before signing, putting the message in an envelope, attaching a stamp and putting it in the post, transmission of e-mail is virtually instantaneous and, once sent, is usually irrevocable. As a result, e-mail correspondence is often in content more like spoken conversation for habitual users — hasty, ungrammatical and rash — and tends to lead parties to say things they would normally not commit to writing and would often not even say in face-to-face interaction with the other party. Psychologically, electronic interaction combines a sort of deceptive distance — one is after all sitting safely behind a terminal in one's own office when writing — with a kind of equally deceptive intimacy. Studies and anecdotal evidence show that e-mail communications lack the body-language, eye-contact, or spoken cues that exist in direct conversation or on the phone, and that prevent the making of inappropriate statements.[5] All this means that those sending e-mail are dangerously prone to making remarks that, once public, turn out to be legally actionable.[6]

5 See T. A. Cutrera, "Computer Networks, Libel and the First Amendment," *Computer Law Journal*, vol. 11, no. 557 (1992), pp. 559-560.

6 Of course in some jurisdictions it is doubtful whether the sending of e-mail by one person to one person only who is the person defamed constitutes adequate "publication" for the purposes of fixing libel liability. This is probably true of England (*Pullman v. Hill* [1891] 1 QB 524) but not Scotland (see Norrie *Defamation and Related Actions in Scots Law* (Butterworths, 1995). It is also possible that even in England an e-mail sent one-to-one may be regarded as an insecure communication, able to be intercepted and read in transit by third parties like a postcard, and therefore may attract libel liability (*Sadgrove v. Hole* [1901] 1 KB 1.)

Usenet newsgroups,[7] noncommercial Web sites and "chatrooms" are even more problematic from the defamation point of view than other zones of the Internet because of the influence of traditional Internet culture. Until relatively recently — roughly, the early Nineties — the Internet was largely the domain of technophiles, students, academics, and workers in the computer industry, principally in the US. These users usually accessed the Internet for free and used it for noncommercial purposes. There was a strong collective sentiment towards anarchy, libertarianism, and free speech rights, and a strong corresponding dislike of corporate, governmental or legal authority or control.[8] In this culture, full, frank, and unfettered discussion known as "flaming," which was often indistinguishable from rudeness and abuse, was not only tolerated but by and large encouraged. The usual remedy for being flamed was not to post a writ for libel but to flame back. It was and is not uncommon for newsgroups to degenerate into "flame wars" — torrents of abusive comments which destroy all sensible discussion in the group. This was apparently acceptable when most Internet users shared a similar cultural background.[9] But in recent years the Internet has ceased to be the domain of such "netizens" and is now extensively used by individuals and organizations from beyond this specialized culture, including family members, children, and corporate interests who pay for Internet access and see the Internet as a field for commercial expansion rather than for unfettered self-expression. For these users, flaming and abuse are not acceptable and preservation of corporate reputation is paramount.[10] It is not coincidental that several of the earliest Internet libel cases to be settled in the UK have revolved around preservation of corporate reputations that have been subjected to online criticism.[11]

7 See, for example *Rindos v. Hardwick*, unreported, Supreme Court of Western Australia, 31 March 1994, where the alleged libelous comment was made on the newsgroup sci.anthropology and was that a certain academic had not been worthy of tenure.

8 "Cyberspace arose out of the academic and research communities and reflects a culture in which axioms of First Amendment jurisprudence became the dominant value. Although 'the First Amendment is a local ordinance in cyberspace, Cyberians throughout the world often invoke its talismanic force against those attempting to hinder free and robust speech." (L. Gibbons, "No Regulation, Government Regulation or Self-Regulation: Social Enforcement or Social Contracting for Governance in Cyberspace," *Cornell Journal of Law and Public Policy*, no. 6 (1997), pp. 475- 485. (Footnotes omitted.)

9 See for example Godwin, "Libel Law: Let it Die" at < http://www.wired.com/wired/4.03/idees.fortes/ letitdie.html >.

10 Hard-copy media interests also have an interest in seeing the Internet conform to non-virtual standards of conduct. See for example comment by Joe Conason in the *New York Observer* in relation to *Blumenthal v. Drudge*, a $20-million libel action filed by a Clinton aide on August 27, 1997 in respect of allegedly defamatory comments made in an online AOL-hosted political gossip column. "Without the regulatory whip of libel, the Internet would become a totally free market for defamation, dragging the rest of the media down to the same level." (Reported in *The Guardian*, March 16, 1998).

11 See the *Western Provident Association v. Norwich Union* dispute, reported in *Scotsman* July 27 1997; and the *Forward Press v. Poetry Society* dispute, reported in *Guardian*, February 15, 1996.

What DiffiCulties Are Caused in Internet Libel Cases by the Transjurisdictional Nature of the Internet?

One of the key problems in Internet libel cases is that a libel placed on the Web or a newsgroup is usually published in every country of the world at once, leaving the alleged libeler open to suit in a multiplicity of courts. An example is instructive here. Tom, a private individual resident and domiciled in Scotland, posts a defamatory comment about the global environmentalist and entrepreneur Anya, also resident and domiciled in Scotland, to the Usenet newsgroup talk.environment. The posting states that Anya employs Third World sweat labor to produce her world-famous environmental cosmetics line. The group is read by subscribers in many countries, including England, Scotland, and the USA. As a result sales of the cosmetics slump throughout the world. Anya wishes to sue. In which country's courts can Anya raise a libel action? In law, this is described as the question of *jurisdiction*. Each country has its own rules as to when its courts will accept jurisdiction, but there are some underlying principles most countries tend to respect. For example, a defender should not be prejudiced by a case being raised against him or her in a country where she or he will be unable to defend him or herself, nor should a plaintiff/pursuer be allowed to raise actions in a court unconnected to the cause of dispute, simply so he or she can take advantage of useful remedies offered idiosyncratically by that court (e.g., punitive levels of damages, or corruptible judges). Ideally, to prevent such "forum shopping," there should be only one country in whose courts a particular action can be raised, and it should be both adequately connected to the action, and accessible to the defender.

For these reasons, the Brussels Convention, which regulates domestic jurisdiction in civil matters in Scotland, and transnational civil jurisdiction in Scotland, England and most of Western Europe, has as its first and overriding principle that jurisdiction is founded in the country where the defender is domiciled.[12] In the above example, that would indicate that Anya should raise her action in Scotland. However the Brussels Convention gives as an *alternate* rule of jurisdiction that the case may be raised in the "place where the delict is committed."[13] Where is a delict such as defamation committed? There are two obvious interpretations

12 Art 1 of the Brussels Convention on Civil Jurisdiction and Judgments.
13 Article 5(3). "Delict" is the civil-law phrase for tort, used in Scotland but not in England.

— first, the place where the remark was originally made (the "source" of the delict); and secondly, the place where the remark is read or made public and has an impact on the reputation of the person defamed (the "target" of the delict). Case-law from the European Court of Justice interpreting the Brussels Convention — notably the recent referral to the ECJ from the English House of Lords in the case of *Shevill v. Presse Alliance S.A.*[14] — seems clearly to establish that either interpretation is a valid alternative for the purposes of fixing jurisdiction. Thus in our scenario, notwithstanding the fact that both the pursuer and defender are Scots, there is jurisdiction in both Scotland, where the posting originates, and in England, where the posting has been read and caused loss to reputation — as indeed there is in every country party to the Brussels Convention where the offending posting could be read, and where Anya has a reputation that can be damaged (which in our scenario she has).

Why does this matter? First, it allows rampant forum shopping. In our example, Anya is perfectly entitled to raise the action in the country whose courts are least friendly, and most alien in law and language, to the defender, and most likely to award her enormous damages. Secondly, *multiple* actions can potentially be raised which are likely to hasten the defender's collapse, faced with ruinously high legal costs, regardless of the merits of the action. This has implications for freedom of expression given that it is hardly unknown for economically powerful parties to use their economic power to bring libel suits as an effective way of silencing opposition from ideological critics and economic competitors.[15] Thirdly, once an action has been raised in a certain country, it will be a matter for the international private laws of that country what law is actually applied to determine the action. Many courts will simply apply their own law. This may mean that a person posting a statement to the Internet in (say) Scotland, finds his or her words judged by the standard of civil comment imposed by the law of (say) China or Singapore. Again this has serious implications for freedom of speech given the variation worldwide in libel laws in matters such as fair-comment defenses, public-figure rights, political or judicial privilege, etc.[16]

---

14 (Case C–68/93) [1995] 2 WLR 499; and see comment by Forsyth in *Cambridge Law Journal* no. 515 (1995).

15 See, for one notorious recent example, the "McLibel" case brought by McDonald's, the fast-food empire, against two campaigners who alleged environmental misdeeds by the plaintiffs (*McDonald's Corp v. Steel (no. 4)* (Unreported, 1997) (QBD).

16 For a comparison of liability for libel and other related civil wrongs across a number of Western jurisdictions, see C. Campbell, ed., *International Media Liability* (Wiley, 1997).

ISP Liability and Internet Libel

Although the above scenario is worrisome in respect of individual litigants, it is the implications in relation to ISPs which cause the most disquiet. As already stated, no one can publish or distribute material on the Net without the aid of an ISP. In the UK, US, and many other jurisdictions, in principle any person who publishes or republishes the defamatory statement of another is as liable for the loss caused to the plaintiff as the original maker of the statement. Therefore it will often be more attractive for someone who claims to have been defamed to sue the ISP as publisher —it is likely to be locatable, with a registered place of business, and probably significant liquid assets — rather than to sue the original defamer, who may have vanished, acted under cover of an anonymous remailer or pseudonym, be living in another country where judgments for damages are difficult or impossible to have recognized and enforced, or simply have no attachable assets. As a result, ISPs, by virtue of their role as gatekeepers to the Internet, find themselves sitting on a liability time bomb. This would be unfortunate enough without going on to consider the nature of the potentially libelous material which ISPs distribute. In the UK these representations resulted in section 1 of the Defamation Act 1996, which provides that a person such as an ISP is *not* to be regarded as the publisher of material originated by others if it is *only* involved in operating or providing any equipment, system or service by means of which that material was made available in electronic form (emphasis added).[17] Once the ISP has established itself in the "nonpublisher" category, it can avail itself of the defense provided by section 1(1), which provides that no liability arises where a person can prove that they took reasonable care in relation to the publication of the libelous material, and did not know, and had no reason to believe, that what they did caused or contributed to the publication of a defamatory statement. In the US, legal protection in respect of libel has gone even further. Section 230 (c) of the Communications Decency Act 1996[18] guarantees immunity to ISPs in respect of liability for content originated by others, and this has been held to exclude the possibility of any claim under common law

---

17 See s 1(3)(c); s 1(3)(e), which also provides a defense potentially applicable to ISP liability.
18 This section was *not* overturned by the Supreme Court in *Reno v ACLU* .

libel against an ISP as publisher of content provided by another.[19] Thus at present it appears that ISPs enjoy much more extensive protection against libel liability in the US than they do in the UK, where there is considerable doubt as to how effectively the provisions of the 1996 Act have been drafted.[20]

LEGAL CONTROL OF INTERNET CONTENT

Although civil liability for Internet content is of deep concern to businesses, and especially to ISPs, it is the question of how the state should intervene in respect of criminally offensive material such as child pornography that has attracted the attention of the general population.[21] The storm of controversy and confusion in relation to this area which has engulfed Internet users and state regulators alike has led Jeffrey Shallit, a US academic and cyberlibertarian, to coin Three Laws of New Media:

 Rule 1: Every new medium of expression will be used for sex.

 Rule 2: Every new medium of expression will come under attack, usually because of Shallit's First Law.

 Rule 3: Protection afforded for democratic rights and freedoms in traditional media will rarely be understood to apply to new media.[22]

As a general principle of Western legal systems, state jurisdiction in criminal matters is territorial. Thus, in theory, there is no legal vacuum in relation to criminal activities online. Each state's laws on pornography, hate speech, blasphemy, etc., apply within its own territory, and will apply to criminal acts perpetrated there and to Internet users and ISPs situated there, just as they do in respect of communications distributed via more conventional media. Most states already have in place rules of criminal law prohibiting the distribution, publication,

19 *Zeran v, America Online Inc.* US District Court of Eastern Virginia, March 21, 1997, Civil Action 96-952-A; and see < http://www.bna.com/e-law/cases/zeran.html >. A case so far unresolved is attempting to claim that even post-Zeran an ISP host can still be liable as a primary content provider rather than a secondary publisher; see *Blumenthal v. Drudge*, DC. DC Civil Action No. 97- 1968 PLF, complaint filed August 27, 1997, reported (1997) 2 BNA EIPR 949.

20 See further Edwards "Defamation and the Internet", *op. cit.*, no. 6, pp. 193- 194.

21 There is more anecdotal evidence than hard statistics as to the nature and prevalence of Internet pornography, but one interesting and comprehensive recent survey is the Carnegie-Mellon study reported in M. Rimm, "Marketing Pornography on the Information Superhighway" *Georgetown Law Journal*, vol. 83 (1995), p. 1849.

22 Taken from J. Shallit, "Public Networks and Censorship," in Ludlow, ed., *High Noon on the Electronic Frontier: Conceptual Issues in Cyberspace* (MIT Press, 1996).

import, and use of child pornography; many also have criminalized racist or hate speech, the other type of offensive content on the Internet which is beginning to command serious attention.[23] Why, then, is the effective regulation and proscription of pornography and hate-speech on the Internet so problematic for states?

New and Stricter Content Rules

Even if existing law can be adapted sensibly to deal with the demands of the new technologies of communication, there remain arguments that more stringent regulation is justified in relation to content on the Internet than in other media. While the content of Internet pornography may be identical to that circulated via other media, the environment in which it circulates is significantly different in a number of ways. The most vociferous arguments that Internet porn is a "new horror" however have been made in relation to the ease of access by children.[24] The fact that access to computers and the Net has become commonplace, combined with the fact that the Net is unregulated by a state or industry governing body or censor (unlike radio, TV, film, and video) led to moral panic in both the US and UK in the early to mid 1990s.[25] Demands were made across the world that children be protected by a clamp-down on Internet content generally.

In the US this led to the passing of the Communications Decency Act 1996, an Act which broadly attempted to impose criminal sanctions on anyone who placed "obscene or indecent" content on the Internet, knowing that it might be read or seen by a person under 18. Since it is generally impossible to know if a child is "lurking" in a newsgroup, or reading a Web site, effectively this criminalized such content even in respect of interadult communication in all the popular forums of the Internet. The Act was attacked, moreover, because it banned not just matter such as child pornography — which was already illegal, whether found in hard copy or on the Internet — but also "indecent" material, which in traditional media had been acknowledged in the US as having some degree of First-Amendment protection. At a more symbolic level, the Act was seen as a

---

23 See, for comprehensive coverage of global developments in this area, Hatewatch < http://www. hatewatch.org > and the Simon Wiesenthal Centre < http://www.wiesenthal.com/index.html >. In the UK, the Jewish Policy Centre (79 Wimpole St, London W1M 7DD) takes a watching brief in this area: see its report *The Governance of Cyberspace: Racism on the Internet* (July 1996); also the EMAIN project reported by J. Craven, "Extremism on the Internet" (1998) 1 JILT at < http://elj.warwick.ac.uk/jilt/wip/98_1crav/ >.

24 Phrase taken from the UK House of Commons Home Affairs Committee First Report on Computer Pornography, HC 126.

25 See T. Gibbons, "Computer Generated Pornography," in *International Yearbook of Law, Computers and Technology*, vol. 9 (1995), p. 83.

declaration of war on the traditional free-speechers of the Internet, and as demonstrating flagrant disregard for the right of freedom of expression online.[26]

The legality of the CDA was challenged by a variety of civil liberties groups and the Supreme Court quashed the offending provisions on June 25, 1997.[27] The rationale that the CDA was a necessary infringement on the freedom of speech of adults to protect the interests of children was robustly rejected.

The kind of judicial scrutiny that was applied is only possible in states such as the US which allow constitutional overturn of legislation. In the UK, for example, despite the impending incorporation of the European Convention of Human Rights (which includes rights to freedom of expression) the doctrine that courts cannot declare statutes invalid is to be preserved. Clearly, constitutional arguments as utilized in the CDA case can and should be marshaled by free-speech activists but will have to be introduced at the level of policy and law creation in the UK and other states without Bills of Rights. It is noticeable that the European Union's ongoing attempts to formulate policy and action relating to Internet content have taken cognizance of the US CDA debacle by seeking to avoid any assertion that adult rights must suffer to protect the interests of children, or that in general state censorship of the Internet which extends the categories of illegal material, as opposed to undesirable material, is acceptable.[28] As we shall see, both the US and EU, in the wake of the CDA, have turned to self-regulation and user-control of Internet content as more fruitful and, it is hoped, more constitutionally sound solutions.

Can Laws Restricting Internet Content be Enforced?

States attempting to apply and enforce their national laws relating to criminal content on the Internet can encounter the fact that the Internet is no respecter of national boundaries. Porn is as likely to be accessed by a Scottish citizen sitting at a terminal in Edinburgh from a server or Web site physically located in

---

26 "The Cyberian community rejected the Communications Decency Act because it was a paradigm for illegitimate government regulation in cyberspace. Accordingly, Cyberians chose the CDA as the issue on which to take a stand." L. Gibbons, *op. cit.*, no. 10, pp. 503-504.

27 *Reno v. ACLU*, June 26, 1997 at < http://www.aclu.org/court/renovacludec.html >.

28 See European Parliament Communication of October 16, 1996 on *Illegal and Harmful Content on the Internet* (*op cit.*, no. 4, chapter 3): "In terms of illegal and harmful content it is crucial to differentiate between content which is illegal and other harmful content. *These different categories of content pose radically different issues of principle, and call for very different legal and technological responses.* It would be dangerous to amalgamate *separate issues such as children accessing pornographic content for adults, and adults accessing pornography about children.* Priorities should be clearly set and resources mobilised to tackle the most important issues, that is the fight against criminal content."

Denmark, or Germany, or the US, as from one within UK criminal jurisdiction. In practice, it is usually both practical and legally possible for national authorities to prosecute and punish the *recipient* of pornographic material even if it is hosted on a foreign server, and also to punish parties who store illicit material on foreign located servers, or supply it by download from such servers, so long as *they themselves* are personally located within the jurisdiction. In the UK, the first such successful prosecution has recently concluded in respect of a student living in Lancaster who stored more than 5,000 indecent photographs of children on a Web site physically located in the US.[29] But the major policy goal for state authorities is generally not to punish individual recipients of porn but to close down those who supply it. Where pornography is stored abroad, this means that international cooperation will be necessary to facilitate extraterritorial law enforcement.[30]

One way to secure international assistance would be by seeking harmonization of global rules on criminal content, probably by some form of multilateral treaty.[31] But it is difficult to imagine consensus being reached as to international standards on obscenity, or indecency, or racist speech, let alone blasphemy, or political speech, even if the participant countries were restricted to Europe, or the West. Even if some consensus was achieved, it might very likely have to be pitched at a lowest-common-denominator level which some states might find impossibly repressive and thus unenforceable, and others, like the US, unconstitutional.

Solutions to the Enforcement Problem

Given the severity of the difficulties of enforcement of rules restricting content across national boundaries, there is a great incentive for states to attempt to pin responsibility for guarding the Internet on the ISPs. Making ISPs responsible can have unfortunate results in which one country's laws permeate another country's territory. In one famous incident in December 1995, a court in Munich, Germany, forced CompuServe in Europe to withdraw certain newsgroups which were

29 "Student given eight month sentence over porn site," *Scotsman* (April 1, 1998). and see also *Cyber Rights and Cyber Liberties (UK) Newsletter*, no. 5 (January 1998), accessible at < http://www.leeds.ac.uk/law/pgs/ yaman.htm >.

30 See "Who Watches the Watchmen: Internet Content Rating Systems and Privatised Censorship", November 1997, at < http://www.leeds.ac.uk/law/pgs/yaman/watchmen.htm >.

31 Mayer-Schoenberger and Foster (*op. cit.*, p. 1) suggest that if international norms as to unacceptable speech were identified then these types of speech might be regarded as illegal under international law using the concept of *ius cogens*. This avoids the need for an international treaty but does not seem to be a wholly practical solution.

deemed to have pornographic content from circulation within Bavaria. Because the software operated by CompuServe was not sophisticated enough to segregate the news-feed to Bavaria from that going to the rest of Europe, the effect was that these newsgroups had to be censored throughout Europe by CompuServe to meet the demands of German law alone. Furthermore, in a judgment that sent shock waves round the world, in May 1998, the head of CompuServe Europe was convicted by the Munich court for helping to distribute pornography and sentenced to two years' probation and a 100,000 marks fine in respect thereof, despite concessions from the prosecutors themselves that it was technically impossible to filter out all such material.

If it is difficult to impose restrictions on content providers who conduct operations from foreign soil, and inappropriate to place the whole responsibility of content regulation on ISPs, what solutions remain? Since the downfall of the CDA, it has become difficult both in practice and in ideology for states to attempt openly to censor content on the Net. Instead, both the US and the European Union have embraced the idea of self-regulation by users via the technologies of content-rating and filtering software. The scheme espoused by the European Union as a potential global industry standard is that of PICS (Platform for Internet Content Selection).[32] PICS works on a principle known as "neutral labeling." PICS "tags" sites with labels which contain different types of information — for example, a tag may reveal that a site contains bad language, nudity, depictions of violence, and racial intolerance. Users such as parents then adjust the filtering software loaded on their computer[33] so that only sites with appropriate PICS tags can be viewed by those using that computer. Sites which do not have PICS tags are blocked, as are sites with inappropriate tags.

While the user-control embodied in PICS is welcomed by most parties to this debate, there are a number of aspects to it which are unsettling to cyberlibertarians.[34] While PICS may be "value neutral," the ratings schemes it uses to block content are not. They necessarily reflect a set of values by means of which decisions as to what content is offensive are made. Depending on what

32 See European Parliament Communication of October 16, 1996 on "Illegal and Harmful Content on the Internet," (*op. cit.*, no. 4, chapter 5); See also *EU Internet Action Plan* available at < http://ww2.echo.lu/legal/en/internet/actplan.html >.

33 PICS now comes as standard with recent versions of Netscape Navigator and Microsoft Internet Explorer, the two most commonly used Web browsers.

34 See L. Lessig, "Tyranny in the Infrastructure," *Wired*, vol. 5, no. 7, at < http://www.wired.com/wired/5.07/cyber_rights.html >; "Who Watches the Watchmen?" *op. cit.* no. 36; ACLU White Paper, *Fahrenheit 451.2: Is Cyberspace Burning?* available at < http://www.aclu.org/issues/cyber/burning.html#Free >

ratings scheme is purchased, its values are then embedded invisibly in the user's software. A rating system devised by the American Civil Liberties Union will not be the same as one devised by (say) the Roman Catholic Church.

PICS is a popular solution for states and conservative interests because it avoids accusations of state censorship but allows questionable sites to be collectively excluded by the users themselves. It also to some extent meets the demands of ISPs to be exculpated from liability. If illegal material does make its way to the user, ISPs can claim it was the user's own fault for not properly using the filtering software. But for cyberlibertarians, PICS is said to replace state censorship with privatized censorship which is applied covertly by the collaboration of the state and the inventors of the ratings schemes popularly in use.[35] Whether the state overtly censors or covertly encourages the use of blocking software, they claim, the result is the same: certain sites, whose content is not illegal but merely offensive to some, find that they are blocked from reaching an audience. On the other hand, some might say that this is no different or more objectionable than the right of any member of the public to choose not to borrow books they find offensive from the library, or not to buy magazines they find disgusting. Where PICS and associated ratings schemes clearly cross the boundaries from personal choice into privatized censorship, however, is where they are imposed on pain of legal penalties by the state on ISPs, on content providers, or on other institutions which give access to the Internet, such as schools and public libraries. In the US, attempts are currently being made to do exactly this. One bill espoused by Senator McCain introduced on March 12, 1998, proposes to link state funding of public schools and libraries to the installation of filtering software on their computers, for the protection of children; while another bill, espoused by Senator Coats and dubbed "Son of CDA," seeks to impose penalties on commercial Web sites which distribute material "harmful to minors" and do not cooperate with rating and filtering schemes. It is clear from the actions of countries such as China and Singapore that if ISPs are commanded by law to implement certain filtering tools, the effect can be a blanket ban on allowing certain information to enter the country in electronic form.[36]

35 The most popular rating scheme currently available for use with PICS is RSACi, which was originally developed in the US to rate computer games.

THE WAY FORWARD?

As this discussion has demonstrated, adopting a regime for regulating Internet content is fraught with difficulty. On the one hand, cyberlibertarians resist any attempts to apply special restraints to Internet access on the apparently reasonable grounds that freedom of expression applies as strongly to the new media as to the traditional media. On the other hand, a variety of other interests, including corporations, parents, ISPs, and state governments, recognize that a number of factors make the Internet a place where special risks arise which have no parallel in traditional media. These circumstances include the anarchic and forthright nature of traditional Internet culture; its untamed nature as an electronic frontier; the ease and cheapness both of access to, and publication on, the Internet; and the difficulty of enforcement of existing national rules imposing both civil and criminal liability given the transjurisdictional nature of the Net. The solutions currently being promoted by conservative interests in the US, whether they are labeled privatized censorship or not, do have an inherent risk of curtailing freedom of expression, and are rather blunt instruments with which to protect children and other vulnerable groups such as racial minorities given the current state of filtering technology. Restraints on content in libraries, in particular, are particularly objectionable given the libraries' role as public repositories of information and as a resource for democratic empowerment. A better and more thoughtful model for dealing with Internet content can be found in the latest Action Plan put forward by the European Union to promote safe use of the Internet. This plan draws a clear division between *illegal* content which is already proscribed by state law; and *harmful* content which, while offensive to some, is not banned but should possibly be restricted in its circulation, particularly for children. In the EU Action Plan, as a primary policy aim, *illegal* content is to be removed from the Net, possibly by cooperation with ISPs undertaking self-regulation by means of a code of conduct. ISPs however are not to be made scapegoats when the providers of original content prove difficult to find or prosecute. *Harmful* content on the other hand is a matter for the personal choice of users who would wish to avoid it. Such users should be empowered to block access to such material for themselves and their children by the provision of appropriate filtering and rating software, tailored to the cultural and linguistic diversity of Europe's heterogeneous population. This would avoid the threat of US-based ratings systems imposing US cultural sensibilities on European users. Finally the EU plan looks to the future with a plan to raise awareness among parents and children of the opportunities and risks of the Internet. The EU plan is not perfect. It provides no real solution to a number of the issues addressed above, not least the fact that the European Union is no more an impermeable island in the sea of the Internet than any single nation state. Illegal content will still arrive in the EU courtesy of foreign sites. Moreover, illegal material as defined by the EU may be considered to be merely harmful elsewhere. But the EU emphasis on making more transparent the values underlying the ratings system — cultural, linguistic, religious, political — and on providing different varieties of ratings schemes, is encouraging. It is certainly an improvement on the PICS software currently dominant in the US. The Internet Watch Foundation, an industry body mainly composed of UK ISPs that supports the EU proposals, recently claimed that PICS lacks only some final tweaking of the available rating systems and that "the ... beauty of this approach is that any adult can see and publish anything they like: the system allows free speech on the Net and free choice to consumers."[37] On the other hand the influential net commentator, Larry Lessig, has suggested that PICS imposes "the most effective global censorship technology ever designed."[38] Both sides have an element of truth. The fact is that in reality neither side of this debate can claim victory. Indeed it remains to be seen whether any system, legal or extralegal, sanction- or software-based, can truly restrict the anarchic conversation and freedom of communication which has become the norm among the growing number of people who frequent the highways of cyberspace.

36 See the list of material recently forbidden entry by the Chinese government in (1998) 3 BNA EIPLR 36.

37 Internet Watch Foundation, *Rating and Filtering Internet Content* (March 1988) at < http://www.internetwatch.org.uk/rating.html >.

38 *Ibid.*, p. 41

ONLINE PORNOGRAPHY: BALANCING FREEDOM OF EXPRESSION AND COMMUNITY VALUES IN PRACTICE

Michael Hudson[1]

This paper is about the migration of pornography into the online environment. It is clear to anyone using the Internet that online pornography is widespread. The Internet already has amplified the amount and accessibility of pornography on a scale that probably exceeds that introduced by the printing press in Europe 400 years ago. It is this increase that has caused a flurry of activity as governments and citizens grapple with questions of regulation, restriction and free speech. But the Internet does not conform to national structures, nor can it be governed by the usual kinds of laws. There have already been many instances where regulation demonstrably failed because of constant and sophisticated attempts to undermine methods of enforcement.

There are many competing interests involved in schemes to control pornography. One of the most conspicuous is the philosophy of freedom of communication that is followed in many countries.[2] There are also legitimate concerns about the harm that may be caused to children by exposure to obscene or offensive materials. Moreover, many believe in protecting all people from material that

1 The author is grateful to Professor Mark Armstrong of the Media and Telecommunications Policy Group at RMIT for thoughtful comments on the text.

2 That freedom is found in written form for example in the United States Bill of Rights, and in Article 19 of the International Covenant on Civil and Political Rights, which 137 countries have ratified.

may have the capacity to corrupt society's morals. Specific cultural and religious policies often include prescriptions about how sexuality and violence, for instance, are to be treated.

The most effective schemes that have emerged so far reveal two changes in the way governments attempt to regulate in this area. First, the emphasis has shifted from local to global. Local laws are an important part of Internet regulation, but they work only if tailored to an international context. Secondly, regulation has become decentralized. A much broader base of participants has emerged to manage Internet issues, such as telecommunications carriers, Internet-service providers and user organizations. Government has become less interventionist and prescriptive and more facilitative. Codes of practice and coregulation are current solutions adapted to this new era.

PORNOGRAPHY GOES ONLINE

One way to discuss various types of online pornography is to use the categories which have been applied to pornography in more traditional forms such as print and film. There are two categories into which pornography is often divided: hardcore and softcore.[3] Distinguishing between the two is a contentious and subjective matter as is distinguishing between forms of hardcore pornography that should be illegal and those forms that should not. Extreme forms of hardcore pornography, which may also include nonconsensual acts, graphic violence, bestiality, or sadomasochism, are banned in many places. Where hardcore pornography is not banned its distribution is generally restricted according to age.

In some countries the task of classifying pornography is performed by a government agency. For example, in Australia, films that are classified "X" are deemed to be unsuitable for sale or exhibition in most Australian states but are not illegal to possess.[4]

Magazines such as *Playboy* and *Penthouse* are usually regarded as softcore pornography. Without attempting a definition, softcore pornography tends to be nonviolent, less sexually explicit and/or less exotic than hardcore pornography. In this sense, unusual forms of sexual behavior such as bestiality and sadomasochism, except in very mild forms, are usually excluded.

---

3 Child pornography is treated as an additional type, below.
4 See for example *Classification (Publications, Films and Computer Games)(Enforcement) Act 1995* (Vic), Part 2.

Unlike pornography in print or cinematographic forms, on the Internet there is no evident effort to distinguish between hardcore and softcore content for marketing purposes or any other reason. This reflects the lack of online regulation. In contrast to traditional forms of pornography, there are few, if any, requirements imposed on the providers of pornographic content. As a consequence content providers do not need to consider the relative character of the material they create for the Internet.

Although pornography is abundant on the Internet, it is rarely encountered by mistake.[5] However, it is readily and freely accessible with the use of the most basic searches. For example, word searches for "sex", "porn", "naked" and even "girl" return hundreds, if not thousands of links to pornography.

Child pornography is a special case. It is probably illegal in every jurisdiction of the world.[6] It may be the only form of material that is universally banned. One of the reasons for that is that it is strongly linked to child abuse and the activities photographed often constitute crimes in themselves. Access to child pornography on the Internet seems mostly confined to closed services such as chat rooms and Usenets.[7] It occurs in both textual and photographic form.[8] The degree of global consensus on the subject matter, the ubiquitous laws, and the penalties mean that it is unlikely to be found on the World Wide Web in significant amounts, and it is unlikely to be discovered by uninformed searching.

PORNOGRAPHY SUCCEEDS ONLINE

"The current concern regarding censorship of pornography is not a recent phenomenon, but dates back to the early days of mass communication."[9]

---

5 Australian Broadcasting Authority, *Investigation into the Content of Online Services: Report to the Minister for Communications and the Arts* (Sydney: July 1996), p. 67, available at < http://www.dca.gov.au/pub/aba/olsfin.doc >. See also findings supported in Reno v ACLU, 521 US, 117 S.Ct. 2329 (1997).

6 Widespread agreement is shown by the support for the European Convention on the Rights of the Child, article 34 of which prohibits the exploitation of children through involvement in pornography, < http://www.unicef.org/crc/articles/a34.htm >. The convention is the most widely ratified human rights treaty in history; see < http://www.unicef.org/crc/conven.htm >. It was unanimously adopted by the United Nations General Assembly on November 20, 1989 and has since been ratified by all countries except the United States and Somalia. See < http://www.unicef.org/crc/status.htm>.

7 Australian Broadcasting Authority, *op. cit.*, p 62.

8 *Ibid.*, p 63. See also Internet Watch Foundation Annual Report, < http://www.internetwatch.org.uk/annual.html >.

9 Goldstein and Kant, *Pornography and Sexual Deviance* (University of California Press, 1973), p 155.

Some would argue that the Internet is doing today what the printing press did in Europe 400 years ago, which is to dramatically expand the dissemination of material. However, the Internet is actually much more than the advent of a new method of content-dissemination. The printing press created the capacity to mass-produce material and therefore widen distribution. The Internet does this but has many additional features which change patterns of dissemination. It can also present and manipulate the content in different forms. Most of these features are well adapted for offering pornography in vivid and arresting form. Rimm considered various factors that make the Internet a convenient medium for transmitting pornography.[10]

▪ "Consumers enjoy considerable privacy on computer networks and can easily avoid the potential embarrassment of walking into an "adult" store to acquire pornography." In addition, the fact that the Internet is available at work or at home at any hour is a convenience that is not matched by books, , videos, or film.

▪ "Second, consumers have the ability to download only those images that they find most sexually arousing. Previously, a consumer had to purchase an entire magazine or video in order to gain access to a few desired depictions." On the Internet the capacity to browse and to select is unlimited. This is an advantage for browsers in places where magazines, for example, can be sold only when contained in a sealed wrapper.[11]

▪ "Third, easy, discreet storage of pornographic images on a computer enables consumers to conceal them from family members, friends, and associates." The technology of encryption enables another layer of concealment to be applied. Images are also easily and discreetly portable on removable disk.

▪ "Fourth, the prevalence and fear of AIDS and other sexually transmitted diseases has helped pornographers to successfully market 'modem sex' and autoeroticism as 'safe' and viable alternatives to the dangers of 'real' sex. Finally, new and highly advanced computer technologies are quickly being absorbed into

10 M. Rimm, "Marketing Pornography on the Information Superhighway," *Georgetown Law Journal*, vol. 83 (June 1995), pp. 1849-1934. (Footnotes omitted.) This article later formed the basis of a cover story article by Philip Elmer-Dewitt, "Coming to a Screen Near You: Cyberporn," *Time Magazine* (July 3, 1995). Rimm's paper was roundly criticized in a paper by Donna L. Hoffman and Thomas P. Novak, "A Detailed Analysis of the Conceptual, Logical, and Methodological Flaws in the Article: 'Marketing Pornography on the Information Superhighway" (July 2, 1995, Vanderbilt University); < http://www2000.ogsm.vanderbilt.edu/rimm.cgi >. The critique sparked a controversial exchange widely reported on the Web. Without entering into the merits of that debate, the author has attempted only to cite apparently undisputed statements and findings from the original Rimm article.

11 In Australia, 'Category 1' publications must not be displayed in an area open to the public unless they are contained in a sealed wrapper (which may be transparent so as to show the cover), *Classification (Publications, Films and Computer Games) (Enforcement) Act 1995* (Vic), section 27.

the mainstream, permitting an ever-expanding audience to gain access to digitized pornography available on the 'Information Superhighway'."

These are not the only key characteristics of the Internet. Discrete services have evolved that are dedicated to pornography and to particular types of pornography. The United States Supreme Court described them as:[12]

"Electronic mail ('e-mail'), automatic mailing list services (sometimes referred to as 'listservs'), 'newsgroups,' 'chat rooms', and the 'World Wide Web.' All of these methods can be used to transmit text; most can transmit sound, pictures, and moving video images. Taken together, these tools constitute a unique medium known to its users as 'cyberspace' located in no particular geographical location but available to anyone, anywhere in the world, with access to the Internet."

These services allow Internet users to find like-minded people all over the world to share ideas, photographs, and stories on topics of interest to them. Products which previously served a small niche market can be very successful on the Internet because their audience reach is no longer geographically restricted. One example is *Wetset* magazine. Produced and coordinated from Australia, the Internet has enabled it to attract an audience and revenue from all over the world.

Another popular feature of the Internet which has powerful implications for the marketing and supply of pornography is its immediacy. For example, a person sitting at a computer in New Zealand could use e-mail to instruct a content provider in Botswana to send images of specified sexual acts. In such cases, the product may be live video, text or still images. It may be made available to anyone connected to the Internet at the time, to members of that site or just to one subscriber.

The Internet is a popular format for the presentation of pornography. The Multiplex site *Where did we go last week?*[13] records the hits made by Australians on a large selection of Internet sites.[14] It publishes the top 100 sites by category as well as in consolidated form. In April and May 1998, around 15 of the top 124 sites were devoted to adult material. Two sites consistently ranked around 30th.[15] Most of the top-30 sites were not dedicated-content services in themselves but, rather, reference or search sites which direct users to other sites of interest.

12 *Reno v. ACLU*, 521 US, 117 S.Ct. 2329 (1997).

13 < http://usrwww.mpx.com.au/~ianw/ >

14 The sample in June 1998 was more than 37,000.

15 < http://www.voyeurweb.com, www.atkingdom.com. > Rankings recorded weekly.

However, for all its apparent advantages and popularity, the Internet is not yet the way to make money. Although there is evidence that operating a business online is more cost effective than operating "offline,"[16] relatively few businesses actually return a profit from online trade. Take one of the most visible and well-known Internet businesses, the bookseller, Amazon.com.[17] It has been cited around the world, and particularly in America, for its phenomenal sales growth. In 1997, Amazon was the third or fourth biggest bookseller in the United States. It had a per quarter revenue of around US$40 million and a share price that had more than quadrupled in the previous year. Amazon has none of the shopfront costs and relatively fewer staffing costs of traditional booksellers. However, despite this "success", it has yet to make a profit. In 1997, it posted a second quarter loss of US$8.5 million and a third quarter loss of US$10 million.[18]

The same is probably true of most businesses trading in pornography online. Business statistics are difficult to find and generalizations or anecdotes about the financial success or financial failure of online-pornography businesses can not be relied on. Organizations that represent the adult-pornography industry, and from whom one might expect such information, are also rare. The Australian EROS Foundation[19] has signed members from most legitimate adult-content providers in Australia but does not yet collect any statistics about their online transactions. Nonetheless, it is apparent that the trade in pornography continues to expand despite social and economic constraints.

The pornography industry is rarely promoted as a means of generating wealth or of improving a country's local or international trade. Its leaders are never held up as examples of successful business people. Government and the community never defend it; although legal, its treatment seems similar to that applied to the trade in "soft" drugs. That is because pornography is an ethical issue and accounts about pornography in society are always accompanied by polarized debates

---

16 Forrester Research found that the cost of an Internet transaction is only one third as much to process as a telephone transaction and that a computer taking orders 24 hours a day, seven days a week, costs less than employing human personnel; < http://promarket.com/pmflyer.htm. >

17 < http://www.amazon.com >

18 Figures taken from Chris O'Hanlon, "Retailers' Spin May Stretch Truth on Web Sales," *Australian Financial Review* (January 23, 1998), p, 52; and Eric Ellis, "Online Bookseller in Frontline of Battle to Make the Net Pay," *Australian Financial Review* (weekend edition, March 14-15, 1998), p. 12.

19 < http://www.eros.com.au/ >.

about ethics. Many countries, rightly or wrongly, are still bound to the values that characterized crackdowns on the trade in erotica in Victorian England.[20] Governments believe that to support the pornography trade is political suicide. In most cases, the safe option is to oppose it or, at most, to be neutral.

On the other hand, it can be just as controversial to impose restrictions on pornography. This is particularly so in countries which support freedom of expression as an important civil liberty. In 1997, for example, the US government lost the battle over the Communications Decency Act (CDA). Among other things, the Act made illegal the "knowing" transmission of "obscene or indecent" messages to any recipient under 18 years of age[21] and prohibited the "knowing" sending or displaying to a person under 18 of any message "that, in context, depicts or describes, in terms patently offensive as measured by contemporary community standards, sexual or excretory activities or organs."[22] On June 26, 1997, the Supreme Court upheld a decision of the District Court which found the CDA constitutionally invalid. The Court confirmed earlier cases which held that where "obscenity is not involved, the fact that protected speech may be offensive to some does not justify its suppression"[23] and that "the fact that society may find speech offensive is not sufficient reason for suppressing it."[24]

Governments around the world are feeling similar restraints. Add to that the practical difficulty of controlling a medium as mercurial and abundant as the Internet and one appreciates the need to reconsider the fundamental approach to regulation. Most of the community and Internet-allied commercial groups support some form of regulation of content. The difficulty is finding something that is effective and enforceable as well as acceptable to opposing interests.

20 For a review of the approach to censorship in the Victorian era, see G. Robertson, *Obscenity* (London: Weidenfield and Nicholson, 1979), and R. Fox, *The Concept of Obscenity* (Melbourne: The Law Book Company, 1967). For general information on Victorian England, see S. Mitchell, *Daily Life in Victorian England* (Greenwood Publishing Group, 1996).

21 Communications Decency Act, title 47 U.S.C.A. ¤223(a)(1)(B)(ii).

22 Communications Decency Act, title 47 U.S.C.A. ¤223(d). There were limited defenses to both these offenses.

23 *Carey v. Population Services Int'l*, 431 US 678, 701 (1977) Consistently with this decision, the Supreme Court in *Reno v. ACLU*, 521 US, 117 S.Ct. 2329 (1997) found that the CDA was constitutional insofar as it applied to "obscene" material but not "indecent" or "offensive" material; pp. 37-39. In the earlier case of *Miller v. California*, 413 U. S. 15, at p. 24, the Court had adopted a three-prong test of obscenity.

24 *FCC v. Pacifica Foundation*, 438 U. S. 726, 745 (1978).

25 Rebecca Vesely, *Wired* (January 21, 1997), < http://www.wired.com/news/topframe/1587.html >. Other general

INTERNATIONAL CONTROL OF ONLINE PORNOGRAPHY

In the last five years much time and money has been spent on investigating ways to regulate the flow of obscene material over the Internet. There have been numerous failed attempts. A nonpornographic example from September 1996 is the German censorship of the Dutch magazine *Radikal*. The magazine, which has advocated the overthrow of the German government by force, is not illegal in Holland. At the direction of German prosecutors, a number of Germany's Internet-service Providers (ISPs) excluded all material originating from the Dutch server, XS4ALL, which hosted the offending site. After the blocking, the publication popped up on at least another 40 mirror sites around the world offering a range of alternative access paths to German citizens. This fact was communicated to the German authorities by letter from XS4ALL. The ban was raised a short time later and described in *Wired* magazine as "like pointing a fire hose at a beehive — instead of quashing the bees, it only scatters them, and makes them more insistent."[25]

Such episodes have led to a broad convergence of views about how obscene content should be managed. Several Asian countries have abandoned initial attempts to rigorously control the flow of information online. Global business incentives and the sheer volume of material work against it. In late 1997, Singapore authorities were trying to filter every transmission entering the country,[26] but as traffic and the potential for online commerce increased, a licensing scheme and a self-regulatory approach were adopted.[27] Malaysia showed support for online commerce in 1997 with the introduction of a package of "cyberlaws" designed to encourage businesses to move online.[28]

The Australian Broadcasting Authority completed one of the earliest and most comprehensive reports on the regulation of online services in 1996.[29] Recognizing

---

references to the ban are at < http://www.xs4all.nl/~felipe/press/global-alert.txt >, < http://www.xs4all.nl/~felipe/germany.html >, and < http://www.wired.com/news/politics/story/3265.html >. Access to the magazine itself may be obtained at < http://www.xs4all.nl/~radikal/ >.

26 Eric Wilson, *Australian Financial Review* (September 26, 1997), p. S14.

27 The Australian Broadcasting Authority, *The Internet and Some International Regulatory Issues Relating to Content* (Sydney: October 1997), pp. 38ff. (This pilot comparative study prepared for UNESCO is known as *The ABA/UNESCO Report*.)

28 < http://www.news.com/News/Item/0,4,17358,00.html >; <http://www.news.com/News/Item/0,4,7351,00.html >; *ABA/UNESCO Report*, p. 38.

29 *The ABA/UNESCO Report*.

the Internet as a global medium, which tends to elude traditional forms of regulation, it recommended that:

"Industry codes of practice be developed by online service providers. This emerging industry group provides an important intermediary function in the online environment and can achieve much in terms of finding practical and workable solutions to address community concerns." [30]

The development of codes of practice and self-regulation has gained support around the world.[31] The most frequently contemplated self-regulatory schemes include the following elements:

▪ A collective body to represent defined classes of business which play some role in the placement of information online. They may include Internet-service providers, content providers, and even carriers.

▪ A code of practice which is the result of agreement between online groups and which specifies the obligations, responsibilities, and penalties for noncompliance which bind each group.

▪ A legislative scheme which provides the authority and measures for enforcement of the obligations contained in codes of practice. It may also grant indemnities from liability where provisions of the code have been followed.

▪ The implementation of rating systems or classification systems for Internet material that allow software installed on users' computers to filter out unwanted Internet content.

▪ A mechanism for communication between the end-users and online businesses or some independent organization. Such a channel is particularly important for the lodging and processing of complaints about online content. Most jurisdictions recognize that the consumer of information is in the best position to locate obscene content and notify appropriate bodies about it.

The ubiquitous nature of the Internet means that regulation cannot effectively be centralized. Codes of practice recognize regulatory roles for a much larger proportion of those who make up the Internet and online community. This means that everyone from consumers to the government must be involved in

---

30 *The ABA Report*, p 10.

31 Examples include the Internet Service Provider Association of Belgium < http://www.a-1.be/en/ispa.html >; The Internet Service Providers Association of the UK (ISPA-UK) < http://www.ispa.org.uk/ >; NLIP, Dutch Foundation for Internet Providers < http://www.nlip.nl/ >; The Australian Internet Industry Association < http://www.iia.net.au/ >; The French Internet code, < http://www.planete.net/code-Internet/index.html >; Information Technology Association of America < http://www.itaa.org/index.html >; and The Electronic Network Consortium Japan < http://www.nmda.or.jp/enc/index-english.html >.

making decisions about content and in eliminating or restricting access to material thought appropriate. Initiatives to achieve this result are under way all over the world.[32]

One of the most successful self-regulatory schemes is Internet Watch (IWF).[33] It established a hotline and began accepting complaints about Internet content on 3 December 1996. In its first year of operation, a total of 781 reports were processed which led to consideration of more than 4,000 items.[34] Around 85 per cent of those were concerned with child pornography; the rest included other pornography, racism and financial scams. The majority of reports referred to Usenet articles with a large proportion on the World Wide Web.[35] Consumers are able to report material by e-mail, fax and telephone.

Online businesses have also begun to use their own methods of regulation, sometimes in parallel with codes. It is in the interests of legitimate providers of adult content to prevent perusal of their material by minors. Many do this by incorporating links to companies offering software filters that give parents and others the capacity to block pornographic content.[36] In any event, many of the sites which offer either hardcore or softcore material allow browsers to see samples without any conditions.

Because the Internet operates above a local level, jurisdictional barriers are hampering the capacity of each country to implement schemes which protect the community from obscene material. This has led to investigations by public and private international organizations, such as the World Wide Web Consortium, the EC, OECD, and UNESCO. It has also spawned mandated groups such as the International Working Group on Content Rating. Collective initiatives such as these are probably the most effective way to arrive at policies that have a multijurisdictional operation.

---

32 For a short list of them, see < http://www2.echo.lu/best_use/advice.html >. In April 1997, the Internet Law and Policy Forum, Content Blocking Working Group, published a report which included summaries of national initiatives on content blocking and details about self-regulatory programs which had commenced around the world; < http://www.ilpf.org/work/content.htm >.

33 < http://www.internetwatch.com >.

34 IWF Annual Report, < http://www.internetwatch.org.uk/annual.html >.

35 Usenet articles represented 45 per cent of reports while the Web represented 39 per cent, IWF Annual Report, < http://www.internetwatch.org.uk/annual.html >.

36 See for example < http://www.sexgalore.com/ >, which gives links to Web Track, Net Nanny, CyberPatrol, Surfwatch Cybersitter, and Safe Surf.

Software Filters and Content Rating

The World Wide Web Consortium (W3C)[37] was one of the earliest collaborative ventures founded to develop common protocols for the smooth evolution of the World Wide Web, not only on content issues. In 1996, it initiated the Platform for Internet Content Selection (PICS).[38] Organizations in several countries established labeling schemes for use by parents and schools which conformed to the PICS standards. The most prominent was the Recreational Software Advisory Council labeling scheme for the Internet (RSACi).[39] The RSACi labeling system addresses the level of violence, sex, nudity, and language on a Web site. Content is given a rating between 0 and 4 on each of these topics. The label operates as a classification of the content on an Internet site rather than making a judgment about its appropriateness for any given audience or purpose and gives users the ultimate choice about what material they wish to see. Such an approach has advantages over those filtering programs that operate on a keyword basis to exclude offensive material as, inevitably, a significant amount of useful, inoffensive content is also blocked. Its major disadvantage is that it is limited to rating controversy, rather than more general information. Consequently, it is not adapted to perform more complex information retrieval searches. SafeSurf[40], Cyber Patrol[41] and Net Nanny[42] are examples of filtering software that can operate with PICS and RSACi protocols.

As an extension of the PICS initiatives, in 1997 W3C created the Metadata Activity, which includes the Resource Description Framework (RDF) Working Group.[43] RDF is a protocol for description of Internet content based on a set of 15 categories of information, known as the Dublin Core.[44] It continues in the PICS tradition of creating data sets about Web pages that may be searched rather than having to scan the contents of pages themselves. In this sense, it is termed "metadata" or data about data. The Dublin Core is not restricted to controversial content such as language, sex, and violence but is sophisticated enough to

37 W3C homepage: < http://www.w3.org/ >
38 < http://www.w3c.org/PICS/ >
39 RSAC homepage: < http://www.rsac.org/ >
40 Safesurf homepage: < http://www.safesurf.com/filter/index.html >.
41 Nortel homepage (manufacturers of Cyber Patrol): < http://www.nortel.net/index.html >.
42 Net Nanny homepage: < http://www.netnanny.com/ >.
43 Press release: < http://www.w3.org/Press/RDF >.
44 Named after Dublin, Ohio where the system was conceived.

consider, among other factors, authorship and source.[45] Obscene-content rating is just one potential use; it has been designed to perform more complex retrieval tasks such as search-engine data collection, and digital library collections.[46] It has not yet been widely touted as an alternative to those schemes that eliminate content on the basis of controversial content alone.

The European Commission Initiatives

The European Commission had explicit concerns about pornography long before the Internet appeared.[47] In recent years, two documents have been at the center of the European Commission's initiatives on the regulation of online content.[48] These papers were both released in October 1996, and aimed to generate public and industry debate about the best approach to adopt for the regulation of online services.

The European Telecommunications Council (ETC) extended the debate about Internet content issues by urging the following measures:[49]

▨ Encourage and facilitate self-regulatory systems including representative bodies for ISPs and users, effective codes of conduct and, possibly, hot-line reporting mechanisms available to the public.

Encourage the provision to users of filtering mechanisms and the setting up of rating systems (for instance, the PICS standard, launched by the international World Wide Web consortium with Commission support, should be promoted).

On November 26, 1997, the European Commission adopted the "Action Plan on promoting safe use of the Internet," which it set out in a communication to the European Parliament.[50] The key points contained in the *Action Plan* were:

▨ Promotion of self-regulation and creation of content-monitoring schemes, including an European network of hot-lines to achieve a high level of protection

45 For a description of the categories, see < http://purl.oclc.org/metadata/dublin_core_elements >.

46 < http://www.w3.org/Metadata/RDF/ >.

47 For example, the European Convention on the Rights of the Child adopted by the United Nations General Assembly in 1989; < http://www.unicef.org/crc/conven.htm >.

48 *Communication on illegal and harmful content*, and *Green Paper on the Protection of Minors and Human Dignity in Audio-visual and Information Services*. Both papers are available at < http://www2.echo.lu/legal/en/Internet/internet.html >, and details of global initiatives at < http://www2.echo.lu/best_use/legal.html >.

49 On November 28, 1996, a working party convened by the ETC submitted an Interim Report ("Interim Report on Initiatives in EU Member States with respect to combating Illegal and Harmful Content on the Internet"; < http://www2.echo.lu/legal/en/Internet/content/communic.html >). It was adopted as an ETC resolution on February 17, 1997; < http://www2.echo.lu/legal/en/Internet/content/resol.html >. On April 24, 1997, the European Parliament also adopted a resolution arising from a report on the European Commission Communication, urging a cooperative approach between countries; COM (96) 0487 - C4-0592/96, < http://www.europarl.eu.int/dg1/a4/en/a4-97/a4-0098.htm> .

50 < http://www2.echo.lu/legal/en/Internet/actpl-cp.html >.

(especially dealing with content such as child pornography, racism, or antisemitism).

■ Demonstration and application of effective filtering services and compatible rating systems, which take account of cultural and linguistic diversity.

■ Promotion of awareness actions directed at users, in particular children, parents, and teachers, to allow them to use Internet resources provided by industry safely and with confidence.

The Action Plan emphasized that the best method to implement these initiatives was through cooperation between users, industry, and government. It distinguished between illegal content on the one hand, and harmful content on the other. In the case of illegal content, it was the principal responsibility of the law enforcement authorities to impose restrictions and penalties. The role of industry was recognized as confined to restricting circulation as far as possible. In the case of harmful content, it concluded that "the priority actions should be in enabling users to deal with harmful content through the development of technological solutions (filtering and content rating systems), to increase parental awareness, and to developing self-regulation which can provide an adequate framework, particularly for the protection of minors."[51]

These documents make it clear that the availability of unrestricted content on the Internet is of serious concern in Europe, particularly in the area of child pornography. It is also clear that the European Parliament does not consider that the regulation of Internet content is something that can be done effectively at a national level. There are express indications that the best method is seen to be the adoption of international cooperative procedures for dealing both with outright illegal content and for the appropriate classification of material that should have a restricted audience. It is thought that the identification, prosecution and penalization of offenders also be undertaken according to an internationally agreed protocol.

International Working Group on Content Rating (IWGCR)

■ The IWGCR was formed at the Global Information Networks Ministerial Conference in July 1997,[52] as a result of collaboration between the Recreational Software Advisory Council based in the USA, the Australian Broadcasting

51 *Ibid.* p. 3.
52 Press release: < http://www.iwf.org.uk/p080797.html >.

Authority, and the INCORE partners.[53] The aim was to design a content rating framework which was consistent with the work which had already been done.[54] Formal meetings were held in September 1997 and following the Online Summit in Washington in December 1997.[55] The IWGCR put forward seven principles for a global rating system:[56]

■ It must be world-wide and open to as many cultures as wish to participate.

■ It must be culturally neutral in its content descriptions, and as objective as possible, to enable broad subscription.

■ It must be easy for users, especially parents, to understand and use.

■ It must meet the needs of content-providers for a simple means to rate content.

■ It must have rigorous quality-control mechanisms to avoid mistakes in rating.

■ It must be based on a matrix of categories and of levels negotiated between different countries. The RSACi system uses only four categories of content. Under IWGCR proposals it is likely that this will be expanded.

■ It must be as adaptable as possible, and work across technologies.

CONCLUSION

If we look back at the past, we shall find that there has always been pornography ranging from the most beautiful erotic art to public rape.[57] Pornography can be traced from ancient civilizations to today. It is subject to varying and continually changing social and legal attitudes. Throughout, the concepts of art, pornography and obscenity have been under constant definitional challenge. Where one finishes and another begins has never found a settled answer. Many authors have

---

53 The INCORE partners are ECO Forum from Germany, the Internet Watch Foundation from the UK, and Childnet International. Childnet International is a nonprofit organization with headquarters in London. It also operates in the USA as an independent nonprofit organization; < http://www.childnet-int.org/who.html >.

54 < http://www.dca.gov.au/aba/unesco7.htm >.

55 Internet Watch Foundation, Report, *Rating And Filtering Internet Content: A United Kingdom Perspective* (March 1998); < http://www.internetwatch.org.uk/rating.html >.

56 Taken from a summary of an address given at the ESPRIT conference in Brussels on November 24, 1997 by Nigel Williams, Director of Childnet International; < http://www.childnet-int.org/ratings/index.html >.

57 David Holbrook, "A Historical Perspective," in *Pornography: The Longford Report*, Appendix IV, (London: Coronet Books and Hodder Paperbacks Ltd., 1972), p. 449.

undertaken in depth explorations of the origins and definition of pornography.[58] The invention of the Internet has had at least two important impacts on pornography in society to date. The first is the scale. The Internet is already prolific and continuing to spread around the world at exponential rates.[59] Like the printing press, the Internet is a communications advance which has already revolutionized and amplified the exchange of information between humans. Unlike the printing press, the Internet has introduced multidirectional traffic on a mass scale. The interactivity of the Internet challenges the distinction between supply and demand by also giving the audience the capacity to be suppliers. This capacity, and the relatively low cost of connection to the Internet, has increased the number of content providers and the types of content. The result is that information on a formidable range of topics, including pornography, is more accessible to more people than ever before.

The second major impact of the Internet on pornography is on content. Again, the interactive nature of the Internet is responsible for this effect. Different forms of pornography have been thoroughly explored for thousands of years but the manner in which they have been represented has always been dictated and limited by the media in which they appeared. The invention of the camera captured pornography in photographs. The invention of film presented it as moving pictures. The advent of communication by telephone provided the means for interactive "phone sex." The technology of the Internet gathers together the old options and creates new ones. Electronic bulletin boards, chat rooms and listservs are three examples. Some pornography sites allow members to interact with the subjects and to request particular material with immediate results. The result of all this is a compelling immediacy.

The amplification of pornography through its migration to the Internet has rekindled debate around the world about the treatment of pornography in society. Because every country sees a need for some control of online content, there are numerous local and cross-cultural initiatives to investigate ways to do this. But a mixture of regulatory failure, conflicting cultural perspectives, and

---

58 Details on these topics are contained in, for example, G. Robertson, *Obscenity* (London: Weidenfield and Nicholson, 1979), chapter 3; B. McNair, *Mediated Sex: Pornography and Postmodern Culture* (London: Arnold, 1996), chapter 4; Goldstein and Kant, *Pornography and Sexual Deviance* (University of California Press, 1973), chapter 1; T. Emerson, *The System of Freedom of Expression* (New York: Random House, 1970), chapter XIII.

59 About 40 million people were using the Internet in mid-1996. That number is expected to increase to 200 million by 1999; *Reno v. ACLU*, 521 US, 117 S.Ct. 2329 (1997).

technological intuition has led to the realization that local action will not be an adequate remedy for perceived problems.

This means that any potential "solutions" must be flexible enough to accommodate laws and cultural philosophies of different countries. Some of this flexibility is built into the most prominent schemes now under serious consideration. These offer a content-rating approach for all Internet content that will allow filtering of material according to defined markings. The ability to define which parameters should be excluded and which should be freely accessible can accommodate cultural differences. Filtering is normally performed automatically by software installed at strategic points along the supply chain.

Filtering schemes call for reliance on a broader base of regulation than has typically been tolerated in most countries. Commonly termed self-regulation or coregulation, this involves greater participation from carriers, Internet-service providers, content providers, and users. By contrast, the technological protocols underpinning these schemes must be uniform. If software filters are going to be effective on material that can originate from anywhere in the world, they must operate on consistent, objective parameters all over the world. At this level, international cooperation is essential.

The Internet demands international thinking in an increasing number of areas. As more social and financial activities are drawn to the Internet, there will be greater need and use of internationally-recognized protocols for regulation. Pornography was one of the earliest and most controversial subjects to move online, but it will become a smaller and smaller part of the global regulatory scheme. In this sense, online pornography has played a valuable role in forcing countries to change the ways in which they address online issues. It was one of the triggers for the formation of cooperative international regulatory groups which are now well-placed to pursue policy development on other issues as they arise.

Local mechanisms are likely to become secondary to global imperatives. The challenge will be for each country to design its interaction and conformity with international protocols so as to protect local culture from impingement by others. The flexibility of rating systems for Internet content can assist this balance. It is clear that there is no simple solution to online pornography. There is no perfect compromise to satisfy proponents of liberalization and proponents of regulation. There is no guaranteed way to protect the values of local cultures from the influence of foreign ones. It is clear that the best approach will be multifaceted.

REPORTS FROM THE FIELD

NEW INFORMATION AND COMMUNICATION TECHNOLOGIES: FREEING INFORMATION FLOWS OR WIDENING SOUTH-NORTH GAPS?

Chin Saik Yoon

THE NEW INFORMATION AND COMMUNICATION TECHNOLOGIES

The Internet is probably the most famous example of the new information and communication technologies (ICT)s introduced over the past decade. It triggered a global trend towards computer-based communication. It also did more to promote the use of computers in homes than any previous application. The excitement generated by the phenomenal growth of the Internet, particularly the World Wide Web (WWW), has over-shadowed a number of other significant innovations within the information and communications sectors. Among these are global satellite television and radio broadcasting, cellular telephones, satellite telephones, clockwork radio receivers, high definition television, publish-on-demand books and newspapers, CD-ROMs, "talking-books", palm-sized electronic information tools, facsimile machines, and more.

Most of these innovations process, store and transmit information in the binary language of computers. The universal adoption and application of the language created for the first time in human history a common platform for the handling of information and cultural material as diverse as text, graphics, speech and music, full motion video, statistical data and many other types of audio and visual products.

Digitization of television and radio programming also made it possible to compress broadcast content into smaller digital packages for more cost-effective transmission over scarce satellite channels. The advent of compression technologies sometimes increased by 10 times the broadcasting capacities of satellites for mass media content. This innovation occurred in tandem with (and probably facilitated) the rapid expansion of a few very large media conglomerates into the establishment of truly global television broadcast services.

Satellite and other forms of long-distance telecommunication links were at the same time used by the print media to transmit high-quality facsimiles and digital versions of their publications around the world. This enables, for example, a newspaper edited, typeset, and designed in Paris to be published simultaneously in Hong Kong, Singapore, Paris, London, New York and San Francisco. Similar technology is used to distribute digital versions of popular local and national newspapers to "publish-on-demand" outlets (such as those found in major North American airports).

The publish-on-demand technology has a small number of users compared with the compact disc read-only memory (CD-ROM) format. On CD-ROMs, the electronic versions of documents are delivered on small plastic platters and content accessed directly via personal computers fitted with appropriate disc-drives and software. The main advantage of CD-ROMs over paper-based publish-on-demand technology lies in the powerful search-and-retrieval software which is delivered with the discs.

The "Appropriate" ICTs

The rapid development of personal computer based technologies overshadowed equally significant innovations in other areas of the communications and information sector. One such innovation is the clockwork radio which is powered by a spring wound up in the fashion of mechanical clocks. The spring is linked to a mechanism which generates electricity to operate the radio. The clockwork radio promises to overcome the familiar problem of obtaining batteries to power transistor radios belonging to listeners living in isolated communities. It should also help the poor who cannot afford to buy regular supplies of batteries.(This clockwork energy technology has since been adapted to power devices ranging from lap-top computers to portable water purification units.)

Over the past decade we also saw the introduction of radio, television and telecommunication services to more parts of the developing world. Although considered "old" technologies in the developed world, these technologies are relatively "new" to these regions. Governments and development agencies often played catalytic roles in the diffusion of these technologies by funding the construction of the infrastructure, setting-up and staffing the organizations responsible for producing the broadcast content or telephone exchanges, and providing radio and television receivers to poor communities which could not afford to buy their own. A notable exception is the spread of the video cassette recorder (VCR) which has been funded largely by local entrepreneurs in the South who use the VCRs and television sets, and electricity generation sets, to operate "video parlours" where they charge small admission fees. In many parts of the developing world, visitors have been surprised to find these video parlours operating in remote villages not reached by other forms of mass media.

The other technology which diffused quickly across the developing world via commercial sales, particularly in the Asian region, is the facsimile machine. The spread of these machines suddenly sky-rocketed in the mid-1980s as a large enough user base was finally established to make the sending and receiving of faxes a universally viable means of communication. The diffusion process within Asia was fueled by the capacity of the machine to handle any of the hundreds of calligraphic scripts in which Asian languages are written.

THE SOUTH'S ACCESS

The developing countries" access to the latest ICTs has been limited. Computer-based and Internet-related technologies require the support of an extensive infrastructure for them to operate. Electricity is required to power the hardware; and stable local and international telecommunications links to make the connections with computer networks which collectively form the Internet. The rural hinterlands of developing countries have largely been denied access to the new technologies because such major infrastructural facilities often do not exist outside major urban centres of the South. This absence of rural connectivity leads sometimes to the conclusion that computers and the Internet is inappropriate to the developing world. The development community often finds itself divided on the relevance of computer networking systems to the short-term needs of the South. This division is deepened by the type of information now available on the World Wide Web (WWW) of the Internet. The WWW content is published predominantly (estimated at 80 per cent) in the English language; and the topics covered very often relate more to wealthy, industrialized societies than the priorities of developing communities.

While the development community engaged in heated debates about the appropriateness of the new ICTs, the private sector has swiftly and quietly proceeded with the introduction of profitable new technologies. This has led to some striking examples of technological leap-frogging. Visitors to the capital cities of some of the least developed countries are frequently surprised by the proliferation of mobile cellular telephones even as conventional telephone service continues to be plagued by engineering problems and the wait for a new subscriber line may be several years. A more startling example is the spread of satellite-based mobile telephones, which are considered exotic even in industrialized communities, in very remote locations of the South where capital cities themselves suffer from chronic infrastructural failures. These services now reach a small group of elite users with the resources to purchase expensive handsets and batteries and pay the high connection charges.

Television programming broadcast directly from satellites is the other technology introduced principally by the private sector. Because the area of coverage (or "footprint") of such broadcasts tends to be broad and non-discriminating, many countries in the South enjoy spill-over broadcast coverage not intended primarily for them. This is the case in Asia where several countries with least developed economic status are situated across the borders from relatively wealthy neighbours.

CONTROLLING ACCESS

Until the advent of many of the new ICTs, governments of the South had near-total control of public information flow and channels of mass communication within their political borders. The mass media were either directly owned and operated by a government department, or indirectly controlled via media companies owned and managed by interests aligned with the political leadership. This ownership structure produced a media philosophy which is the complete opposite to that found in industrialized countries. Northern media has long positioned itself as relentless watch-dogs of their governments and private sector; their reportage and commentary are frequently combative and confrontational. Such critical and openly hostile journalism is held up as their chief indicator of a free press and their special contribution to the democratic process.

The media in the South see themselves as partners of government in improving the quality of life of the people and the economy and security of the country. Southern media see their role very much as educators and mobilizers of the citizenry towards realizing national aspirations visualized by the national leadership. They argue that limited resources and energies in the South are too scarce and precious to be spent fueling potentially devastating conflicts, and should be focused instead on furthering common interests and nurturing the fragile nationhood of their countries. This philosophy of Southern media permitted policymakers and politicians to exert far-reaching influence on national mass communication systems until the new ICTs appeared on the scene and effectively disrupted the comfortable monopolies and oligopolies enjoyed by the national media up to that time.

FORCED ENTRY BY TRANSNATIONAL MEDIA CONGLOMERATES

The advent of direct satellite broadcasts worried the Southern political leadership because they saw themselves and their constituencies losing control over news reportage and, political and economic commentary. Foreign-owned and offshore- based news services acquired, overnight in some instances, a self-appointed right to take vigourous part in the national agenda of foreign countries via critical and often adversarial editorial commentary. The vast financial, production and human resources of the foreign media quickly won over Southern audiences with their superior design and editorial techniques, as well as blunt commentary styles which reflected the watch-dog philosophy of their Northern managers. Several governments in the South had knee-jerk reactions to this and promptly passed legislation to ban the means of accessing these foreign broadcasts. Ownership of satellite antennas and related decoding hardware was outlawed. Many later softened their policies to accommodate the medium by licensing locally owned television stations and cable services to relay the foreign broadcasts.

As the world became their audience, satellite television companies quickly developed their news gathering capabilities to cover the planet. Portable news studios were built which could be quickly packed into the cargo containers of aeroplanes for despatch to far corners of the world to cover breaking news. A trend then developed where celebrity anchor-persons moved to remote centres of major news events for extensive on-the-spot coverage. Such saturation coverage was targeted at the lucrative North American media markets and reflected a North American bias.

The presence of foreign news crews also frequently acted as "lighting rods" for local political opposition to the established powers. Dissidents quickly learnt the power of a dramatic sound-bite and an arresting news-clip. They often staged incidents for the foreign news cameras to draw attention to their causes. It is interesting that this manipulation of the foreign media by dissidents gave the South reverse access to the new media in a powerful way which brought formidable pressures to bear on the Southern political leadership.

Satellite television brought not only news and commentary but also entertainment into develping regions. Made-up of music videos, situation comedies, soap operas and sleekly-crafted advertisements, this content is considered "harmless" and generally ignored by policy-makers and media gate-keepers. But many community leaders and media critics in both the South and North are alarmed by the popularity of this material with local audiences. They fear these foreign productions will undermine local cultural and social values in profound ways, producing a new and very subtle form of "colonialization". Cees Hamelink[1], a prominent international communication researcher based in Amsterdam, calls this the "McDonaldization" of culture leading to the creation of a standardized form of global culture which not only erodes indigenous cultural identity but also promotes an alien lifestyle which is not sustainable.

The long-term implications of a supply of global cultural products being dominated by a few sources extends well beyond basic gate-keeping and commercial interests into the very survival of whole cultures and all the economic and political interests which they support.

RESULTS OF FORCED ENTRY

The arrival of the transnational media conglomerate caused one positive impact upon the South. The fierce competition they caused shook-up generally complacent national media organizations. Alarmed by the rapid loss of audiences and readers to the foreign-owned media, many governments and Southern media managers have been motivated to liberalize their domestic communication policies. National media is being given greater freedom to practise more forthright journalism and to adopt more attractive production and editorial formats. Some media organizations have also been provided with much needed financial resources to improve their production, distribution and broadcast infrastructures. Funds are also being allocated to train and upgrade the skills of their media professionals.

1 Cees J Hamelink, *Trends in world communication: On disempowerment and self-empowerment* (Penang, Malaysia: Southbound,1994) pp 111–114.

But not all the domestically generated changes have been desirable. One trend which attracts concern is the tendency of national media to emulate the production formats of the international media. We now see the proliferation of music video and game shows, soap operas, and situation comedies which are basically local language clones of international productions. Whether such cloning of standardized global media formats is any better than the foreign productions themselves remains to be researched.

SOUTH-NORTH FLOWS

Transnational media conglomerates comprising global television, radio, newspapers, magazines and book publishers have always been owned and managed by media moguls, press barons, and para-statal organizations from rich industrialized countries because of the vast financial resources needed to establish and operate them successfully. The South, with its limited financial resources and almost non-existent high-technology base to handle most of the new ICTs, has been kept out of the global big media sector. As a result the flow of information and cultural products remains predominantly from North to South.

What is more startling is that even South-to-South information flows continue to be routed through the North. We see this happening on a daily basis in news coverage where one national television station in the South may obtain news footage about events happening in a neighbouring Third World country via a transnational media conglomerate based in Paris, London or Atlanta.

Asia offers some examples of experiments to by-pass this dependence on the North. In television news gathering, the Asia Vision news exchange programme which is based in Tokyo, Japan and Kuala Lumpur, Malaysia, has brought together national television stations to swap television news footage with each other.[2] The Asia Vision initiative is undertaken by the Asian Broadcasting Union which has also organized and managed several co-productions for television focusing on the cultures of member states.

The other interesting initiative is the DEPTHnews Features Service operated by the Press Foundation of Asia. The service commissions features and reports from

---

2 Chin Saik Yoon, "Asian development communications in the 1990s," in David Nostbakken and Charles Morrow, *Cultural Expression in the Global Village* (Penang, Malaysia: Southbound, 1993), pp 119-120.

Asian journalists which are then edited by Asians based at their editorial offices in Manila before being sent via regular postal service to subscribers in the region.

But the advent of the Internet, and particularly the network"s World Wide Web (WWW), has presented the South with its first significant opportunity to reverse some of the heavily lopsided information flow. The technology employed is relatively affordable, and the cost of operating a WWW site is also within the means of most national or provincial groups in the South. While the skills and knowledge required to connect to the Internet and publishing on the WWW remain in short supply in the majority of developing countries, a critical mass of such talent appears to be developing quickly. Communicators in the South have been quick to realize that while the WWW will remain an inappropriate technology for serving grassroots communities within the South, at least for a time, it is potentially a powerful and cost-effective medium for reaching the elites and policy-makers in both the South and North. Civil society in the South may have discovered an appropriate and potent instrument for advocacy.

Apart from technological access, the WWW offers a surprisingly level "playing-field" on which information providers of both the South and North can compete fairly. Because of the need to design content which can be accessed quickly over regular telephone lines, WWW publishers around the world adopt basic, technical production values for their Web sites. This has helped avoid the situation faced by the South in television broadcasting whereby transnational media conglomerates using cosmetically more attractive program packaging are able to win audiences away from Southern media which can only afford to adopt basic production approaches.

COMPETING FOR CONTROL OF THE DIGITAL FRONTIERS

The Internet has remained until now a global model of a participatory medium open to all users in the South and North. A big part of its attractive philosophy can be traced to the active role played by the academic community in pioneering its growth and setting an altruistic tone of operation. In recent years commercialism has crept into the network as greater numbers of commercial users have changed some of the Internet"s norms and concerted efforts are being made to convert the network into a superhighway for electronic commerce.

The governance of the Internet now faces fundamental changes. Contrary to popular description of the Internet as a truly decentralized computer network without any controlling hub, such a nerve-centre does exist in the form of a small putty-coloured plastic box measuring 18 inches square and just over seven inches high sitting on a small aluminum shelf in a squat brick office building in Herndon, a town about an hour"s drive east of Washington D.C.[3] The box is a high-speed personal computer which operates the "A" root server, the meeting point of all computer networks linked to the Internet. Without this box the Internet will not work. The maintenance contract of the root server by a U.S. private sector contractor expires in April 1998. The National Telecommunications and Information Administration of the U.S. Department of Commerce has proposed a new long-term plan for not only the maintenance and operation of the "A" root server but also the governance of the Internet. The proposal is described in a paper popularly referred to as "The Green Paper".[4] It has attracted much concern outside of the U.S. for its suggestion that the U.S. Government retain "oversight" of the operation of the Internet.

The Internet Society (ISOC), a non-profit, non-governmental international organization which has provided leadership in the management of Internet related standards, educational, and policy development issues, responded to The Green Paper by stating that "the US government would be well-advised to leave the details ... to be defined in a self-determination process..."[5] The ISOC also asserted that "...if the Internet is ever to reach its fullest potential, it will require self-governance. If any one entity attempts to control or govern the Internet, it is likely others would protest. It then follows: if consensus is not reached, the Internet could very well become fragmented and, accordingly, cease to exist as we now know it".

Political interests are not the only factors behind current attempts to control the Internet. A gold mine of commercial profits is waiting to be tapped. The some-

---

3 Monte Paulsen, "Raiders of the last ark,"< http://www.NewHavenAdvocate.com/articles/raiders.html >, accessed on 19 March 1998 .

4 US Department of Commerce, "A proposal to improve technical management of Internet names and addresses," < http://www.ntia.doc.gov/ntiahome/domainname/dnsdrf.htm >, accessed on 30 January 1998.

5 Internet Society "Comments of the Internet Society in regards to the Department of Commerce, National Telecommunications and Information Administration, 15 CFR Chapter XXIII [Docket No. 980212036-8036-01], Improvement of technical management of Internet names and addresses ['Green Paper']," (March 17, 1998), < http://www.isoc.org/internet/news/isocgreen.shtml >, accessed on March 19, 1998.

what arcane issue of "Internet names and addresses" hides the fact that the current U.S. contractor managing the "A" root server receives about US$8.75 million each month from the assignment of names and addresses.[6]

Even as ISOC and similar organizations strive to influence the development of the Internet, interested parties are raising questions about the representation of users from the developing countries in its governing organizations. Izumi Aizu, a Japanese user who has followed the growth of the Internet from its early days, has argued for the "need for more balanced geographic participation" in the decision making process of the Internet. He opposed moves to the commercialize the names and addresses registration process. He also points out that out of the current total of 87 authorized registers of names and addresses, less than 10 are from developing countries.[7]

ATTEMPTING TO CONTROL THE SOURCE OF A NEW NIGHTMARE

Many regulators in those parts of Asia which were affected by the melt-down of the foreign exchange and stock markets in the second half of 1997 have identified the adoption of new information technologies by the international money markets and stock exchanges as a contributing factor. While they do not deny that the new technologies have made the markets more efficient in confirming transactions and disseminating market intelligence, they point out that the same technologies were skillfully deployed by market manipulators to drive the business and banking communities into a mad stampede which robbed the region, over a matter of weeks, of advances that had taken decades to achieve. At the height of the panic triggered by the manipulators, investors and bankers in North

6 The ethno-political conflicts are undoubtedly organized by groups of elites who are either defending existing political and financial interests, or who perceive political or financial advantages arising from such conflicts. These conflicts are therefore rooted in the mobilization of groups of people on the basis of religion, language, caste, ethnicity, or other cultural markers. Claims for legitimacy of such cultural identities are made on the basis of historical or mythological events popular with the groups that are being mobilized. For instance the extremist sectors of the Bharatiya Janata Party (BJP) of India legitimize the Hindu identity on a national scale, and claim such identity as coincident with being an Indian. Minority groups such as Muslims are perceived as invaders or foreigners who have, through conquest or deceit, forced their way to centers of power. Such communal consciousness refuses to accept the plural, culturally-differentiated reality of Indian society. See Pradip M. Thomas, "Media and Politics of Revivalism in India," *Media Development*, vol. 39, no. 3 (1992), pp. 28-31.

7 Izumi Aizu, "My comments on Green Paper," a posting distributed via owner-anr-talk@magritte.netizen.or.jp on March 19, 1998.

America and Europe treated all the economies of South East Asia in one big lump and indiscriminately dumped currencies and stocks of both strong and weak economies within several hours of feverish trading driven in part by hysterical round-the-clock economic reportage disseminated by the new ICTs. Some regulators have argued that using the older technologies, trades would have taken a little longer to confirm and that the slower pacing would have enabled the financial sector in the affected countries to clarify their positions and very possibly brought some more responsible decision-making back to the international market place.

MEDIA IN THE INFORMATION HIGHWAY: FREEDOM OF EXPRESSION IN THE AGE OF GLOBAL COMMUNICATION[1]

Anura Goonasekera

New communication technologies are creating new types of communities. They are variously referred to as intelligent communities, smart communities, parasocial communities, virtual communities, and cyber-communities. The social relationships among the members of these communities are not necessarily based on physical proximity. Strategic locations such as transportation crossroads, easy access to raw materials and labor, which were very important for the emergence and sustenance of communities in earlier periods of history, are no longer the deciding criteria for the emergence of intelligent communities. New telecommunication technologies have made it possible for business to produce, consumers to purchase, and workers to interact without the need for a common physical location.[2]

[1] Some of the material in this paper was presented at the 28th Annual Conference of the International Institute of Communication (IIC), Sydney. Australia, in October 1977, and at the conference on *Internationalizing Communities* at the University of Southern Queensland, Toowoomba, in November 1996.

[2] International Center of Communication, San Diego State University, *Building Smart Communities: How California's Communities Can Thrive in a Digital Age* (1997).

While an entirely new form of civic organization is emerging as a result of the impact of new communication technologies, the policies governing these social processes are still influenced by an old mode of thinking. Even the scientific community has not been very helpful in this regard. Social scientists, researchers, and popular writers use metaphors borrowed from earlier periods of history to describe futuristic developments in the field of communications. We speak of global villages, electronic superhighways, multimedia supercorridors, etc. These metaphors are much too simple and commonplace to capture the momentous changes that are taking place in the intelligent communities. However, policies continue to be influenced by this thinking. We bring in regulations, deregulation, and reregulation which may be entirely irrelevant to the processes that are going on in the newly emerging communities. There appears to be a vast chasm between the needs of new communication technologies and the policies that are used for their social applications. This is clearly the case in policies that govern the transnational media. It has serious implications for freedom of expression in an age of global communication. And this is compounded by issues involving the representation of different cultural interests by the media.

What is significant in the changes that are brought about by new communication technologies is that the traditional centers of control are withering away. This has obvious implications for freedom of expression. Mass communication under the previous modes of production, both capitalist and socialist, used to be controlled by a group of functionaries. It was easy for the owners of the media to design policies to control the media, including its content, at various stages of production. The owners could be media moguls or governments. However in the intelligent communities, linked to the information superhighway, such direct controls through ownership are becoming increasingly difficult. Internet service providers, for instance, cannot monitor the content of the messages that are transmitted using their on-line services. Furthermore the traditional distinction between different kinds of media, such as print, broadcasting, and film, is getting blurred. Multimedia is becoming the vehicle of the future. Old-fashioned censorship will now be very difficult to impose. With the advent of new communication technologies the medium, the message, and the audience will not be discrete entities. They are interacting and merging to become parts of civil society — an intelligent community. A different morality will emerge. The question is what kind of a morality will this be? Will it support values such as openness, freedom, and tolerance that are needed for civil life in any human community? Or will it bring about a hegemony that will be a threat to smaller communities and their cultures? Freedom of expression in the new communication era is closely involved with this emerging new morality.

TRANSNATIONAL MEDIA

Modern communication technologies are creating unprecedented opportunities for cultural contacts between individuals and communities living in remote parts of the globe. Transnational television broadcasting is the most conspicuous medium that brings about these cross-cultural contacts. However, there are other media both traditional and new which impact on societies. Electronic networks, e-mail, electronic databases, cellular networks, faxes and telephones are all putting people into contact with each other in an historically unprecedented manner.

Because of modern information technology, media are rapidly becoming internationalized. They seek wider markets than those in the countries of production and immediate distribution. And unlike the case of Hollywood movies, such foreign sales are not a bonus but a main source of revenue. Television is a front-runner in the quest for global audiences, but newspapers are not far behind. Not only are these media locating correspondents and stringers in a large number of countries, but the management of these media organizations and their modes of production are being diversified. CNN is opening bureaus in Asia. The *International Herald Tribune* (*IHT*) is published from Singapore. BBC World Service has commenced program production in India. Rupert Murdoch's StarTV, not satisfied with Asia-wide audiences for its English-language programs, is now looking for regional-language audiences within Asia in communities that speak different Asian languages. Principally these are Chinese-language, Malay-language, and Indian-language audiences. While communication technology has created the potential for global media, cultural interests and the logic of the market are fragmenting the global media in Asia into regional, geolinguistic areas. These geolinguistic areas cover more than one country. They are supranational and represent a multiplicity of mores, customs, laws, and traditions. This is a situation hitherto unknown in the media history of the world.

The internationalization or globalization of media has raised important issues. One such issue is about freedom of expression in a culturally plural environment. These issues raise questions not only of freedom of expression in multinational media but, more importantly, questions of politics (i.e., of power); questions of law, both domestic and international; and questions of international commerce and economics. More often than not politics, law and economics are intertwined. This essay will examine the issues of media globalization in Asia as a process of meaning creation necessitated by a clash of interests between leaders in Asian countries and the owners of multinational media — a clash between the imperatives of nation building and rapid economic development through authoritarian governance, and the ideology of the capitalist, confrontational press of the Western democracies. It is a power struggle principally between the owners of multinational media and the rulers in Asian countries. Questions about freedom of expression are intertwined with these issues. These will get resolved only after the major contenders agree to a set of international covenants governing the conduct of global communication.

THE ROLE OF INTERNATIONAL MEDIA

During the years 1986/87, the Singapore government restricted the circulation of *Time*, *Asian Wall Street Journal* (*AWSJ*), *Asiaweek*, and *Far Eastern Economic Review* (*FEER*) — all having wide circulation in Singapore. The restrictions were imposed by a *Government Gazette* notification, under the Newspaper and Printing Act, and hence this procedure is referred to as gazetting. The disputes with *Time*, *AWSJ*, and *Asiaweek* have been over the right to reply, considered by Asian leaders as an integral part of freedom of expression. All three publications had carried stories about events in Singapore which the Singapore government said were factually incorrect. The government replied. *Time* and *AWSJ* refused to publish its statement. *Asiaweek* published the reply but, unknown to the Singapore government, edited the reply and attributed the edited version to the Singapore government.

FEER's report was alleged to be not only false but defamatory of Mr. Lee Kuan Yew, the Prime Minister of Singapore at that time. The government wrote twice to *FEER* to either substantiate or withdraw the allegations. *FEER* refused, on grounds of editorial prerogative. Its circulation was restricted from 9000 copies to 500 copies and a libel case was filed in Singapore courts.[3]

The manner in which Hong Kong and Macau settled their differences in transborder broadcasting highlight the different ways in which economic interests could impinge on such decisions.[4] At the center of the differences between Macau and Hong Kong was the need for Hong Kong to secure its internal market for Cantonese TV broadcasts. The moment Hong Kong's local Cantonese TV market is adversely affected, local program operators such as TVB, ATV, and Warf Cable will apply pressure on the Hong Kong Government to secure this market In 1991, Macau TV (TdM), which is government owned, decided to boost its signals to cover vast areas of Hong Kong. This would make TdM virtually another free-to-air TV station in Hong Kong without getting a Hong Kong license. Furthermore, one of the TdM channels broadcast in Cantonese. This would affect adversely the incomes of local program operators. The advertising standards in Macau were freer, with few restrictions on cigarette and alcohol commercials. This would result in loss of advertising revenue for local TV stations. Consequently pressure was brought on the Hong Kong government to stop Macau from broadcasting to Hong Kong. In the absence of any covenants, laws, or understandings governing transborder broadcasting, the Hong Kong government had no formal way of addressing this problem. It used economic pressure on the Macau government to get it to stop the intended TV expansion. It did this by threatening to legalize casinos in Hong Kong. Legalization of casinos in Hong Kong would affect adversely Macau's most important source of revenue — gambling. People in Hong Kong are the major customers of Macau casinos. If Hong Kong was not a major source of revenue to Macau, probably the Hong Kong government would not have been able to persuade Macau to drop its intention to

3 The article in question was about a Marxist conspiracy revealed by the government in which some members of the Catholic Church were implicated. The report was about a meeting held between Mr. Lee and Catholic leaders led by Archbishop Yong. In his suit, Mr. Lee alleged that the article depicted Mr. Lee as being intolerant of the Roman Catholic Church and that he set out to victimize Catholic priests and workers (*The Straits Times*, Jan. 1988). The Singapore courts found all four defendants guilty of ill-will, spite, or wrong or improper motive. It awarded Mr. Lee $230,000 in damages. Eight years after this incident *FEER* remains gazetted under the Newspaper and Printing Act. However, after many years, the permitted circulation has been increased to 4000 copies.

4 Paul S. N. Lee, "Foreign Television in Hong Kong: Little Watched but Favourably Received," in Anura Goonasekera, ed., *TV Without Borders: Asia Speaks Out* (Singapore: Asia Media and Communication Centre, 1998), pp. 141-170.

boost its TV signal. There was no legal basis on which the two countries could have settled their differences.

What conclusions can we draw from these cases? Many of these cases highlight the different expectations that people may have regarding the concept of freedom of expression. Many leaders in Asia consider the right of reply as an integral part of this freedom. However this view is not shared by the editors who consider such a right to be subject to editorial judgment or editorial prerogative. Some others believe that cultural and commercial considerations take precedence over the free flow of information.

It has also been argued that the international media which report events in individual countries are not reporting these only for an audience outside of these countries, say people in Britain or US. In fact, these reports are also meant for people in the countries about which the news item is written. English is spoken and read by influential people in these countries, and therefore these reports have an impact on an important section of the population. Local-language newspapers pick up these stories and give them wide publicity, even among people who cannot read English. In short, the international press has become an off-shore press to be read and consumed by the people in Asian countries. The *AWSJ*, based in Hong Kong, reports not to readers in America or Europe but to Indians, Malaysians, and other Asians. Such newspapers are like domestic presses of these countries, but owned beyond their shores or territorial boundaries. In this situation, the leaders of Asian countries sometimes see the correspondents of the international press as acting like journalists do in America or Europe — taking sides to determine the outcome of events. In other words, Asian leaders see journalists in the off-shore press as interfering in the domestic affairs of their countries.[5]

The permission given to international media to operate in an Asian country is a privilege granted by the government of the Asian country on its own terms. The basic understanding is that these foreign journalists report events in these countries as outsiders for outsiders. In short, they do not become participants in the domestic debates of these countries. These journalists cannot assume the role

---

5 It is even argued that the purpose of such interference is to bring an outcome favorable to the international media organizations for which they work, or to the interests of Western countries in general. This they do in many ways: by setting the agenda for influential groups in these countries, for instance, or by publishing stories that question the honesty and integrity of government leaders, thereby making such leaders fearful of the foreign media. This is a strategy to soften their stand against such media. Freedom of the press is seen as battle cry to impose Western hegemony in emerging Asian nations. Refusal to publish rebuttal of their stories by international media, which is controlled by companies based in Western countries, is seen as cultural arrogance.

that American journalists play in America. They cannot become examiners, adversaries, and inquisitors of the government. No Asian country can withstand such an insidious and irresponsible onslaught from the foreign press. The foreign correspondents are temporary guests in the countries where they are stationed. Most of them have little or no understanding of the language, history, culture, or forms of governance in the countries that they try to report on. Some of these journalists approach their subject with a cultural arrogance and superiority which is resented in Asia. In foreign countries these journalists should be observers, not participants.

The libertarian ideology of the press is not a universal model that is applicable all over the world, and at all times in every country. The libertarian view is that the press should be free to publish or not to publish what it chooses, however irresponsible or biased its actions may seem to be. In this model, the audience is seen as freely choosing in the market place of ideas. The logic is that where the media are free, the market place of ideas sorts out the irresponsible from the responsible and rewards the latter. But this model cannot be applied to all countries. In different countries, the press has grown out of different historical traditions and political experiences. Consequently, it will play different roles. The free market place of ideas in multicultural, multiparty democracies in Asia can result in a heightening of racial and religious tensions, a mobilizing of sectional constituencies, and an arousing of emotions. In this situation, partisan media can flood the market place with racially divisive information, confuse people, and set the country on a course of racial strife and civil war. In such a media environment, basic issues such as economic growth and equitable distribution are rarely tackled by the press. Instead easy solutions are peddled for complex problems that require hard political decisions. In this situation, the free market brings about confusion and violent dissension rather than enlightenment and consensus.

ETHNICITY IN THE GLOBAL VILLAGE

While it is true that telecommunications, satellites, computers, and transnational media have brought the world together, and provided unprecedented opportunities for the establishment of closer cultural linkages and identities among nations, this potential for cross-fertilization of cultures has also created apprehensions regarding the erosion of cultural identities of indigenous people. National leaders have voiced fears of the loss of cultural identity due to the intrusion of foreign cultural products and their accompanying values. As such, the communication superhighway is viewed by some Asian leaders more as a threat to cultural identities than as an opportunity to create a more consensual culture among neighboring people. Such fears, whether correct or not, have had their influence in creating policy regimes which attempt to contain the flow of information that is considered harmful to the cultures of these countries.

Furthermore upswings in ethnic politics, religious fundamentalism, communalism, and nationalism have taken center stage in the world today. National minorities in many countries have become militant activists. For most of these activists, local autonomy and sovereignty take precedence over multicultural co-existence and integration into a global village. Freedom of expression is limited by a "higher" morality based on fundamentalist principles. Some sociologists and political commentators have described the current spate of ethno-political conflicts in the world as being rooted in the history, culture, and traditions of these countries. These conflicts are seen as movements of revivalism, or nativistic movements.[6]

While it is true that the mobilization of communal groups by elites is based on identities such as religion, language, caste, or ethnicity, these by themselves do not make such groups revivalists of something from their past history or culture. In fact the distinguishing characteristic of modern day religio-ethnic movements

6 The ethno-political conflicts are undoubtedly organized by groups of elites who are either defending existing political and financial interests, or who perceive political or financial advantages arising from such conflicts. These conflicts are therefore rooted in the mobilization of groups of people on the basis of religion, language, caste, ethnicity, or other cultural markers. Claims for legitimacy of such cultural identities are made on the basis of historical or mythological events popular with the groups that are being mobilized. For instance the extremist sectors of the Bharatiya Janata Party (BJP) of India legitimize the Hindu identity on a national scale, and claim such identity as coincident with being an Indian. Minority groups such as Muslims are perceived as invaders or foreigners who have, through conquest or deceit, forced their way to centers of power. Such communal consciousness refuses to accept the plural, culturally-differentiated reality of Indian society. See Pradip M. Thomas, "Media and Politics of Revivalism in India," *Media Development*, vol. 39, no. 3 (1992), pp. 28–31.

is the weakening of traditional cultural values that bind the individual to the group and insulate them, thereby minimizing the tendency for disorientation. Having weakened and eroded the traditional cultural ties, no alternative ways of binding the individual to his community is provided.

One important reason for the breakdown of traditional group identities is the suicidal rate of population growth in some countries and the consequent mass migration to the slum cities. Individuals are detached from community, ethnicity, temple/church, and caste associations. Their dependence on impersonal channels of communication such as mass media is heightened. Large groups of unemployed and floating people are available to be mobilized for innumerable causes by the elites in these countries. Multiparty politics make such mobilization of groups part of political expediency and strategy. In this situation contentious issues proliferate, and the political process gets fragmented with increasing numbers of people advocating various group-related issues. The process leads to the emergence of weak political regimes, leading in turn to political stalemate, public disenchantment, apathy, and the rise of extremist groups. The process becomes a vicious circle with political regimes becoming increasingly weaker, and social disorder, riots, and assassinations becoming endemic in society.

Ethnic and communal conflicts in the contemporary world are therefore specifically modern phenomena rooted in contemporary socioeconomic and political conditions. They are part and parcel of the process of globalization. The very same forces that helped create intelligent communities have also given birth to the exact opposite — inward-looking fascist communities in which the rights and freedoms of the individual are sacrificed in the name of higher fundamentalist goals of the community as a whole. While such movements use metaphors from the past to mobilize groups and communities, these are nothing less than modern political conflicts played out on an ethnic, religious, or communal plane. The use of metaphors from the past must be understood as symbols used by the elites to manipulate and mobilize the people for the elites' own ascent to power.

What we see in the world today are the twin and opposite forces of internationalization and localization playing on each other. Communication has linked the world in an hitherto unprecedented manner, and has laid the foundation for the emergence of intelligent communities. At the same time, it has also created apprehensions about the survival of cultures, making communities look inward, and become protective and closed. It has not resulted in creating anything like a global village. It has created a world of information-super-rich; it has also created a world of information-poor. And the two worlds are drifting far apart. It has not contributed much to consensual understanding. Modern communication technologies have given the opportunity to develop a consensual culture by putting people in close contact. However the emergence of such a culture would require international understandings, agreements, and co-operation based on equality and fairness. This is yet to emerge. What has emerged are deep divisions, mutual suspicions, and perceptions of unfairness.

INTERNATIONAL AGREEMENTS

It is clear that many of the areas opened up by transnational communication require or envisage agreements among states in order to gain mutual benefits such as potential access to markets. These can take the form of international conventions or bilateral agreements. Such agreements are particularly important in relation to international trade in cultural products. In the absence of such agreements countries have been forced to settle issues of transborder broadcasting on their own, and at times in very unconventional ways. The manner in which Hong Kong and Macao settled their differences in transborder broadcasting, described earlier in this paper, highlight the different ways in which economic interests could impinge on such decisions.

Recently some of the issues in this area have been the subject of international debate and negotiations. In the Asia-Pacific region it is difficult to envisage transnational television or any other type of communication as the means of establishing a common culture. Unlike those in Europe, the countries in the Asia-Pacific region have different traditions and historical experiences. These countries are far more diverse, suspicious of each other, and jealous of their indigenous cultural heritages.

In 1994, the General Assembly of the Asian Broadcasting Union (ABU) met in Kyoto, Japan and adopted a resolution specifying guidelines for transnational satellite broadcasters in the Asia-Pacific region. The objectives of the guidelines were similar to those of the EC directive but the contents were very different. Unlike the European Directive, the ABU guidelines placed emphasis on respecting the cultural diversity in the Asia Pacific region rather than on creating a common transnational culture in this region. In its introduction the guidelines say that the development of satellite-television services will undoubtedly foster the free flow of information in the Asia Pacific Region. At the same time the document asserts that there is serious concern that this situation could have a deleterious effect on the values and cultures of the countries of the region. A series of similar guidelines, called *Guidelines on the Programme Contents of International Satellite Television Broadcasting in the Asia-Pacific Region,* were also adopted at a Tokyo meeting of government policy makers from 21 Asian and Pacific countries. These guidelines reiterated the need to respect the principle of the free flow of information, and to protect the sovereignty and domestic systems of those countries where the satellite signals reach.[7] It is quite possible that such guidelines would eventually provide a common ground for the development of a pan-Asian TV culture. However, in order to achieve this it would be necessary for the members of ABU and the relevant government agencies to work out a consensus or a common vision among the countries involved. This will require, at some stage, international covenants to bind the countries to a common course of action.

There are many other areas which need such international understanding or agreements. All these have relevance to issues relating to freedom of expression in an age of global communication. Liberalization of trade in cultural products consequent to GATT/WTO decisions is one such area.[8] There was a time when cultural products such as movies, performing arts and music were exempt from trade liberalization. The 1989 Free Trade Agreement between the USA and Canada specifically exempted cultural products such as films, videos, TV, radio broadcasting, sound recording, and print media. In many countries foreign ownership of media of communication is either prohibited or severely restricted for reasons of national security, and because of social and cultural considerations. However under the Uruguay Round of Talks in 1986, the sector of trade in services was brought under GATT commitments to the open market and subjected to GATT discipline. The rules of GATT/WTO[9] will now apply to cultural products and services as they would apply to all other services.

---

7 Hoso-Bunk Foundation, "Asia Speaks Out: Towards Greater Programme Diversity in Asia," (1996), a report on the proceedings of a forum held August 1-2, 1996, in Kuala Lumpur, Malaysia.

8 General Agreement on Trade and Tariffs or GATT. World Trade Organization (WTO). GATT was replaced by WTO in 1995.

9 There are 27 separate legal agreements and 25,000 pages of liberalizing commitments on market access for goods and services which entered into force in January 1995 together with the creation of WTO.

If trade in cultural products is liberalized — that is, if cultural protection is withdrawn — will this result in the flooding of markets with products from the more powerful economies, particularly the US? From the point of view of international trade what opportunities do the WTO trade discipline provide for harnessing new markets in cultural services and products?

While it is true that GATT/ WTO rules make no special distinction between cultural products and other goods, this by itself does not open up hitherto restricted markets in cultural products. This is because of the GATT/WTO principle of allowing individual countries to make commitments in the market-access areas. This mechanism gives all countries considerable flexibility in handling cultural products and services. Each country can decide whether it wishes to offer market opening guarantees for any particular cultural product or services. "In addition GATT provide particular flexibility for developing countries wishing to open fewer sectors or liberalize fewer types of transactions in future negotiations, thus making explicit their rights to extend market access in line with their development situations."[10]

TRIPS

From the point of view of international trade in cultural products perhaps what is more significant is the agreement on intellectual property protection (the TRIPS agreement), which obliges all member countries that wish to benefit from membership in WTO to apply Berne Convention standards, enforceable through a dispute-settlement mechanism. For instance, producers of sound recordings must be granted an exclusive rental right — the right to authorize or prevent the commercial renting of their work. Protection provided for performers and producers will be effective for at least 50 years, and will apply to all signatories to the agreement. The agreement also contains detailed obligations on governments to provide effective enforcement including criminal sanctions against copyright piracy. GATT signatories are obliged to provide remedies under their municipal law to guarantee that intellectual property rights can be effectively

10 M. A. Kakabadse, "The WTO and the Commodification of Cultural Products: Implications for Asia," *Media Asia* (Singapore), vol. 22, no. 2 (1995), pp. 71-77.

enforced by foreign nationals who hold such rights. These very detailed and strict provisions, it is expected, will increase investor confidence, leading to more trade in cultural products in the international market.

Despite this, intellectual property rights remain a major concern. This is a particularly sensitive issue in Asia. One reason for this is the relatively weak and ineffective legal and policing mechanisms. It has been claimed that violations of software licenses in Asia-Pacific alone amounted to losses exceeding US$2 billion in 1994.[11] Without protecting intellectual property rights and building inventors' confidence in the protection of their patent rights, Asian countries will be unable to attract business, and particularly to attract investments in research and development. Laws and regulations necessary for the enforcement of WTO decisions are still not in place in some of these countries.

Furthermore, decisions of national courts have become quite important in relation to satellite broadcasts in recent times. The StarTV decision in Sri Lanka and the Indian Cable Act are instances of cases in which, in the absence of international agreements, local laws were used in the determination of issues relating to international broadcasting.

The important point is that a body of legal decisions, customs, conventions, and treaties is continually evolving. Transnational communication is being regulated in one form or another. It is increasingly important to elucidate the principles on which such regulations are being made. Cultural considerations and commercial considerations seem to be competing with each other in the evolution of these principles. Free flow of information at present depends much more on national policies than on international agreements. Systematic research is needed to elucidate these processes.

Another concern in relation to international trade is the proliferation of international electronic-networks. "Internet," for instance, is fast becoming a household word in South East Asia, particularly in the more affluent countries in this region. This has opened a vast area of contentious issues raging from cybertrade, cyberdollars, cyberporn, and consequent demands for censorship. Many governments in Asia see it as their moral duty to preserve core cultural values, and protect society from what these governments perceive to be corrupting foreign in-

11 Linda Low, "Social and Economic issues in Information Society: A South East Asian Perspective." A paper submitted at the *Workshop on Chances and the Risks of the Information Society: Its Social and Economic Effects in Europe and South-East Asia* organized by the School of Communication Studies, Nanyang Technological University, and Fredrich Ebert Stiftung, and held September 18-20, 1995, Singapore.

fluences. This fear of foreign cultural domination is fueled by the historical antagonism between the colonized, subordinated countries of Asia, and the colonizing and hegemonic imperial powers. It has been reinforced by the popular discourse of media imperialism, which became a powerful intellectual theme in the 1960s. Western media products were perceived as culturally and morally harmful to the well-being of Asian countries.

Few if any would argue in favour of pornography on the Internet, but in other areas there is much room for debate. For instance, it often happens that material that is legal in one country may be illegal in another. Because cyberspace is seamlessly global, it has been argued that cyberspace censorship requires stricter laws (*The Straits Times*, April 12, 1995), but application of such laws becomes very difficult, particularly when it involves electronic mail. It is difficult to frame laws to control and censor information considered offensive and also, at the same time, allow a free flow of information.

MARKET COMPETITION

Cybertrade is another area of concern. Such activities could lead to building up of currency and credit beyond the control of national governments, and could create problems in the implementation of monetary policies. Imposing import duties and sales taxes could become increasingly difficult, leading to losses in government revenue.[12]

As the trend toward transborder satellite multichannels in the Asia-Pacific region increases, competition for market shares is likely to intensify. Most of the current satellite programs are in English, Chinese, and Indian languages. Japan and Korea are likely to enter this market. In addition to the current commercial transborder broadcasting services by private companies, several governments in the region have also launched international services or are planning such services. Notable among these services are CCTV international of China, Korea Channel, and the Japanese international TV broadcasts. These telecasts are for the nationals of these countries living abroad.

12 *Ibid.*

GENERIC CULTURAL PRODUCTS

We are also seeing changes in the very concept of multinational media programs. Earlier we could identify such programs on the basis of the countries of origin. The USA was identified as providing the bulk of these media programs. It could be argued that in future the world will see generic entertainment software, created by the confluence of capital from USA, Japan, Europe, and other nations, servicing the newly deregulated and privatized media systems in Asia and elsewhere. In the future, it may not make much difference if an increasingly generic cultural product is owned and produced by companies in America, Japan, Europe, or Asia. The challenge is to identify a path towards autonomous national cultural productions in a system that is increasingly catering to the marketing imperatives of transnational companies. Perhaps encouraging independent producers of media for niche audiences in local languages is the answer. The emergence of regional markets for cultural products is an indication that, despite these overarching developments in global media, some room remains for autonomous national cultural productions.

The clear message of globalization is that we live in the same world. But different groups see different meanings in this world. Communication across cultures facilitated through advanced technologies makes for more informed, more aware persons with, possibly, a less parochial outlook. It can promote unity among diverse peoples, and contribute to the emergence of a more tolerant, consensual culture across national borders. Trying to shut oneself off from the intrusion of foreign cultural influences may, perhaps, be like blinding oneself in the hope that one may walk with more safety in a jungle of pit and precipice. The global spread of media is here to stay. We must learn to live with it. In order to harness its potential for good, one should look on it as an opportunity to open one's eyes through education and experience, not to blind them in fear and ignorance.

INDONESIANS USE THE NET TO FIGHT CENSORSHIP

Andreas Harsono

In mid-June 1996, about 40 newspaper editors and television executives were invited to a luncheon in a military building in the capital city of Jakarta. They were addressed by a spokesman for the military, Brigadier General Amir Syarifudin, who asked the editors "not to exaggerate" their coverage of opposition leader Megawati Sukarnoputri.

Gen. Syarifudin also suggested the editors use the name Megawati Kiemas when referring to the chairwoman of the opposition Indonesian Democratic Party (PDI), after the surname of her husband, rather than the name she is commonly known by, Megawati Sukarnoputri, after her father, the charismatic President Sukarno whom the current leader, President Suharto, replaced in 1965.

The general also asked the editors "to defend the dignity of the government," specifically denying earlier media reports that the military had been behind a meeting held in Medan in northern Sumatra to replace Megawati with a government-sponsored leader.

The following day, most Indonesian media drastically toned down their coverage of street rallies in which thousands of pro-democracy activists clashed with riot police.

It was relatively easy for the military-led regime of President Suharto, who came to power in 1965 after an abortive coup blamed on the communists, to discourage major news organizations from covering the protests. But that was as far as conventional censorship could go. Indonesians still got the news through the Internet and international radio broadcasts. Demonstrators who gathered at PDI headquarters in Jakarta distributed print- outs taken from the Internet-based "Indonesia-L" mailing list. They also faxed these uncensored news reports to their provincial offices and plastered them on walls for the public to read.

When the military forcibly occupied PDI headquarters the following July 27, the Internet played an even more crucial role in penetrating the government's information blockade. Its importance was underlined when the military took a number of measures to deal with it. For instance, a lecturer at Duta Wacana Christian University in Yogyakarta, about 500 kilometers east of Jakarta, was arrested at his home by soldiers and charged with photocopying e-mail messages relating to the 1996 riots.

POLITICAL BACKGROUND

It is widely believed here that the armed forces toppled opposition leader Megawati following a proposal that she contest the 1998 presidential election. Such a challenge to Suharto, who has been re-elected six times without opposition, would have been unprecedented.

Although Suharto has transformed Indonesia into one of the economic leaders of the Pacific region, at least before the recent economic crisis, critics complained that he ruled Indonesia with an iron fist. No opposition is allowed, and attempts to oppose his policies have provoked violent crackdowns in regions such as East Timor, Irian Jaya, and Aceh.

The Christian-nationalist PDI is the smallest but most outspoken of the three political parties in Indonesia. Most PDI supporters are located in the central and eastern part of Java and on the island of Bali as well in the eastern part of Indonesia where the majority of the country's Christian population lives.

Political turmoil in recent years has often meant turbulent times for Indonesian news media.

The military-backed government has in the past closed dozens of newspapers. In June 1994, for instance, it shut down three news weeklies and later jailed four journalists working for underground media who protested the closure.

Allegations of biased reporting at one point provoked Megawati's supporters into burning a number of newspapers and staging a protest in front of the RCTI, the largest privately-owned station in Indonesia. Protesters pointed out that the station, owned by President's Suharto's son, had ignored their public meetings while promoting the military-sponsored congress.

The military has also prevented local stations from helping such foreign news agencies as Reuters, Associated Press Television, Worldwide Television News (WTN), Cable News Network, Australian Broadcasting Corporation, and Channel 9 of Australia from transmitting their television reports abroad. In most countries it is normal practice for visiting television journalists to use the facilities of domestic broadcasters to edit and transmit their reports. An official of the state-owned TVRI said this courtesy would not be provided for reports of street demonstrations. Electronic media in Indonesia were also prevented by the military from broadcasting similar material.

Although censorship, intimidation and harassment of news media are not new in Indonesia, dating back to at least 1745 when the Dutch closed down the *Bataviasche Nouvelles* tabloid, new information technology is now providing new techniques for evading suppression of the news and enhancing freedom of speech.

OFFICIAL CENSORSHIP AND THE INTERNET

The "Indonesia-L" mailing list, popularly known as "apakabar" after its mailing address,[1] is a good example. Moderated by an American, John MacDougall, it provides its subscribers with daily news reports from both Indonesian and for-

1 apakabar@clark.net

eign newspapers and underground news agencies as well as from individuals willing to provide material. Another example is a news agency called PIPA, which literally means "pipe." It was established by professional journalists unable to place their reports in mainstream media. Although these reports are professionally written, based on facts and frequently used by Jakarta-based foreign journalists to write their own reports, they are always anonymous.

The Indonesia-L list and unlicensed news services on the Internet became extremely popular after the government closed down news weeklies *TEMPO*, *DeTIK* and *Editor* in June 1994. These decision touched off street protests and clashes with soldiers, often involving younger journalists. When some of the protesting journalists later created an independent union, they often lost their jobs. The government-controlled Indonesian Journalists Association (PWI) put pressure on editors to dismiss these journalists, arguing that the Indonesian law recognized only one compulsory journalists' organization. "Those who are out of the organization are not allowed to work as journalists," said PWI Secretary General Parni Hadi, who is also the chief editor of the daily newspaper *Republika*.

Journalists who found themselves on the street had a new option after 1994 when Indonet, Indonesia's first Internet commercial provider, began operation. Some of them began to publish on the Net. One of the most influential of these unlicensed "magazines" was the *Suara Independent*. Its journalists were encouraged by Human Rights Watch/Asia which issued a report in May 1996 drawing attention to the absence of laws, regulations, or ministerial decrees concerning the new medium. Under Indonesian law, for example, a prospective publisher must apply for a license from the Information Ministry and receive recommendations from various official agencies going into business. No such restrictions raised barriers to publishing on the Internet.

Indonesia now has more than 20 independent Internet service providers. No official statement has been released on the number of Internet subscribers but providers in Jakarta estimate that Indonesia now has about 30,000 e-mail users. This is a relatively low number compared to a population of 195 million but the number is growing rapidly.

Not surprisingly, in view of all this, the banned *TEMPO* magazine reappeared on the Internet on March 6, 1996, and established a Web site called TEMPO Interaktif. There was no immediate government reaction. In fact, Information Minister Harmoko, who had closed down the print version of the weekly, said he did not see anything wrong with its home page. He was quoted as saying, "Anybody can go on the Internet. There are no regulations against it."

The inaugural Internet edition of the magazine ran a controversial story about the government's decision to give special privileges to a car manufacturer run by Hutomo Mandala Putra, President Suharto's youngest son.

Within four months, *TEMPO*'s Internet magazine had more than 5,000 registered subscribers. The server where it was located was being accessed by up to 10,000 users daily. One of its editors speculated that "perhaps our home page is the most popular Indonesian Web site dealing with Indonesia."

More recently, the Indonesian military has attacked the Internet as a channel for subversive ideas. A senior general said a number of prominent figures, including an Indonesian scholar living in exile in Australia, were using a "communist method" to propagate leftist views through the Internet.

Internet providers have also been reporting visits by military officers searching for the names of users. According to Feraldi W. Loeis of the Internet provider Radnet[2] which counts more than 3,000 users, requests for names have been refused so far on privacy grounds. "We haven't been asked to censor anyone," said Mr. Loeis, reporting that Radnet had been asked to curb the distribution of what government officials considered pornography but had not been asked to censor political material. The military has now suggested to the Information Ministry that some sort of "gate" is needed to identify and weed out news that could damage Indonesian culture or affect security. It has also suggested registering Internet users. An interdepartmental team has been set up to study these proposals.

Meanwhile, according to journalists, military intelligence agents are searching editorial offices in an effort to journalists who have been using the Internet to publish reports critical of the government. Gen. Syarifudin himself is busy trying to locate journalists who continue to write uncensored news reports. The army has reportedly assigned some of its intelligence force to search office by office, editor by editor, to find Internet-based journalists who reported to the outside world that the ruling military officers in Indonesia have not been entirely open and candid in their dealings.

2 < http://www.rad.net.id >

FREEDOM OF EXPRESSION, PUBLIC SERVICES, AND TECHNOLOGIES FOR DEMOCRATIC AND HEALTHY SOCIETIES: A LITHUANIAN PERSPECTIVE

Vytautas Butrimas

I am writing this article from one of the countries that was once occupied by the former Soviet Union. During the period of occupation which lasted from 1940 to 1990, Lithuania was cut off from the rest of the world. This period of occupation had an adverse effect on the development of freedom of expression, public services, and technologies in Lithuania. In this article I argue that the new possibilities provided by recent developments in information and telecommunication technologies should be welcomed as tools to empower citizens with choice and control over their lives. However, the potential dangers of creating a new category of "have not" nations should not be underestimated. The new technologies can provide opportunities for democratic growth, for job creation, and for creating healthy societies. These boons should be made available to all countries and not limited to the usually favored traditionally developed countries.

WHAT AN INFORMATION SOCIETY SHOULD NOT BE

I made my first trip to Lithuania in 1977 to visit relatives. At that time Lithuania was behind the "iron curtain" and a very remote place to me. Eventually this trip led to other trips and finally to my decision to move here five years ago and to start working for the Ministry of Communications and Informatics.

Lithuania in 1977 had an information society of a kind which was far from what we now think of as an information society. Information was under strict state control. Radio and TV stations were carefully managed by the state and broadcast only approved information. This also held true for print media. Newspapers printed official news and only officially approved authors were able to publish their books. This was an information society that was directed from the top down. Information was used by Lithuania's rulers to steer people's minds along a selected path. Lithuania was cut off from the rest of the world in terms of information. The dynamic interchange of ideas going on in the west was closed to the Lithuanian people. There was no *New York Times* best-seller list, no films from Hollywood, and no western magazines (except perhaps those provided to Party leaders).

The country I visited then seemed to be an unknown civilization waiting to be discovered. The technology I saw being applied in everyday life was out of date. The telephone system was probably 25 years behind the times and the stores and shops relied heavily on the use of the abacus. The backwardness was largely caused by the oppressive control of the flow of ideas and information. This stifled the creativity and synergy that happens when people are allowed to be creative and to communicate freely. This state of affairs was the exact opposite of what was going on in the west.

Why did the system crumble?

In my opinion, this was caused by advances in information and telecommunications technology which tended to dissolve the iron curtain. The flow of information across our borders became unstoppable, and with this information came a new awakening on the part of our people in regard to the way they should live their lives.

The leaders of the totalitarian system feared this flow of information and for this reason did all they could to stop it. This was expressed in many ways, from press censorship to the jamming of western radio broadcasts. Even the use of information and telecommunications technology was kept under strict control. Special regulations governed the use of typewriters and photocopy machines. Telephone calls to and from the west were difficult to arrange and usually had to be re-routed through Moscow.

Technological innovation and its results were reserved for the military-industrial complex. The citizen-consumer was usually forced to make do with a poor selection of products characterized by poor quality control and obsolete technology. Computers and communications equipment were manufactured in Lithuania but were manufactured with the military or government market in mind and not the average consumer.

CONVERGENCE AND THE INTERNET

The latest advances in information and telecommunication technologies are daily changing our individual lives, working conditions and the communities we live in. At the same time there is a convergence of technologies occurring. Look at my computer. When I started working at the Ministry of Communications and Informatics almost five years ago I used my computer only for correspondence and to do translations of documents. My workstation was a lone computing island. My collaboration with my colleagues was done verbally or by sharing diskettes. Later my PC was connected to the Ministry's network (LAN) and I was able to send my documents electronically to other departments. Then came a connection to the Government's larger networks (WAN) where I was able to communicate electronically with other institutions. Eventually I could access more sources of information through the Internet via e-mail and the World Wide Web. Recently a new audio/video card was installed on my PC's motherboard for evaluation. This new card makes it possible for me to place phone calls over my PC and even to video-conference with my colleagues.

As a result of this convergence of services our computers are no longer just word processors or database and spreadsheet tools but are functioning as personal libraries and telecommunications centers. This means more efficient use of our time and resources. For example, if one needs to quickly find some information, it is no longer necessary to leave one's office or apartment to look for a knowledgeable person or to travel to a library for the information. Much of the information one may need is already available on the Internet. Another example: it is now possible to find out what one's bills for utilities and other services are and to pay them electronically. No longer do we need to waste time filling out burdensome and time-consuming forms by hand at an institution (and then wait in line to submit and process them). All this makes it possible to save time for better things: recreation, reading, theater, family, and community life. The minimum requirements for participation in all these wonderful things that are becoming available in the information society are a computer and access to the Internet.

HASTENING THE DEVELOPMENT OF DEMOCRACY

One may ask what does this all have to do with democracy?

We all learned in school that it was the Greeks who came up with the idea of democracy. If we look more closely we find that theirs was not a true democracy in the modern sense.[1] Only those who were aristocrats, had some property, or had some special interest were able to vote. The others (women, slaves, and foreigners) were left out of the process altogether. Greek democracy, it can be said, benefited only a few. In our time, however, a healthy and functioning democracy requires that all participate. The key to having a healthy government and democracy is an informed citizenry.

A poorly informed citizenry is one of the greatest dangers to democracy in the Baltic Countries today. As we prepare to elect new leaders and make decisions about our future, it is important to have access to accurate information that is readily available. This is one of the major reasons why the information society is so important to us. In my opinion it is the main reason why the European Union is requiring all new applicant states to create information societies.

---

1 See < http://www-adm.pdx.edu/user/song/greekciv/politics/jamie/changes.html >.

I cannot let this opportunity pass without commenting on our current sources of information: press, television, and radio. No one can doubt the vital importance of these media as sources of information. Nevertheless, they should not be considered as the only sources of accurate information. It is not enough, for example, to base one's understanding of Lithuanian affairs on the information provided by one newspaper or by the same radio or TV commentator. In order to make a sound judgment on any matter, people have to have access to other sources of information, documents, and opinions. One of the best ways is through the Internet.

There are many ways to misinform or only partially inform our people today. It is my view that our journalists are themselves aware of the public's poor access to accurate and unbiased information, and this encourages inaccurate, biased, or sloppy reporting. If our journalists knew that people themselves could access information about their officials, they would try much harder to provide accurate information to the community. The result would be a better press and a better informed citizenry.

THE INTERNET AS A LIBERATING FORCE, AND THE KEY TO SUCCESS IN THE 21st CENTURY

The Internet phenomenon should be viewed as a democratic triumph that has not reached its full potential for changing our world for the better. Lithuania has over 3.5 million inhabitants: only 20,000 have access to the Internet. I call these 20,000 the privileged few or the "haves". These "haves" can freely use their computers to access information from many sources located throughout the world. These people already know what it is like to be a member of the Lithuanian, European Union, and world information societies.

It is almost 50 years since the United Nations Declaration on Human Rights. I think that it will not be long before an amendment will have to be added to the Declaration. It will be an amendment that recognizes the right of every individual to access the Internet. This will be necessary as we more and more begin to measure countries not so much by their economic indicators as by their level of Internet use.

The ability to access information in a timely manner is required more and more in our increasingly competitive environments. One must remember that the world is a rapidly changing place. The countries that will keep up and stay ahead of these changes will have the information available for decision-making at the right time and will be the real winners. Those countries that are isolated or are unwilling to actively pursue policies meant to provide their students, scientists, and businessmen with this information will be the real losers or "have-nots" of the twenty-first century. The successful nations with flourishing economies and healthy societies will be those that promote the free flow of information and provide the latest technologies to their people.

There is some concern over the decline of the individual in relation to big business and the state. If I go back to what I said about the new capabilities available in today's computers, one can argue that each individual now has a powerful tool to make one's point of view known. The new technologies are empowering people from the bottom up. Take publishing for example. If you have a computer, access to the Internet, and a web page builder, you can publish anything: a work, an opinion, a photograph, or anything else that can be presented in digital form. The individual no longer has to feel powerless. He or she can make his or her views known to a world audience.

Being able to freely make one's views known and to know about the views of others is a necessary element of democracy. The individual does not necessarily have to be diminished by technology. He or she has everything to gain from it if it is made available at a reasonable cost and with regulations that promote its use.

DANGERS TO AVOID

With the rapid adoption of the Internet as an accepted mechanism for the distribution and exchange of information, there have been some sour notes. One such problem is the concern over unacceptable content being carried on the Internet. The Internet until now has been subjected to very little regulation. This is probably the reason behind its astounding rate of growth. But now it is being viewed by governments with some concern. The issue of censorship has surfaced again. Calls for censorship have been largely based upon the issue of the regulation of pornography and other unacceptable content being distributed over the Internet. Another issue is data security. These are issues that will have to be addressed. The regulation of content should be studied carefully. Arguments in favor of controlling the distribution of pornography should not lead to further restrictions in other areas. The content issue is also important for the creation of new business and jobs. Most of the world's cultural heritage is stored away in vaults for want of exhibition space. The capability of artifacts and even out-of-print books to be published over the Internet should not be overlooked. The content industry has a great potential to flourish over the Internet. It is estimated that electronic commerce revenues, both direct and indirect, will increase to 200 billion ECU worldwide by the year 2000.[2]

In the concern over data security over the Internet we should be careful not to let our governments use this as an excuse to limit citizens' access to information about government. If this happens we run the risk of returning to a one-sided distribution of "official" information very much like the system in Lithuania during the Soviet period.

Another concern relates to the cost of membership in the information society: i.e., a computer, modem, and an Internet-service-provider contract. This is especially so when one compares the computing power one can obtain today with what could be obtained 10 years ago for the same money. However, the initiation fee (roughly US$1,800), if we may call it that, is far too high for the majority of the people living in the world today.

Governments should not be afraid of the promise of these new technologies. Computers need to be made available to as many people as possible. A good place to start would be to make them available to the public in significant numbers in our libraries, schools, and government institutions. In time the new technologies will stimulate job creation. It has been estimated that by the year 2010, 50 per cent of the world's economy will be based upon the service and applications sector.[3] Job creation will be a benefit resulting from investment in a nation's information-society development program.

2 European Commission Green Paper, "On the convergence of the telecommunications, media, and information technology sectors, and the implications for regulation," Brussels, December 3, 1997.
3 From "Key Actions For a More User Friendly Society," a speech given by George Metakides, Director Information Technologies, European Commission DG III - Industry, at the *Telematics, Advancing the Information Society* Conference, Barcelona, February 6, 1998.

INFORMATION SOCIETY POLICY

In Lithuania we have made significant strides in developing our telecommunications infrastructure and developing data transfer networks. However there is much work that still needs to be done To create a healthy democracy we also need an information society. To do both we need access to information already stored in our databases and registers. We have passed all the laws we need to make this possible but our government institutions still do not cooperate with each other effectively. A spirit of cooperation and willingness to enter into a dialogue is required by those who manage our registers of information; they control a major part of the information required for the information society. These managers need to think not only about their own institutions' needs and interests but about the needs and interests of other institutions. Access to information is the key to having a healthy government and democracy. It was President Thomas Jefferson of the United States who said, "Whenever the people are well informed, they can be trusted with their own government. Whenever things get so far wrong as to attract their notice, they may be relied on to set them to rights."[4]

The Ministry of Communications and Informatics is tasked by the government with implementing the State Communications and Informatics Development Program. We call on the public, members of our government, private institutions and the academic community to work with us to make the information society a reality in Lithuania. We also look forward to cooperating with other countries in creating a true global information society that is open to everyone, promotes the free flow of information and exchange of ideas, helps countries to be competitive in the world market, and creates new jobs.

---

4 Thomas Jefferson to Richard Price, 1789; cited in < http://pages.prodigy.com/jefferson_quotes/jeff0350.htm >.

CULTURE AND ENTROPY AT THE INTERFACE OF FREEDOM OF EXPRESSION AND THE NEW COMMUNICATIONS TECHNOLOGIES

Fredric M. Litto

When the Portuguese "discovered," in 1500, the land which eventually came to be called Brazil, they brought with them the values and mores which oriented their lives back home. Hence, for more than 300 years, the inhabitants of Brazil did not have the right to publish newspapers, books had to be printed in Portugal only after receiving official approval, and institutions of higher learning were prohibited in the colony. It was only with the arrival in Brazil in 1808 of the Portuguese Emperor Dom João VI and his Court, fleeing from the armies of Napoleon, that the communications structure of the modern world began to take form, albeit under close religious and political supervision.

Full freedom of expression is relatively recent in Brazil, dating essentially from the end of the military regime which governed the country from 1964 to 1984. Censorship of theatrical and cinematographic activities, as well as journalistic censorship, were severe during that period, but since they had always existed in the country in one form or another, tightening or easing up depending on the regime in power, Brazilians took censorship in stride, trying to find the lighter side of the phenomenon so as to stand the pressure. There was even a difference of opinion among some intellectuals as to whether censorship should continue to be carried out by the Ministry of Justice or should be transferred to the Ministry of Education so that questions of linguistic and cultural "accuracy" in translations and adaptations of literary and artistic works could be included with the usual filtering of religious and political "offenses."

Most curious of all, perhaps, for those interested in the history and sociology of censorship, the leading newspaper of the city of São Paulo at the time, the sober, business-oriented, and right-of-center *Estado de São Paulo*, regularly placed in the spaces reserved for news stories, but which had been cut by the censorship, excerpts from the works of the Portuguese poet Luís Vaz de Camões (1525-1580), or exotic recipes. So, all readers *knew* that the censors had been at work. This lighter side of things should not in any way distract our attention from the fact that hundreds of journalists, artists, scientists, intellectuals, students and union leaders were tortured during the period, some losing their lives, others fleeing the country, never to return.

Nevertheless, the ways in which Brazilians reacted, and continue to react, to censorship offers some insight into the phenomenon in a specific cultural setting. It is my belief that as the world moves in the direction of a society increasingly dominated by technological artifacts, procedures, and mind-sets, different cultures around the world will react in different ways. Like a quilt made of patches of different materials, some closely woven and not permitting much penetration of light or air, others loosely woven, at once resilient and permeable, the world scenario for freedom-of-expression will be varied and constantly challenging.

THE LOW-DEFINITION FUTURE

I believe that it is possible to describe some cultures as being "high- definition" (in the sense of photographic resolution, i.e., with clearly delineated lines) and others as being "low-definition" (lines with a fuzzy, diffuse appearance). In high-definition cultures, if a meeting is called for 9:00 a.m., it begins at 9:00 a.m. If three participants are expected to have reports ready for the group, three reports will be forthcoming. And during the meeting if someone says "A," there is no doubt in anyone's mind that by saying "A," the speaker meant "A," and not "B" or "C." On the other hand, in low-definition cultures, if a meeting is called for 9:00 a.m., it usually can only get underway at about 9:30 or 9:40, when all the participants have finally arrived and finished their customary greetings. If three participants are expected to have reports ready, the group is lucky, indeed, if at least *one* of the reporters has even a prolegomenon to his report ready. And during the meeting, if someone says "A," it is generally understood that by saying "A" he *might* be meaning to say "A," but it could also be that he wishes us to infer from his words meanings "B" or "C."

It is all a question of capacity for toleration of ambiguity, of innate flexibility, and of a consistently variable perspective. Brazilian culture definitely falls into the category of "low-definition," and although such a category may appear inefficient, intolerable and unmodern to those who view it from the perspective of "high-definition," I believe that it will be the low-definition cultures which will have the greatest success in confronting the hurdles which surely lie before us as the new communications technologies increasingly alter our domestic and professional lives. I also believe that *entropy*, here signifying the constant augmenting of the numbers of people, messages, bits, and bytes filling the universe, will have a salutary effect on human communication, making censorship of any kind increasingly difficult; perhaps, eventually, impossible.[1]

My convictions arise in part from personal experience. Though I have lived in Brazil for the last 27 years, my earlier years were spent in North America, which I left both to take up a full professorship in Brazil's leading university, and also because I was profoundly disappointed in the "system".[2] Little did I know, ingenuously transferring myself to Brazil in 1970, that an entirely new environment awaited me, one replete with police spies in the classrooms, persecution of faculty peers caused by ideological differences, and the closing down of newspapers and radio stations which refused to temper their criticisms of those in power. Brazil survived those difficult times, and I did, too. But I learned several lessons in the process.

---

1 For an account of how this concept from physics can help us understand the changes occurring in contemporary society, see Jeremy Rifkin, *Entropy: A New World View* (New York: Bantam, 1980).

2 William I. Oliver, "The Censor in the Ivy", *The Drama Review* (New York), vol. XV, (fall 1970), pp. 31–55.

GETTING AROUND THE CENSOR

One was that there is a physical limit to the censorship that can effectively be levied against a group. For example, during the 1970s and early 1980s I frequently received mail from abroad which had been clumsily opened, inspected, and then crudely taped up again and stamped with a the seal of the postal censorship authority. But there was no rhyme or reason to the procedure. Some pieces opened and sent on to me were innocuous and inoffensive; but other mail never was inspected. All in all, I considered myself protected by the fact that there were 150 million Brazilians at that time, and that it was unlikely that "low-definition" censors would get a fix on my reading habits.

As I look at the Internet today, its steady growth and increasing complexity, I cannot imagine *any* system of censorship capable of detecting and denouncing with complete success the communications and habits of large populations. You may say: "Aha! But today it's far easier to censor electronic media: just put word-spotting and voice-recognition filters into the principal nodes of data channels, and you'll catch the "offenders" every time." But it is not so easy. Here again, the Brazilian experience rings loud. During the most repressive period of the military regime, Brazilian popular music continued to express the mind and mood of the vast majority of the population. And the writers of this music were geniuses in developing a coded language which expressed protest against the regime and its policies but which appeared, on the surface, to be about romantic hopes and needs, especially about fallen-out lovers. Everyone understood, except the censors, who let such songs pass. My favorite of the period, liberated by the censors, was Chico Buarque de Holanda's lines in one of his many sambas with a hidden protest message, *"Apesar de você, amanha há de ser, outro dia... Voce vai pagar com juros, juro."*[3]

The mixture of Puritanism with questions of high-and low-definition cultures is especially worthy of comment. When Brazilians read in the press about North American school boards and school principals who suspend from class a six-year old boy for having *kissed* a six-year-old girl, they can only lament, with profound sadness, the meanness, the emptiness, the desperation of such acts and such people. Brazilians love to hug and kiss. In the ten years that I have directed a

---

3 "Despite you, there will be another day tomorrow... You're going to pay with interest [for what you've done], I swear."

university laboratory concerned with computers in education in Brazil, I have never heard of a school placing foul-word-searching software on the school's server, a common censoring phenomenon in North America. On the contrary, although it's not written anywhere, the general feeling in schools here seems to be: let the young ones use foul language and seek out pornographic images on the Internet for a few weeks because by so doing they'll eventually become bored by it and will then turn their interests and attention to more serious, less alluring, subjects. It is known that prohibited subjects carry a fascination greater than their reality. Pornography on the Internet is infantile and boring. And nobody is obliged to watch it.

POLITICAL CONFORMITY AND REALITY

Culture determines world view, which in turn generates behavior, which in its turn generates stereotypes. And in Brazil, everything is permitted, even those things which by law are prohibited. In Brazil, some laws catch on, and others don't. In such an environment, it is hard to imagine the establishment of, or respect for, laws governing the use by average citizens of electronic networks. If the standards for what is "indecent" are hard to pin down in other countries, they may well be impossible to ascertain in Brazilian culture. There is no mania concerning the question of "political correctness" as it is known in the northern hemisphere, and no one has even raised the idea of V-chips in television sets to censor violence or sexuality. Since the end of the local military regime and the fall of the Berlin Wall, there is no longer any political "patrolling" from either the right or the left.

Hence, when Brazilians learn that 13-year-old students in McKinney, Texas were recently suspended from school because they had created Internet sites with parodies of school authorities or silliness of a highly imaginative, if irreverent kind, they are grateful that such problems (the censorship; *not* the students' creativity) do not exist here.[4] Once again, a cultural value is at play here: in Brazilian schools there is no sense of *in loco parentis*. That is, in the four hours in which a student typically attends class each day, the school does not consider itself a

---

4 Tamar Lewin, "Schools Challenge Students' Internet Talk", *New York Times* (National Report, March 8, 1998), p. 16.

substitute parent. Nor should it. This is not to say that the "moral intelligence" of children should be off-limits in school activities. On the contrary, it is important that what it means to be a "good person" as opposed to a "not-so-good person"[5] permeates formal and informal learning at all age levels. The question is how to do this without censorship, without losing our "negative liberty,"[6] which allows men, women (and children) the "freedom to act diversely and to make their own mistakes."

Even when there is a majority vote in favor of reducing liberty (or "regulating morality"), it is not necessarily right, as we saw in June of 1997, when the U.S. Supreme Court struck down the law, unanimously approved by the Congress, to ban distribution of "indecent" material to Internet sites that could be accessed by young people under 18 years of age. Likewise, attempts to "filter" content, through special software, such as PICS (Platform for Internet Content) or Surf Watch, are difficult to apply comprehensively and bring, embedded with them, other problems. Although Surf Watch sold 3.4 million copies in the period from May, 1995, to March, 1997, banning 30 thousand of the Internet's 300 thousand available sites in the same period, its approach seems doomed to failure since its filter is based on a site's name and not on its content; names can change, and apparently innocuous discussion groups can arbitrarily change course at any time. The PICS solution, similarly, seems impossible to apply since it would require that *all* sites be rated, and would apparently create a "filtered society," which could be manipulated by school boards, school principals, employers, and governments at will.

TEACHING WITH NEW TECHNOLOGIES

All of these questions are important to Brazil as it reconquers the position it held in the 1970s as one of the world's foremost users of distance-education, and subsequently lost as a result of government discontinuity. There are presently 34 million children enrolled in public and private primary schools and 6 million in secondary schools. But another 200,000 adults, who never finished their primary

5 Robert Coles, *The Moral Intelligence of Children* (New York: Random House, 1997).
6 Isaiah Berlin, *Two Concepts of Liberty* (1957).

and secondary school education, are participating in Telecurso 2000, whose delivery-system uses a combination of open-circuit television, Internet, and textbooks sold at newspaper stands throughout the country. These students receive instruction at home or at one of 6,200 teleclassrooms in factories, construction sites, prisons, churches, and community centers. Thousands of engineers throughout the Southern state of Santa Catarina receive continuing education through a sophisticated program combining teleconferencing and the Internet. And 150,000 secondary-school students in the State of Ceará, in the poor Northeast region of the country, receive enrichment courses through open-circuit television.

Why do we want children to use the new interactive communications technologies? It is because we want them to see themselves in new ways, to be creative in new ways. We want them to navigate successfully in the new environments created by these technologies, exploring multiple viewpoints and their multiple selves, and sensing new contexts. Sherry Turkle of M.I.T. reported that one teenager she interviewed reported that "real life" is "just another window."[7] We also want to break down the walls of the classroom and place pupils and teachers in new spaces for learning, "unfiltered" spaces.

For example, in 1994 and 1995, researchers in the laboratory I direct at the University of São Paulo ran a most interesting project linking, through the Internet, four elementary schools in São Paulo with four elementary schools in Lisbon, Portugal. The project, entitled "Cultural (Mis)Encounters Brazil/Portugal," called for the students to exchange on a weekly basis messages concerning the histories of Brazil and Portugal, and similarities and differences in their cultures and folklore. Among other topics, the children from Santos, in the State of São Paulo, one day wrote to their Portuguese peers that "...in 1889, slavery was abolished in Brazil." In a message the following week, the children from one of the schools in Portugal asked for an explanation, because neither their textbook, nor the teacher's discourse in class, had ever mentioned this phenomenon. And so the children in Brazil had to teach the children in Portugal about slavery, and the Portuguese participation in that kind of commerce. The episode makes one wonder if instead of censoring the Internet to protect children from certain ideas, we should eliminate every kind of censorship so as to protect children from the false information of the adult world. In the same project, the students learned

---

7 Sherry Turkle, *Life on the Screen: Identity in the Age of the Internet* (New York: Touchstone, 1995).

from each other the important lesson that the same historical facts sometimes permit different interpretations: each country, understandably, teaches its young people completely different motives as to why Brazil separated from Portugal in 1822.

KNOWING HOW TO EXPERIMENT

One thing about the use of the Internet in education concerns me, however, and that is the need to give structure to the activities of young people when they communicate electronically. Mere chatting has little educational value; in fact, it is the opposite of what we should be trying to teach in schools: structured discourses using arguments supported by evidence. This will be hard for us in Brazil, where there is no tradition in structured, argumentative discourse; there are no debating teams in schools or colleges, no *Robert's Rules of Order*,[8] and televised "debates" are mere shouting contests. Though it is true that Brazilian children, as those elsewhere, enormously enjoy chatting on the Web, taking advantage of anonymity to speak their minds, with nothing to be held against them, I still believe that through activities structured by teachers who are motivated, well-prepared, and honest with their charges, these new technologies can offer young people heretofore unparalleled educational experiences.

When I report that Brazilian society and Brazilian educators are not concerned with the issues already referred to here, it could be that, as I affirm, cultural differences are the cause. But it could also be that a certain cultural/technological lag is the real cause. For example, although the free distribution of textbooks in public schools in North America began over a hundred years ago, it was only some 25 years ago that it began in Brazil. And surely Brazil will not meet the U.S. goal of having 90 per cent of its schools linked to the network by 2002. It is, however, clear that Brazil and the rest of the world are entering into new times and new challenges. We don't really know how "push technology" (distributing information automatically to addresses on the net, instead of waiting for users to "pull" it down) and "cookies" (software coming from a distant site which surrep-

8 Henry M. Robert, *Robert's Rules of Order* (New York: Berkley Books, 1993). See < http://www.constitution org >.

titiously enters one's computer to "see" what information one uses) will affect children at home and in the classroom.

We say that we are in favor of children using these new technologies to gain local knowledge *and* global wisdom, but we may find that we have among us some who wish to filter that experience. It is likely that we will see a fragmented world, interconnected though it may be through technology, solve its problems in a fragmented way. As each culture has its own accumulated wisdom, its special values and its preferences, each will decide *how* to use technology to promote learning, and thereby create conditions for greater social justice, total freedom of expression, and sane, sustainable development. Perhaps that's the best we can hope for.

THE JOURNALISTIC EXPERIENCE IN LATIN AMERICA

Luis Suárez

Since the proclamation of the Universal Declaration of Human Rights by the United Nations' General Assembly 50 years ago, communication and information have gradually become components, not only of the right to freedom of opinion and expression, but of all individual and social rights. It should first be recognized that freedom of expression in journalism is linked with the freedom of people and individuals. It is more limited when the people's freedom of expression is limited, although the press seems to enjoy a greater degree of tolerance, or to depend more on journalists' arrangements with the powers that be. Through the years, the concept of freedom of expression has been defined varyingly, depending on the society's level of development. These definitions, mostly incomplete, undergo constant refinements in the more advanced societies, which have larger means and in which new challenges arise even before the old ones have been met.

New technologies alter the form and content of communication and information. Hence, the debate on a model of journalism which would be dedicated to the progress and freedom of society, and yet would also be imbued with a sense of social responsibility derived from traditional ethics — which some find too constraining.

Both the media and journalists seek to reconcile these two poles, amid the contradictions wrought by the amazing development of technologies. Therein lies my experience. As an official of Latin-American journalists' associations, I have felt the irrepressible force of these phenomena. I believe that both media and information professionals support the statement issued by the 20th General Conference of UNESCO, in Paris, November 28, 1978, about their contribution to international peace and understanding, the promotion of human rights, and the fight against racism, apartheid, and incitement to war.[1] The transposition of these basic principles in a national setting, and the interdependence of international centers, which own and control the new technologies, force us to qualify this debate on the freedom of expression, as globalization appears inevitable.

PARTICULARITIES

To better understand the peculiarities of the Latin American continent, where there is an enormous gap between the media of urban and of fringe areas, a distinction has to be made between communication and information, without restricting either.

"Technology warrants a distinct use of communication means ... the new communication technologies help shape relations which force us to revise the classic concepts and characteristics of the object of study of our discipline [...] the application of the concept is also clearly influenced by circumstances that are not exclusively scientific. I would like to draw attention to the confusion resulting from the translation of the terms of our discipline, for instance, the concepts of 'communication' and 'information'. Thus, the AIERI/IAMCR (Association internationale d'études et de recherche sur l'information / International Association for Mass Communication Research) translates 'information' by 'mass

1 *Human Rights Collection of International Documents* (New York: United Nations' Publications, 1988).

communication' in its title. Surely, it is inaccurate to use 'information' and 'mass communication' as if they were synonyms."[2]

Had the extraordinary potential of technology not been tapped, it is obvious that information would lag far behind its current state of development. At the same time, the uneven distribution of technology, its instantaneous character, and the haste imposed by media competition are sometimes a cause of misinformation and excesses that affect the educational and cultural development of national publics. It is not without reason that UNESCO paid special attention to information in the International Convention on the Right of Correction, ratified December 16, 1952, and enacted August 24, 1962. The convention deals in detail with the various aspects of information, the professional responsibility of correspondents and agencies, etc.[3]

The advent of new technologies first has a disruptive effect. There is an imbalance between the potential output of technologies and the ability of the media to exploit them. Today in Latin America, we see communication and information centers equipped with the latest technologies, linked to the world's most advanced centers, and editorial rooms full of computers with every possible accessory. But many journalists only make a very basic use of them just to be up-to-date, and do not venture further. This is not to mention journalists who remain attached to their old mechanical typewriters, adamantly resisting the new techniques. These old journalists, in their time, humanized the profession. They are now fading in a romantic aura which has the merit of counterbalancing the dehumanization and exclusiveness forced by the demands of new technologies and their promotion in the communication market.

The new generations are irresistibly drawn into this jungle called the "information society" or the "information age." They believe that those who do not exploit its resources, or at least those deemed essential to the profession of journalism, are in fact "illiterate," even though they may write flawlessly.

In addition to journalists, millions of us subscribe to communication networks, use the Internet, and rely on computers to do our work. We are fascinated by the new technologies, and without taking the time to understand them, plod forward. The new challenges do not stem only from the practical applications of

2 Miguel Rodrigo Alsina, "Redefiniendo el Concepto de Informacion," *Voces y Culturas, Revista de comunicación* (Barcelona, Spain), no 7, first semester, 1995.
3 *Human Rights*, 1988

the new technologies. They involve moral, educational, cultural, and behavioral risks, calling for a reflection on many issues.

TECHNOLOGICAL ADVANCES

In the meantime, technology leaps forward so rapidly that every new product supersedes those that were still novelties only yesterday. This phenomenon is not true everywhere, however. There are less-developed nations, which do not generate new technologies and do not have the financial resources to acquire them. For them, yesterday's products, obsolete in highly-developed and exporting societies, still represent modernity. Quite apart from their general state of technological development, they run a risk in exploiting this new knowledge, and a greater risk still in ignoring it. "Risk without knowledge is perilous, but knowledge without risk is useless."[4]

Let me cite my own case, which is halfway between these extremes. A journalist of many years experience in every branch of the profession, I have learned through empirical methods and, overcoming my bias, came rather late to the use of computers and related technologies. I came to it in the hope of becoming a more complete journalist, up to date with my contemporaries. I came to it also with an eye on the future, because I would have been displaced by this revolution, which challenges the nobler values of journalism, values we ought to preserve and insert into the new technologies instead of letting ourselves be marginalized by them. Otherwise, sooner or later, technology, and with it society and the new generations, will exclude us from the practice of a trade that remains as beautiful today as it was yesterday.

Gabriel Jaime Pérez,[5] referring to some ethical aspects of communications which he deems useful to meet the challenges of journalism, quotes Bill Gates: "I heard about the Iron Age and the Bronze Age, periods of history named after the new materials used by man to make tools and weapons. They were specific ages. Later, I read that academics predicted countries would fight for the control of information rather than natural resources (...) I imagined absurd conversa-

---

tions in an office of the future: 'How much information do you have?' (...) 'I heard that the information price index is on the rise.' These sentences do not seem to make any sense because information is not as concrete nor measurable as the materials that defined previous ages, but information has become an increasingly important material for us. The information revolution is only beginning. The cost of communications will diminish as fast as did the cost of computers. When it is low enough and combined with other technological advances, the 'information highway' will no longer be just the buzz word of greedy managers or emotional politicians. It will be as real and dominant as electricity."[6]

Until the decrease in the cost of new technologies makes them more accessible, their massive exploitation — not the limited use made by individuals or some corporations, but that of written or electronic media — will continue to entail high costs in remote areas, especially in Latin America. In any case, these media lose creative autonomy. They are forced to reduce their regional or national content and globalize their information at the expense of issues that directly concern their community.

In entering McLuhan's global village we run the risk of losing the significance and contours of our own village, be it a locality, a region, or a nation. Reflecting on the current communication society, Gianni Vattimo, one of the best-known representatives of the postmodern school of thought, theorized that "the intensification of communications, the acceleration of information up to the simultaneity of direct television — and McLuhan's *global village* — do not represent one aspect of modernization, but the very heart and meaning of this process. The assumption refers of course to McLuhan's thesis that a society is defined and characterized by its technologies, not in a generic sense, but in the precise sense of communication technologies."[7]

6 Gabriel Jaime Pérez SJ, at the Symposium on Regional, Communal and Rural Press Citizen Participation, organized by the FELAP with the support of UNESCO, May 13, 1997, quoting Bill Gates, *The Way of the Future* (1995).

7 Gabriel Jaime Pérez, *idem*.

TOWARDS GLOBALIZATION

The great technological advances coincide with the media concentration caused by globalization. It is another factor that gives contemporary journalism its uncertain character, influencing and often threatening the employment of journalists, which is a source of conflict in the profession.

Everywhere, media concentration reinforces empires or increases dependence. The main examples are well known: Springer, in Germany; Hersant Rossel, in Belgium; PRISA, in Spain; Hersant, in France; Berlusconi, in Italy; Murdoch, in the United Kingdom. The negative influence of concentration on journalism is all the more serious since "80 per cent of the flow of audiovisual communication in the world is controlled by the United States... (T)he problem may be posed in terms of quality as well as ethics."[8]

Armand Mattelart, the author of many works on the subject, traces the origin of the process of globalization as follows: "In the 1980's, I believe, the globalization of finance was the starting point [...] changes in the world's financial system brought about one of the early applications of real-time data processing. Globalization was first a geopolitical, and even a military concept. This is an issue that communication workers generally overlook. In the 1980's, we began to talk about world enterprises, world communications, world advertising, always from the point of view of corporations which sought to legitimize their world strategy, like Coca-Cola, Saatchi and Saatchi, etc."[9]

It was unavoidable that this globalization — of technologies and finance — would destroy some of journalism's traditional attributes of objectivity and independence. As objective and responsible as they are, journalists today have a hard time remaining neutral in reporting events that affect their country and the world. Concentration also restricts the clash of opinions and makes it virtually impossible to create truly national publishing and broadcasting firms that look after the cultural and information interests of their people.

Ignacio Ramonet, the editor of the *Monde diplomatique* says: "Any journalist, by definition, belongs to the field of communication. He is a mediator between the transmitter and the receiver, with this difference that in networks the transmis-

8 Pierre Musso, Ignacio Ramonet, and Lucien Sfez, "Un Encuentro en Torno al Dictionnaire critique de la communication," *Voces y Culturas, Revista de Comunicacion*, vol 7, no. 1 (1995).

9 Armand Mattelart, interviewed in Barcelona on June 6, 1994 by *Voces y Culturas*.

sion of messages implies a preparation that can in no way be neutral. Journalistic objectivity consists in the ability to 'translate' an information from certain parameters that permit to inform. Today we are seeing [...] a transformation of the concept of information in the press. The traditional model, based on 'who says what to whom,' with what intention, what consequences, etc., has given precedence to a new parameter based on the immediacy of the event. The idea is more to place the spectator in the middle of the event, to confront one with the other, so that the intermediary between the two disappears. In other words, the journalistic function as we knew it is about to disappear."[10]

THE NEOLIBERAL CONSENSUS

Among experts, researchers and polemicists looking for an answer to the contradictions and confusion wrought by the invasion of new technologies and their concentrating effect, there seems to be a consensus that the main political derivative of economic globalization is what is called *neoliberalism*. Thus, neoliberalism — as it is understood and practiced in Latin-America — is a radical conception of capitalism which tends to make an absolute of the market and see it as the beginning, the middle, and the end of any intelligent and rational human behavior. This conception subordinates to the market the lives of persons, the behavior of societies, and the politics of governments. This absolute market does not accept any rules in any area.[11]

The partisans of excessive neoliberalism do not accept any rule in communication and information. For fear that rules limit the freedom of information, one of the most highly-valued human rights, or more likely that they affect their near absolute power to dictate what is to be published or broadcast, a group of publishers belonging to the Inter-American Press Society (IPS) claims that "the best press law is no press law." They reject any code of ethics, in the belief that regulating principles in the press are inherent to the condition and role of the media, which of course they control.

10 Pierre Musso, Ignacio Ramonet, and Lucien Sfez, "Un Encuentro en Torno al Dictionnaire critique de la communication," *Voces y Culturas, Revista de Comunicacion,* vol 7, no. 1 (1995).

11 "*El Neoliberalismo en América Latina, Aportes para una Reflexión Común,*" a document prepared by the Provincial Superiors of the Company of Jesus in Latin America (Mexico, 1996). Published in *Revista Javeriana,* no. 633 (April 1997).

The absence of legislation induced by those who control information and communication technologies leaves the media and media workers — and, in the end, society — at the mercy of the governments' domineering ambitions. The 7th Iberian-American Summit of Heads of States and Governments of Latin America, Spain and Portugal showed how stubborn is this resistance to any regulation as they opposed the use of the qualifier in the notion of the right to true information. It was considered that the qualifier was superfluous as it is of the essence of the trade and the power to inform to be true.

These conditions give rise to paradoxical situations like the anachronistic Mexican law. Article VI of the Constitution of the United States of Mexico stipulates that "the State guarantees the right to information," by virtue of an amendment on the freedom of expression introduced in the 1970s. But this article of the constitution has not yet been followed, like all others, by a subsidiary or regulatory law determining the concrete form of its application. In the meantime, an outmoded law called the Law on Printing, dating back to 1917, continues to apply while the writing and printing of written media as well as radio and television are by and large computerized.

Speaking to the media owners who champion the absence of codes of ethics or regulations, I said that while we had differences, we were also all in the same boat. "We are all interested in the health of journalism. There are common values if we accept a shared and convergent social responsibility, apart from other issues [...] Neither I nor other salaried journalists want corporations to disappear. I don't want to be without work nor do the thousands of journalists of Latin America whom we represent here. In terms of law, we recognize that there are more statements of principle than concrete applications. Universal standards, like the Universal Declaration of Human Rights, which entrenches the right to information in Article 19, are general statements. Governments subscribe to it like many others, but they have their own opinions and first obey internal motives, even pleading sovereignty, to avoid putting into practice the commitments they make at the international level ... On our continent, the application of the right (to information) is a legal quagmire. Legislators waver. Governments wash their sometimes very dirty hands of the matter. While States fade away, governments leave it to the media to come to an arrangement. They push us to the confrontation that we have seen here and we cannot achieve anything concrete. It is good therefore that we prolong the debate [...] To the questions of where, when, how that we teach journalism students as the model of the trade, we should add, given certain facts, this most agonizing question: Why?"[12]

In summary, the few aspects of the situation I have exposed here show that journalism is changing. Prospects are uncertain because we do not know how journalism will meet the new challenges facing it. We see that there is little relation between the academic training of journalists or social communicators and the practice of journalism and social communication. I have often been in a position to see this in discussions with students. They neither question nor validate the content of their study program. On the other hand, they ask plenty of questions about my experiences as a journalist on special assignment for the coverage of events like the Vietnam war, the Dominican and Nicaraguan revolutions, or the tribulations of Che Guevara in Bolivia.

I conclude that there is a gap between the schools of social communication and/or journalism and the reality awaiting their graduates. It seems to me urgent to update the content and pedagogical methods of courses in the three languages of current and future journalism: written, spoken, and visual. The media will continue to change. To meet the new challenges and ensure the concrete application of one of the most important individual and collective human rights in our contemporary and so-called postmodern society, we have to overcome many of the obstacles and confusion I have raised in this empirical work of a journalist with a long and full, if not always successful past.

12 The author, speaking at the *Iberian-American Forum on Communication*, organized by UNESCO in Caracas, Venezuela, June 30 to July 1, 1997.

DIRECT BROADCAST TECHNOLOGY: A MIDDLE-EASTERN PERSPECTIVE ON A NEW DOMAIN OF CONFLICT

Hamdy Hassan

The technology of direct broadcast is considered the most important single factor that has affected media-government relations during the past decade in Third World countries. This new technology represents a special revolution in the Arab World where broadcasting activities have been a governmental domain, while the print media have been subject to considerable influence, and even censorship. There is a noticeable trend among media researchers to suggest that this new technology will reshape the relationship between media, government and the audience.

Since the invention of the printing, no other social innovation has had such momentous effects as broadcasting. "Despite all that has been written about broadcasting, we still underestimate its significance. This underestimate is itself a clue to its peculiar historic power."[1]

---

1 Daniel J. Boorstin, "The Significance of Broadcasting in Human History," a talk given at *The Symposium on the Cultural Role of Broadcasting*, October 3–5, 1978, in Tokyo, sponsored by the Hoso-Bunko Foundation, pp. 9–23.

"He who first shortened the labor of copyists by the device of movable types," in Thomas Carlyle's familiar observation, "was disbanding armies, and cashiering most kings and senates, and creating a whole democratic world: he had invented the art of printing."[2] But with radio and television, we came to experience the most democratic of all forms of media. Broadcasting is the great leveler, going without discrimination into the homes of rich and poor. No prerequisites, no skills are needed, and no questions are asked to enter TV-land and to have a front seat for all its marvels.

The most significant symptomatic feature of the television age was the speed with which it arrived. This speed was the most important and most neglected clue to the revolutionary meaning of television for the common experience. Television and its social effects arrived during the lifetime of one generation. It required two centuries at least for the social effects of printing to emerge, and many centuries passed before the invention of language and writing had social effects. Television was a quantum leap in the experience of every man, woman and child, and of the whole community.

ACCESS TO A LITTLE MEDIA FREEDOM

The preceding decade has represented a new stage, not solely in the history of television but in all human media. The eighties saw major modifications in the frequency and speed of the media that transcended all progress achieved since television was introduced in the fourth decade of this century.

Coping with these changes today is probably the broadest challenge to face the television industry in all countries as well as in the international community. No media system will be able to ignore these changes. If it tries to do so, that system will add nothing to the formation of this industry's new characteristics which are expected to infringe on all information systems in the world.

Not a single media system in our era is able to be fully self-reliant in the provision of first-class television programs. Because of this, global developments in the television industry were a deciding factor in shaping national television performances.

2 *Ibid.*

For some peoples of the Third World direct broadcasting technology now introduces a new period in the history of human media, a period that proclaims the regaining of a freedom that had been lost to their mass media. Despite the countless advantages of conventional mass media, their most conspicuous flaw was that, more than any other type of communication, they could easily be controlled by imperialist and national governments. Every human society has had its traditional channels of communication. Part of its cultural and social systems, traditional channels were adequate for the delivery of information on a societal basis because they existed at the local level and could reach any social class. One of the foremost benefits of traditional media was that they let information circulate in society with notable freedom.[3]

With the advent of mass media, Third World peoples entered an unprecedented area of media monopoly that was marketed under different labels such as "national unity," "total economic growth," or " summoning up all strengths to take up internal and external challenges."

As a result of mass media technology, opportunities to communicate information to people through traditional means dwindled sharply The general public was increasingly turning to mass media channels, which had, amongst other roles, the assignment of influencing social and political priorities in adherence to government policies. In the case of television, over more than 40 years, experience showed that a mass medium could easily be controlled and oriented. Television's huge influence became its major disadvantage. Television emerged as the paramount device in the hands of government for the control of information diffusion within society. An overwhelming majority of people preferred television over other public media for political, social, cultural and entertainment programs and information. Therefore, it was common that television remained the typical manifestation of state monopoly. In many Third World countries, television remains one of the ultimate strongholds to be relinquished by government.

Direct broadcasting technology has been, potentially, one of the outstanding agents of transformation to intervene in the relationship between governments and television, particularly in Third World countries. In this respect, three factors can be distinguished that affect this relationship significantly:

3 These channels were efficiently used for political opposition in many Islamic societies due to their high rate of credibility compared to that of the state-run mass media. Hamdy Hassan, *Islamic Sermons as a Channel for Political Media in Egypt: 1961-1981* (Al-Azhar University, Cairo: 1986).

■ For the first time, television became an interstate, widespread international means of communication. This change in TV's role initiated radical changes in the political, social, and cultural content of broadcast information. This new technology led to the breaking up of TV's huge general public. In that way, not only did this new technology terminate the state monopoly on information broadcast in society, but it reduced the government's ability to mobilize huge audiences with a single concerted slogan.

■ The increase in the number of accessible channels reduced the importance of television, from a media with a huge general public to a media with a smaller audience. Thus, from a supreme media, TV became an average information media[4]. McLuhan's prediction about a "Global Village" is being realized in the way he had imagined. These latest changes are reinstating a world of many villages except that, today, this division does not take place on geographical, racial or religious grounds but on a fairly new basis which is significant for human history. This pattern persuaded some people to propose a new kind of citizenship: TV citizenship.[5] This breaking up of the TV public, greatly diminished the prevalent influence of slogans and, for the first time in many societies, encouraged a variety of opinions and thoughts. This must be regarded as meaningful progress for the Third World.

■ This new technology spread very quickly and this precluded the television industry and governments from carrying out appropriate measures to accommodate this new revolution. It deeply influenced not only overall aspects of the television industry but also other mass media, especially print media. Governments of many countries were compelled to re-examine their policies of information, not only in regard to TV, but also for print media.

4 The most obvious trend during the 1990s in the Arab World was the breaking up of the traditional mass television audience into fragmented segments of smaller audiences, a Western phenomenon during the 1980s. See Marc Doyle, *The Future of Television: A Global Overview of Programming, Advertising, Technology and Growth* (Illinois: NTC Business Books, 1992), p. 2.

5 *Ibid*, p. 173.

DIRECT BROADCASTING AND STATE MONOPOLY

The second Gulf war has possibly been the single prominent event that has had a decisive influence on mass media in the Middle East.[6] This war unveiled two important aspects of the media in this region.

■ The war has strongly drawn the attention of leaders and professionals to the consequence of news and information in this specific region of the world.

■ The war revealed the crucial professional insufficiencies of local news agencies in obtaining and publishing information. Middle Eastern people and even leaders were following the crisis and the evolution of military operations through foreign media, particularly CNN.[7]

In that way, the years after the second Gulf war saw extensive progress in the region's TV industry. The most perceptible was the rapid increase of satellite TV stations directed at peoples in the Middle East and North Africa and operating inside and outside of the region.

On December 12, 1990, the Egyptian satellite channel ESC started broadcasting, primarily as an Arab satellite channel. Less than one year later, the Middle East broadcasting channel MBC began transmission from London. Thereafter, a stream of satellite broadcasts started to flood the Arab World via Arab and non-Arab channels.

In 1994, there were 21 satellites covering the Arab region, transmitting via 145 channels that could be seen all over the Arab World.[8] The public for these new channels was growing too. This happened, regardless of the contrasting positions of Arab governments, with some prohibiting and others authorizing the acquiring of receiving dishes to view the satellite channels.

It is difficult to provide an accurate estimate of the number of people using satellite channels. Some put their number at approximately 10 million Arab viewers, inside and outside of the Arab World. Others affirm there were 2,5 to

6 Christine Ogan, "The Middle East and North Africa," in John C. Merrill, ed., *Global Journalism: Survey of International Media* (Longman, 3rd edition, 1995), pp. 189-207.

7 The major changes in delivery and control of information in the Middle East come through the electronic media See Hamdy Hassan, "Major Trends in World TV Industry and its Effects on Arab TV Industry."

8 Part Kuperus, *Satellite Broadcasting Guide, 1994* (New York, Amsterdam: Bellboard Books), pp 207-286.

3 million dishes in 1994, out of which 400,000 to 500,000 could be found in Egypt[9] and 1,300,000 in the Persian Gulf area. The Annual Report of the U. S. State Department mentions 300,000 dishes in Saudi Arabia.[10]

Prior to the launching of military operations against Iraq, the Arab region had never experienced any private ownership of television stations. These had remained a state monopoly since the end of the fifties. Government ownership was part of a general information policy that included, apart from TV, radio stations and nearly every copy of newspapers, magazines, movies, and books. Videocassettes probably remained one of the restricted fields where Arab citizens could still exercise a liberty of choice; but that liberty was confined to entertainment. Government information policies supported the political regimes in power and the social values approved by those regimes.

Still, voices of political opponents could be heard inside the Arab World , particularly on religious channels, an avenue to reach a public that was experiencing social and political frustration. Since the start of the 1990s, the Arab World has been the scene of a constant competition between governments and the public over the development of TV direct broadcast channels via satellite. The public was anxious to access these channels in order to escape the government's traditional information blockade, particularly as successive crises in the Arab world convinced the general public that it was told only half the truth at most. People noted a sharp discrepancy between what was broadcast by local and foreign media.

VIEWERS AND THE DIRECT BROADCAST SYSTEM

Before the start of direct broadcasting, a tense societal deliberation was held in Arab countries about the social, cultural and ethical effects to be expected from direct TV broadcasting. Popular concern mainly emphasized the cultural and moral not the political aspects; there were alarms about a collapse of prevailing

9 Safran S. Al Makati, *DBS in the Arab World, A Descriptive study of DBSIS Impact in Saudi Arabia* (a dissertation submitted in fulfillment of the requirement for the Doctor of Philosophy, University of Kentucky, 1995), p.110.
10 US State Department Annual Report, Feb 1997.

social values as a result of direct broadcast programs, which, at the time, were believed to originate only from the West. But the Arab public elite, who would normally listen to and view foreign media, welcomed the new technology for two main reasons:

■ They saw these new channels as an effective means of escaping from the low professional levels and poor performance of local media, which were obeying official orders. The elite also regarded these channels as a chance of breaking the state monopoly on news and information in its society and allowing plurality of opinions on local and world events, thus bringing about, in the long run, a change of the prevailing political tone.

■ This new technology could well renew traditional social values in society. The elite considered those values to be an obstruction to the achievement of genuine growth. The elite was convinced that governments had no real intention of changing these values and ways of life because they guaranteed the stability of political regimes.

The overwhelming majority of people who opposed this new technology did so for ethical reasons, while the elite's encouragement was political in motivation. Halfway between moral fears and political support was a silent majority in the continuing debate. This majority's silence implied that it would predominantly join the new channel supporters eventually.[11]

Aside from the three above-mentioned classes of viewers, there was a large public that could not join the satellite TV audience because of the cost of the receiving dishes. The average price of satellite-receiving equipment is US$1,000.[12] However, the desire of a large sector of the public to view the new channels led to the appearance of collective viewing in cafés and also to collective subscription in order to buy centralized reception equipment.

11 For more details about the characteristics of DBSs in some Arab countries, see H Baitulmaal, "Reception of Satellite Channels in Saudi Arabia: A Case Study Riyadh Inhabitants," *Gulf Television Review* (Jan. 12, 1994); Atef A. Al-Abd, "Pattern of Viewing Satellite Channels in UAR," *Media Research* (Cairo, 1994).
12 Safran S. Al Makati, *op. cit.*, (1995).

LONG- AND SHORT-TERM EFFECTS

Direct broadcast technology brought quick changes in relations between the public and the media. Any current evaluation of these effects should take into account various phenomena engendered by eight years of direct broadcast:

■ The number of foreign non-Arab channel viewers in the region is limited. This is due to linguistic, cultural, and social barriers and also to the existence of more than 34 accessible Arabic channels.[13] Many studies showed that the percentage of public viewing the non-Arabic channels does not exceed five to seven per cent of satellite channels' total audience.[14] For example, the proportion of CNN viewers in Saudi Arabia is five per cent of the satellite channel's total public.[15]

■ The program content of Arabic channels remains similar by reason of the cultural and political homogeneity of the viewing public on one hand, and the submissiveness of all these channels to government guidelines, on the other hand.[16] In the same vein, a high percentage of Arabic programs originate in a limited number of production centers, chiefly in Cairo, and, and to a lesser extent in Kuwait, Syria and Jordan.

■ Foreign information and news channels likely to initiate changes in traditional political, intellectual and cultural traditional values, were primarily intended for an elite wishing to participate in international society and New Age culture.

■ Most satellite-channel viewers are part of the silent majority that depends on direct broadcasting for amusement, entertainment, and escape from reality (75 per cent of the general public).[17] This craving for amusement and distraction created competition between satellite channels to produce more programs. The law of supply and demand governed the relation between the general public in the Arab World and satellite channels. This led to the creation of what could be called an information market, one supplying information made up of trivial topics posing no risk at all to prevailing values.

---

13 Hamdy Hassan, "News and Information Usage of Foreign Satellite Channels," *Media Research*, no. 8 (June 1997).

14 M. Al Yassiny Moawad, "The attitudes of Kuwait viewers after liberation," *Faculty of Arts Periodical*, vol. 15 (1994/1995), pp. 14–15.

15 Safran S. Al Makati, *op. cit.*, p.110.

16 There is no Arab satellite channel that is not following one form of another of governmental guidelines.

17 Al-Abd, *op cit.*; Baitulmaal, *op. cit.*

AUDIENCE LEADS THE MEDIA

During the last 10 years, the spread of satellite dishes attained a level of growth probably higher than that experienced during the original introduction of television into this region. This phenomenon could be explained only by the urge to escape from an unsatisfying and frustrating information reality. The freedom to receive and select channels was in itself one of the most prominent factors that shaped the new relationship between the public and television. This newly acquired freedom was one of the rare examples of Arab citizens discovering the meaning of freedom. The use of remote-control devices for channel-hopping was and still is a new-found pleasure for the Arab viewer. The liberty of channel-hopping will inevitably lead to the rewriting of the relationship between the public and other media, particularly print media. The liberty of receiving and selecting creates a new value and is expected to influence the ownership of newspapers, magazines, and even local TV stations in the long run.

The liberty of receiving and selecting has provided unique occasions for drawing immediate comparisons between performance levels, program content and the amount and quality of information shown on local and foreign channels. Probably for the first time in the Arab world, these instantaneous comparisons initiated a general push to improve the performance of local TV stations. These pressures have succeeded so far in altering the content of TV programs almost everywhere in the Arab World. These pressures will also apply to print media. For this reason, in many Third World countries, the general public has been taking specific action to improve national media — an exceptional event in these countries.

Freedom of selection among many accessible channels jeopardized the state monopoly on information delivery. Egyptian President Husni Mubarak declared repeatedly during the last Iraqi crisis that no Arab ruler could today endorse US plans to strike Iraq, and observed "People became well informed through satellite channels."[18] This statement is an indication of the remarkable increase in the importance and influence of public opinion. It represents also a critical change when compared to Arab media assertions in 1990, before direct broadcasting was started in the Arab region.

18 *Al-Ahram*, February 23, 1998.

As Stephen Franklin observed: "The Saudi media was remarkably unchanged even by the events of the Gulf War. The news of the Iraqi invasion was ignored for several days, and even then was described as 'Iraqi Aggression'. Throughout the war, journalists followed their long-term policy of not reporting on sensitive affairs until the government has first formulated its policy regarding these affairs. The freedom of reception and selection that replaced the government monopoly has to be considered a remarkable achievement in the area of media arena during the past eight years in the Arab World."[19]

GOVERNMENT REACTIONS

Direct broadcast technology sounded the knell of government monopoly on information within society. However, Arab governments did not surrender unconditionally to that new situation. Today, they are attempting to make use of this technology to uphold part of their influence in regulating information passing their borders. Arab governments took advantage of particular features of the satellite industry such as the control of Arabic channels. Until now, all these channels are either government property or subservient to government orders. Referring to the targets of the Egyptian satellite channel, the Egyptian minister of information declared: "This channel aims at being an alternative for the Arab viewer at a time when foreign satellite channels are expanding; this channel aims at preserving Arab identity as well as Arab heritage and culture."[20]

To counterbalance foreign news channels, Arab news channels were being created. But to this day, there are only two: The Arabic Peninsula channel broadcasting from Qatar, and ANA channel. The first has achieved popularity because of elaborate and thorough free discussions of many intellectual and foreign political but not local political issues, which in the past were prohibited on local channels. Egypt is getting ready to launch another news channel; and there is the MBC network, owned by King Fahd's son-in-law and based in London, England.

---

19 Stephen Franklin, "The Kingdom and Its Messengers," *Columbia Journalism Review* (July/August 1991), p. 24.
20 *Al-Ahram* (May 28, 1994).

In spite of government endeavors to check the growth of satellite channels, freedom of reception and selection has become a permanent reality in the Arab World. No government efforts aimed at restraining exposure of the public to these channels can ever succeed, unless an acceptable alternative, including daily comparisons of information and news content and diversity of opinions presented on local and foreign channels, is made available. Experience shows that Arab channels intended to perform as substitutes for news and current affairs on foreign channels will not soon be operational.

NEW MEDIA AND DEMOCRATIC VALUES

There is, however, no certainty that the new media technology will lead to a totally different new age with still more freedom of expression. There are even signs showing opposite trends.

Despite errors and failures, traditional media have been playing an important and vital role in bringing forward and delivering massive quantities of information. These media settled priorities for us, reassembled us around the same goals, and achieved the meaning of the unanimity of the Umma, the global community of Muslims.[21] The multiplicity of channels now available to the public in the Arab World resulted in a fragmentation of this public and the severance of ties instituted by traditional media. New channels have created a new type of citizenship: TV citizenship. There is a dark side to this continuous flood of entertainment and information items. As Neil Postman put it "this leads to an explosion and flood of superficial items which shall numb our perception of reality instead of inciting us to understand it."[22]

There is another fear: that this new technology will broaden the gap between those who are over-informed and those who lack information. The expected consequence, in this case, would be further fragmentation of society which could induce a strong feeling of alienation and a permanent distrust in governments and other institutions that need a minimal feeling of consensus to be effective.

21 Wilson Dizard Jr, *Old Media, and New Media: Mass Media in the Information Age* (Longman, 2nd edition, 1997), p. 25.

22 Neil Postman, *Amusing Ourselves to Death: Public Discourse in the Age of Show Business* (New York: Penguin Books, 1986).

Those who are well informed will be better connected to the foreign world than to the country in which they live. As for poorly informed people, they will seek subjects of entertainment rather than cultural programs that enrich their background and personal experience. Freedom of expression does not depend exclusively on media. Current levels of economic growth, political structure, economic organization, degree of political awareness, and external pressures largely determine it. These are the factors that generate ideas and opinions requiring means of expression.

Under the New World Order, Third World governments are, to a certain extent, compelled to alleviate restrictions their media. However, most of these governments have also the means to moderate the impact of this freedom. Unless this freedom of expression is bolstered by political and social structures, it will be nothing more than a freedom to make ineffectual noises.

This kind of situation is promoted by great powers that exert varying and selective pressures on Third World governments. International pressure has succeeded in bringing about a relative liberalization of economic activities and international trade but the same pressure has not been applied with equal persistence in the field of politics. In certain cases, these pressures gave birth to mutilated and ugly regimes, economically liberal for the purpose of looking after the interests of great powers but politically authoritarian and despotic.

For these reasons, the abundance of information available from direct broadcasting channels, will not always be a sign of healthy development. It could even increase alienation, and aggravate negative trends in some societies, encouraging people to take refuge from reality in entertainment channels.

MISADVENTURES ON THE INFOBAHN: INFORMATION TECHNOLOGY IN A SOUTHERN CONTEXT

Wayne Sharpe

A colleague who runs a freedom of expression organization in Nairobi, Kenya, sent me this story. While you are crossing the street, you witness the police shooting dead an unarmed person. No questions are asked of witnesses. To the best of your knowledge, it would have been more sensible to apprehend the man, if indeed he was a suspect, than to shoot him in cold blood. The following day, the government-owned newspaper runs a screaming headline: "Police shoot down one of Kenya's most wanted criminals." The story then continues something like this: "Police yesterday gunned down one of the most wanted criminals in the country as he and four others attempted to rob a bank. The man, who was armed with an automatic pistol, was shot dead after he defied a police order to surrender and instead engaged police in a fierce shoot-out."

Of course you know all this is fabrication but you have no right to contradict the police who "know better". You are bitter, you want to tell the world the truth, but what do you do? Owners of the media organization where you work are afraid of carrying the story lest they get reprimanded.

If the world is to know about your story you have few options. You can fax it outside the country but this is expensive. The government recently directed that international communication charges be tripled to discourage people from sending abroad "negative" stories about the country. You can phone but this would be even more expensive than faxing. Worse still, the line may be tapped. If you are caught, you may be accused of keeping tourists away through alarmist reports. At times like this you wish you were connected to the Internet. You wish you had a computer, a modem, and a telephone line, even an unreliable one. You wish you had a way of evading censorship and bureaucracy.

Simply put, the moral of this story is that the Internet can do for Africa what Glasnost did for Russia.

As we know, even Glasnost encountered some bumps along the road, and so it is with information technology in Africa. This same colleague in Nairobi admits that having the technology, and getting it to work, are two very different matters. Government monopoly of telephone systems, exorbitant hook-up and long distance rates, and frequent power outages make information technology a gamble in many parts of the African continent.

GLOBAL INFORMATION INFRASTRUCTURE

The rapid spread of information technology has led the World Bank to coin a new phrase — the "global information infrastructure."[1] But the term "global" is an exaggeration. Parts of the planet may now be wired, but the main terminals are certainly not located in places like Kenya.

Another colleague, who runs a similar press-freedom organization in Ghana, has had a hard time plugging into the "global information infrastructure." His problems are cost and access. The Post and Telecommunications Corporation (PTC)

1 Eduardo Talero and Philip Gaudette, "Harnessing Information for Development — A Proposal for a World Bank Group Strategy," (Washington, DC: World Bank, Telecommunications and Informatics Division, Industry and Energy Department, 1995).

in Ghana was until recently entirely government-owned. Internet service cost US$100 a month with a $200 annual registration fee. He was also required to buy a modem from the government utility at a comparatively high cost. "Then came the real problem," he said. "We applied for a telephone and it never came. We were informed there were no more telephone numbers. We thought it had something to do with the area ... so we relocated. That did not help."

Government policy on communication in Ghana has been more security-driven than commercial. The PTC was until recently run by a favored military officer. My friend got his telephone line only after the Malaysians became shareholders in the PTC and took over its management. "One cannot be sure what the problem was," my Ghanaian colleague reflected, "whether it was the fear that we were going to use the service for 'subversive' activities or that there really were no lines — we have not been able to know the true story to this day."

The deterrent costs of communication, red tape, censorship, and governments' resistance to change have caused many freedom-of-expression groups to turn to the Internet, and yet for many this is only the beginning of their problems. As my Kenyan friend told me: "The authorities in Africa have many different ways of incapacitating freedom-of-expression and human-rights groups, including exorbitant bills for permits and government services, denial of registration for organizations, apathy, retrogressive legislation, and arrogance."

INFORMATION 'HAVES', INFORMATION 'HAVE-NOTS'

"Today, the principles of open knowledge and the free circulation of goods and ideas have established themselves so firmly in the West that any reservations on that score are usually seen as politically and intellectually radical."[2]

"The information highway may well run the risk of delivering an information aristocracy rather than a digital democracy."[3]

These two quotations touch upon the two inadequacies that threaten to keep the developing world mired in the democratic and technological "dark ages"

2 Roger Shattuck, *Forbidden Knowledge: From Prometheus to Pornography* (London: St. Martin's Press, 1996).
3 Torben Krogh, President of the Council, UNESCO, quoted in Hans d'Orville, "UNDP and the Communications Revolution — Communications and Knowledge-Based Technologies for Sustainable Human Development," (New York: United Nations Development Program).

described by my friends in Kenya and Ghana. While the free circulation of ideas is a right guaranteed to by the Universal Declaration of Human Rights, which has been signed by scores of nations since its inception in 1948, in reality the free flow of ideas is a controversial, if not illegal, concept in many regions beyond the Western world.

It could be said that the one success of the West's international-development initiative over the last four decades has been to expose the less-developed world to the concepts of free expression and democracy, even if poverty and high mortality rates have persisted. And yet, despite the hope of recent years, we have recently seen experiments in democracy abandoned or crushed in Africa and Eastern Europe.

What gains these regions have made in the areas of free speech, free expression, and a free press are in danger of disappearing as the tide of democracy ebbs. At the same time, the information-technology revolution, which represents a lifeline for freedom-of-expression advocates around the world, could be just beyond their reach.

While technical advances accelerate in the West, more than half of humanity has never made a telephone call. According to the United Nations Development Program (UNDP), there are more telephone lines in Manhattan than in all of Sub-Saharan Africa. Per 10,000 population, there are 2,500 computers in the United States, 1,070 in Singapore, and 7 in India. The world average is 250. While media are converging over phone and cable lines in the West, the rest of the world has found it hard to even get a connection.

Times are changing but slowly. By the early 1990s, the World Wide Web had become the most frequently-visited region of the information highway. What is most encouraging is the direction of Web activity. In 1995, the UNDP estimated there were 56 million Internet users worldwide, mostly in the United States; by 1999 this figure is expected to rise to 200 million people. More than 50 per cent of current Net users are outside the United States and this percentage is rising. By the year 2000, less than 20 per cent of all Internet users are projected to be in the US. Eliminating the distinction between information-rich and information-poor countries is critical to eliminating other inequalities between North and South. The spread of the Internet and computer technology beyond the developed world gives hope that the developing world can catch up.

Satyan Pitroda writes: "As a great social leveler, information technology ranks second only to death... High technology can put unequal human beings on an equal footing, and that makes it the most potent democratizing tool ever devised."[4]

But how level is the playing field? In 1995, only seven African countries (Zambia, Mozambique, South Africa, Egypt, Zimbabwe, Namibia, and Tunisia) had direct links to the Internet. Today, over three-quarters of the capital cities in African countries have developed some sort of Internet access — 47 of the 54 nations on the continent. While the number of Internet users in Africa is on the rise, it is important to look at how well usage is distributed across the continent. Current estimates put the figure at between 700,000 and one million in a total African population of 700 million. Of that one million, however, 600,000 live in South Africa.

TECHNOLOGY AND TRUTH

"Advances in the technology of telecommunications have proved an unambiguous threat to totalitarian regimes everywhere," said media financier Rupert Murdoch speaking to members of the UNDP.[5] Maurice Strong has observed: "Knowledge now plays such an important part in the process of development, that development itself is being redefined in terms of the ability to generate, acquire, disseminate, and employ knowledge, both modern and traditional."[6] Information technology, as the vehicle for knowledge dissemination, has become a key component for development in an information age. Yet the ability to communicate is meaningless if it is not accompanied by the freedom to communicate. Freedom-of-expression advocates are embracing technology as quickly and completely as they can because it enables them to act as "global whistleblowers" with a potential audience of 200 million at their fingertips.

4 Satyan Pitroda, "Development, Democracy, and the Village Telephone," *Harvard Business Review* (Nov./Dec., 1993).

5 Rupert Murdoch, cited by Hans d'Orville, *op. cit.*

6 Maurice Strong, "Connecting With the World: Priorities for Canadian Internationalism in the 21st Century," a report by the International Development Research and Policy Task Force, November 1996, p.17.

Experience has shown us that new technologies are invented in the North and reach the South through a type of "trickle down" process. Experience also tells us that new technologies are often used to control people, not to liberate them. Governments use them to control their people and corporations use them to control their workers and influence their political environment. The Canadian Committee to Protect Journalists has documented several case studies of government control of information technology.[7] In Zimbabwe, Internet service providers (ISPs) and the state- owned communications company (PTC) are feuding over control of the entity that registers new Internet sites. The ISPs claim that the PTC wants to assume control of the country's top-level domain and that the government, through the PTC, is attempting to monopolize the Internet service business so that it can, among other things, control who gets registered and who does not. In another southern African nation, Malawi, privately-owned ISPs also fear that the government is creating an information monopoly to serve its interests. Their concerns were expressed after the government in 1997 rejected several ISPs' applications and instead granted one to the state-owned Malawi Post and Telecommunications Corporation (MPTC).

INFORMATION FEAST AND FAMINE

Much has been written about the "information drought" in the developing world. In the United States, more than 46 per cent of GNP is related to knowledge, communication, and information work. By the year 2000, the information sector is expected to grow to 60 per cent of the European GDP. But information is critical for the developing world as well. Discussing the phenomenon of information poverty, the United Nations Center for Science and Technology declared: "The distinction between information 'haves' and 'have-nots' is the basis for the dichotomies between developed and developing, rich and poor … It is within this context that the concept of development might be understood in information terms."

7 David Cozac with David Tortell, "Censorship and the Internet: Challenges for Free Expression Online," an Issues Identification Paper by the Canadian Committee to Protect Journalists (Toronto: November, 1997).

The revolution in information technology delivers tremendous capability — vast information storage, fast and inexpensive communication channels, and links between different media — at comparatively low and steadily declining costs. But by itself, information technology achieves nothing. Developing countries need the free flow of information in order to take full advantage of the technology they now find within their reach.

Six years ago the world's leading freedom-of-expression organizations gathered in Montreal to discuss ways they could work together and avoid duplication of effort as they strive to protect persecuted writers and journalists throughout the world. The Montreal meeting was hosted by the Canadian Committee to Protect Journalists and attended by groups like Human Rights Watch from the US, Article 19 from the UK, and Reporters sans frontières from France. With the emergence of electronic mail as an inexpensive, fast, and reliable method of communication, the technology barrier that had plagued earlier joint-action efforts was overcome.

The result of these meetings, the International Freedom of Expression Exchange (IFEX), has grown from an initial membership of 11 to 30 member organizations today. The growth of this organization tells us a great deal about the direction of growth in the freedom-of-expression activities. Of the original 11 groups that met in 1992, only two were from the developing world. This imbalance is even more striking when you realize that over 80 per cent of all reported freedom-of-expression violations occur in the South, or in nations in transition. But look at the IFEX network today. You will see that of its 30 organizations, nearly half are situated in the developing world. No longer are groups in the West collecting the information, disseminating the information, and "controlling" the news on free expression in the disadvantaged South. The South, more and more, is collecting, disseminating, and controlling information flows in its own backyard. The cheap, efficient, and immediate information technology that is now within the grasp of grassroots activists in the developing world has made this happen.

The road from information "have not" to information "have" is long and full of potholes, but at least there is a road. It is a testament to the tenacity of Southern activists that, despite the high costs and government restrictions that plague the information technology revolution in the developing world, they still find a way.

ACCESS TO INFORMATION, UNIVERSAL SERVICE, AND GLOBALIZATION: SOUTH AFRICA IN THE AFRICAN CONTEXT OF INFORMATION TECHNOLOGY

Jane Duncan

Since the late 1970's, the banking and financial services sectors have become increasingly important in the global production picture, overtaking manufacturing as key sectors.[1] These changes are linked to the fact that commodities markets began to expand beyond the confines of the nation-state in their search for new terrain, requiring the development of a range of global financial services. These developments in turn required faster and more reliable methods of communication to aid the mobility and liquidity of capital. In fact, international financial and corporate services have become the most intensive users of telecommunications and computer networks, leading to remarkable leaps in

---

1 J. Hog and J. Miller, *Information Technology in South Africa: The State of the Art and Implications for National IT Policy* (Working Paper no. 3, Development Policy Research Unit, University of Cape Town, February 1997), < http://wn.apc.org/nitf/dpruwp.htm >.

technological innovation.[2] Foreign direct investment (FDI) has mimicked these trends, with a great deal of investment being directed to telecommunications.

It has been argued that far from connecting vast numbers of people to a shared global information superhighway, the information technology "revolution" has facilitated the development of new centers, world cities, and of peripheries between and within countries. Those countries that were wealthy enough to have achieved universal access in these areas (that is, a telephone within walking distance) are now coping with the mounting cost of maintaining these services, whereas there are vast numbers of countries that have not even achieved universal access, especially in Africa.[3]

Even though Africa accounts for 39 per cent of the world's population, it accounts for only 3 per cent of output in cash terms. About 80 per cent of FDI goes to the economic triad of the United States, the European Union (EU), and Japan, with negligible amounts flowing into African countries.[4] In spite of these alarming statistics, development paradigms advocated by African states have shifted noticeably from an emphasis on command-style state intervention in the economy and development program to a panoply of market reforms that confine the state to only the most "necessary" areas of activity to facilitate foreign investment. In responding to these pressures, states have engaged in cutbacks of social spending and privatization of industries, in conformity with structural adjustment programs developed by bodies such as the International Monetary Fund (IMF), World Bank, and the World Trade Organization (WTO). These policies have been widely criticized as a form of recolonization of the continent according to a new set of regulations, representing primarily Northern interests, designed to further impoverish and marginalize it.[5] In fact, at the 1993 Uruguayan round of trade negotiations Africa's needs and problems barely featured.[6]

2 S. Sassen, "The Spatial Organisation of Information Industries: Implications for the Role of the State," in J. Mittleman, ed., *Globalisation: Critical Reflections* (International Political Economy Yearbook, vol. 9; London: Lynne Reinner Publishers, 1996), p. 34.

3 G. Goggin, "Universal Service" (Unit 6), *Advanced Postgraduate Certificate Programme in Telecommunications and Information Policy* (Pretoria: UNISA, Macquarie University [Sydney], Communications Law Centre), p. 9.

4 F. Cheru, "New Social Movements: Democratic Struggles and Human Rights in Africa," in J. Mittleman, ed., *Globalisation...*, p. 148.

5 There is a great deal of literature on this subject. See, for example, G. Adler, "Zambia's Second Subordination: Re-colonisation Through Neo-Liberalism," *South African Labour Bulletin* (SALB), vol. 21, no. 3, pp. 51–54. Also see a series of articles in *Southern Africa Report* entitled "Whose Globalisation?" April 1996. Titus Alexander also deals with multinational institutions; see T. Alexander, *Unravelling Global Apartheid: An Overview of World Politics* (London: Polity Press, 1996). Also see F. Cheru. "New Social Movements...," in J. Mittleman, ed., *Globalisation...*, pp. 146–153.

6 F. Cheru, "New Social Movements...," p. 150.

South Africa is in a relatively better economic position. In fact, its total Gross Domestic Product (GDP) is more than the GDP of all other Southern African countries put together.[7] However, its position in relation to the Northern super-powers is still tenuous, and recent policies have placed emphasis on the need for the country to become internationally competitive. This policy shift has led to conflicts with sections of civil society and it is to be expected that these tensions will sharpen as the country approaches the second set of democratic elections in 1999, posing an unprecedented test to the democratic government's commitment to freedom of expression.

DE-REGULATION OR RE-REGULATION? TELECOMMUNICATIONS, AFRICA, AND SOUTH AFRICA

The General Agreement on Trade in Services (GATS) has provided a framework adopted by the International Telecommunications Union (ITU) to advocate particular types of changes in African telecommunications sectors. These involve the creation of a regulatory framework in each country to ensure competition, the establishment of a regulatory body for the telecommunications sector, the corporatization and privatization of state-owned national telecommunications operators and their separation from postal services, and other measures for encouraging private sector participation in the industry.

Connectivity in Africa varies vastly from country to country, and within countries between the urban centers and rural peripheries.[8] This picture does not seem to be improving significantly, in that Africa's annual average growth in main telephone lines is dropping, as opposed to the improving situations in Latin America and Asia.[9] At the same time, it is becoming more difficult for sub-Saharan Africa to reach its targeted teledensity of one line per 100 inhabitants by the year

---

7 "Whose Globalisation?" *Southern Africa Report* (April 1996), pp 1-2.

8 See information on African Internet Connectivity at < http://demiurgewn.apc.org:80/africa/index.html >.

9 Latin America's growth in main telephone lines grew from a teledensity of 62 to 10.3 per cent from the period 1986-1990 to 1991-1995; Asia's teledensity grew from 12.3 per cent to 31.5 per cent for the same period; whereas Africa's dropped from 8.0 to 7.9 percent. See M. Minges, "The beginning of change in the African telecommunications landscape?" *Communication Technologies Handbook 1997* (Johannesburg: BMI-Techknowledge, 1997).

2000: in 1996 it would have had to find an extra US$3.1 billion to achieve this target, and will have to treble this figure for 1998 (US$9.4 billion)[10].

South Africa occupies a central position in the connectivity web of the continent. The country boasts the largest telecommunications operator in Africa. Called Telkom, it is 70 per cent state owned with a revenue in 1994/5 nearly four times that of the second largest operator, Nitel (Nigeria).[11] Given its ability to offer low-cost leased lines and fiber links to the Northern centers, it has become the Internet hub for the region, and this role is likely to expand.[12] Therefore, its decisions regarding telecommunications development will impact on development in the whole region.

Its emergence as a key telecommunications force was further reinforced by the fact that it hosted the Information Society and Development (ISAD) Conference in May 1996.

South Africa's intervention in the conference emphasized two core objectives: to redress the inequalities of the past and to become globally competitive through a process of liberalization. With regards to the first, it focused on the country's development needs, while arguing that all available resources must be mobilized to increase the country's ability to compete in global markets.[13] A crucial question that needs to be addressed is to what extent these objectives are compatible.

NATION-BUILDING AND GLOBALIZATION IN SOUTH AFRICA'S TELECOMMUNICATIONS POLICY

Even though the telecommunications industry in South Africa was constituted as a "natural monopoly" until very recently, its main goal was ensuring universal access for whites.[14] Under apartheid, telecommunications was regulated by the Minister of Posts and Telecommunications.

10 M. Minges, "The Beginning of Change...," p. 29.

11 The revenues of the 10 largest telecommunications operators in Africa in 1995 were (in millions of US$): Telkom (South Africa) — 3,6747; Nitel (Nigeria) — 867.8; ONPT (Morocco) — 659.4; ARENTO (Egypt) — 639.5; KPTC (Kenya) — 294.5; Tunisie Telecom (Tunisia) — 263.2; MPT (Algeria) — 203.7; CI-TELCOM (Côte d'Ivoire) — 138.2; PTC (Zimbabwe) — 134.9; and Sonatel (Senegal) — 106.3. From "The Beginning of Change", p. 33.

12 African Internet Connectivity; < http://demiurgewn.apc.org:80/africa/southafr.htm >.

13 See *The Information Society and the Developing World: A South African Perspective* (Draft 5; April 1996); < http://wnapc.org/nitf/pptoc.htm >.

14 G. Goggin, "Universal Service" (Unit 6), *Advances ... Postgraduate...*, p. 10.

Since 1994, the country has initiated a number of activities in order to redress this picture. Following the GATS framework, emphasis has been placed on providing a stable regulatory environment to attract investment, involving de-regulation and liberalization of the industry as a whole, and the privatization of Telkom. This environment is mapped out in the Telecommunications Act of 1996. The importance of the Act was emphasized during Parliamentary debate, with the Minister referring to it as "one of the most important economic bills to come before parliament, because it will provide the information backbone for the achievement of the macroeconomic plan."[15]

The Act created the legal framework for the separation of policy and regulatory functions in the industry — policy-making powers would be vested in the Minister, while regulation would be the responsibility of a new body, the South African Telecommunications Regulatory Authority (SATRA). Another body, the Universal Service Agency (USA) was also established by this statute.

In addition to these activities, there are developments being set in place to give effect to the constitutional rights of access to information, freedom of expression, and government accountability and transparency.[16] These development involve usage of the Internet to facilitate government transparency. Government has a large presence on the Internet, although this presence is not coordinated by a central structure. As a result, government use of the Internet is uneven across departments, and between national, provincial and local governments. A Government Communication and Information Service is being set up to coordinate government communication services, and it is envisaged that this structure will develop and implement strategies for Internet usage by government.

15 G. Hartley, "Naidoo tables legislation 'Vital to Securing Telkom Equity Partner,'" *Business Day* (Tuesday, October 8, 1996).

16 The freedom of expression clause is as follows:
"16 (1)   Everyone has the right to freedom of expression, which includes -
        (a) freedom of the press and other media;
        (b) freedom to receive and impart information and ideas;
        (c) freedom of artistic creativity; and
        (d) academic freedom and freedom of scientific research"
However, the constitution does not extend protection to propaganda for war, incitement to imminent violence, or advocacy of hatred that is based on race, ethnicity, gender or religion, and that constitutes incitement to cause harm.
The clause of access to information is as follows:
"Everyone has the right of access to -
(a) any information held by the state; and
(b) any information that is held by another person and that is required for the exercise or protection of any rights.
2. National legislation must be enacted to give effect to this right, and may provide for reasonable measures to alleviate the administration and financial burden on the state."

One significant project has been the launching of a web site by the South African parliament as part of its commitment to "make Parliament more accessible, [and] to make the institution more accountable, as well as to motivate and facilitate public participation in the legislative process."[17] In addition, the Parliamentary Monitoring Group was established in 1995, an initiative of three South African NGOs[18] with the aim of monitoring parliamentary committee meetings so that effective lobbying can take place on various pieces of legislation and other matters of democratic concern. The PMG has set up a web site, making available such relevant information as minutes of Parliamentary meetings, draft legislation, and providing e-mail and telephonic access to parliamentarians.

These activities are supposed to be complemented by the promulgation of an Open Democracy Act (generally referred to in other countries as a freedom of information act), which has been redrafted innumerable times since it was initiated in 1995. It has been proposed that IT could play a vital role in facilitating access to information by encouraging government to make information about its activities available proactively, rather than simply responding to information requests.[19]

Schools are also developing an on-line presence in South Africa. Most of the country's nine provinces have established on-line networks, and in November 1997, a national body called the South African Schools Network was formed with the aim of coordinating the implementation of information and communications technologies in schools. With over 400 schools already connected to the Internet, the intention is to triple or quadruple this figure in 1998. The network plans to do this by lobbying government and the private sector to ensure that more schools have access to basic services necessary to ensure connectivity, such as electricity and telephones.[20]

These development projects run alongside plans to lay 3 million telephone lines in the next five years, with 2 million of these being in underserviced areas. If these targets are not reached, fines will be imposed on Telkom. One million existing

---

17 Parliament of South Africa, < http://wwwparliament.gov.za/ >.

18 The Human Rights Committee, the Black Sash, and the Political Information and Monitoring Service of the Institute for Democracy in South Africa (IDASA).

19 See Report from Working Group 4 entitled "Communication Mechanisms to Address the Development Needs of Communities and Citizens in the Open Democracy Bill" at the FXI's *The Open Democracy Bill - Central Controversies,* Conference held at Mabula Game Lodge, January 26-28, 1996; < http://wnapc.org/fxi/odb/group4.htm >.

20 See SchoolNet SA < http://wwwschool.za/schoolnet/about.htm >, and "Schools Networking in South Africa Set to Go" (press release), December 10, 1997; < http://www.school.za/schoolnet/pr971210.htm >.

lines are supposed to be upgraded to digital operation (currently, about 71 per cent of Telkom's network is digitized).[21] Currently the disparities in access to telephones are stark. In wealthier areas, there is a telephone penetration of 50 per 100 people: however, the figure drops as low as one telephone per thousand people in the poorest areas. The national average is 9.5 lines per thousand people, placing South Africa well above the average African figure of one phone for every 500 households.[22]

Internet connectivity is quite impressive. South Africa now ranks as the 18th most connected country in the world[23], although the bulk of its users are to be found in academic institutions.[24] In fact, it is estimated that one in 65 people have access to the Internet, compared to elsewhere in Africa, where the average is nearer to one in 5000 people.[25]

In order to achieve these targets, Telkom has been granted a five-year exclusivity period in its 25-year license to lay out and operate a public switched telecommunications network (PSTN).[26] Once the ideal of universal access has been achieved, PSTNs will be opened to competition. In line with the liberalization route taken by other countries, Value Added Network Services (VANS) are already open for competition[27], as is the cellular telephone industry.[28]

However, the most rapid delivery of national infrastructure is related to the installing of a high-speed fiber-optic link between the capital city, Pretoria, and all provincial capitals. This project should be completed late in 1998, and may be

21 "The Revolution Continues: Telkom SA Moves into Change Mode," *Communication Technologies Handbook,* p 73.

22 R. Chalmers, "Plan to Give all Access to Phones," *Business Day,* (May 19, 1997), and J. Naidoo, "Action Vital for Global Wisdom," *Sowetan,* 17 July 1997.

23 P. Fourie, "The Three Holes in the Telkom Ruling," *Electronic Mail and Guardian,* < http://www.mg.co.za/mg/news/97oct2/17oc-internet2.html >.

24 B. Nielson, "Internets, Intranets, ETC-Nets," *Communication Technologies Handbook,* p. 786.

25 "Africa Swarming to Net, but You Still Take Chances in the Bush," *Sunday Independent,* (March 1, 1998).

26 Telkom's exclusivity in respect of the following areas will be maintained: national long distance and international services; local access, public pay phones and infrastructure for VANS; fixed lines for use by mobile cellular network operators; and infrastructure for private networks other than Transnet and Eskom Subject to affordability, Telkom must supply on demand the following: a basic telephony service, a public pay-phone service, emergency services, and services to disabled people. These services will be subject to a fairness vetting procedure. Information from "Changing the Guard: SA's Statutory Regime for Communications," *Communication Technologies Handbook,* pp. 51–52.

27 According to Telkom's licence, VANS have been defined as including, but not limited to, the following: electronic data interchange; electronic mail; protocol conversion; database access; managed data-network services; voice mail; store and forward fax; video conferencing; and telecommunications related to publishing and advertising services, whether electronic or print; and electronic information services, including Internet-service provision VANS are not allowed to carry voice traffic. See "Changing the Guard...," p. 54.

28 Presently, there are two cellular networks licensed by SATRA, Vodacom, and MTN, with the possibility of a third license in the offing

extended to rural areas at a later date. The aim of the network is to increase government efficiency and counter growing tax fraud. These lines may also be leased to the private sector.[29] What needs to be monitored is whether these developments are being pursued at the expense of the roll-out of basic services to underserviced areas given that it is estimated that the cost of installing a telephone in a rural area is as much as 30 times higher than in urban centers, these dangers are real.[30]

UNIVERSAL ACCESS AND PRIVATIZATION: A MARRIAGE MADE IN HEAVEN OR HELL?

Parallel to these developments, the government is also implementing market reforms as outlined in GATS. Telkom is being partially privatized after having undergone a separation from its postal arm. In 1997, 30 per cent of Telkom was sold off to a consortium of two companies as Strategic Equity Partners (SEPs): SBC Communications and Telekom Malaysia. The sale netted R5.58 billion, making it the largest privatization deal ever in Southern Africa.[31] An extra 10 per cent of the company has been earmarked for black-empowerment concerns.

It remains to be seen what impact this privatization program will have on Telkom's ability to deliver on its universal access obligations: in the words of one commentator, "The issue facing the interested parties is to balance likely universal service obligations against the needs for the SEPs to earn a return on their investment".[32] The exclusivity period has been interpreted as a "sweetener" for the SEPs to assist them in achieving such returns, given their obligations to roll out services in non-economically viable areas.

In South Africa, the tensions between equity priorities and the market could be seen recently in relation to the Internet, where Telkom claimed that Internet provision fell within its exclusivity rights — more especially the provision of Internet Protocol that carries low-level Internet traffic — in that it could be defined as a basic service. The Internet Service Providers Association (ISPA) was

29 G. Gordon, "Government Seeks the Hyperspace Slipstream," *Sunday Times*, (March 15, 1998).
30 "Cellphone Industry Takes on the Problem of Rural Access," *Business Day*, (August 11, 1997).
31 S. Lunsche, "Win-Win Deal as SA Puts Privatisation on Course," *Sunday Times*, (March 30, 1997).
32 "The Revolution Continues...," p. 73.

formed in response to Telkom's move into the Internet market through its South African Internet Exchange (SAIX), established in 1996. The ISPA challenged the formation of SAIX on the basis that Telkom was using its monopoly position to cross-subsidize SAIX, thereby undercutting the markets of private ISPs by offering cheaper services. It also contested Telkom's definition of the Internet as a basic service, arguing that it is in fact a VAN service, which opens it up to competition and protection against anti-competitive practices such as cross-subsidization.

The ISPA took the matter to the Competitions Board early in 1997, which decided that SATRA, and not Telkom, was empowered by the Telecommunications Act to interpret whether the Internet was a VAN or a basic service, and referred the matter to the Authority.[33] SATRA ruled in October 1997 that the Internet was a VAN, and that therefore private operators could continue to buy bandwidth from Telkom and re-sell it to end-users. However, SATRA insisted that service providers should apply to it for licenses to operate VANS, one of the conditions being that they should pledge to provide universal access across the country. The specific obligations to be placed on ISPs still have to be decided.[34] Telkom is currently contesting this ruling.

These conflicts between the needs for redress and standards for creating a competitive economic environment are an increasingly important feature of the South African landscape, and we have much to learn from countries which have stood at similar crossroads at earlier points in their histories.

THE GLOBALIZATION OF TELECOMMUNICATION AND SOME CHALLENGES FOR FREEDOM OF EXPRESSION

Currently there are no attempts to censor the Internet on the part of the government, although the question of whether the medium should be "regulated in the public interest" has been raised in the context of a broadcasting policy review now underway.[35] While these developments needs to be monitored, a general

---

33 P. Furber, "Telkom Goes All Out to Control Internet Market," *Sunday Independent*, (April 27, 1997).
34 L. Stones, "Free Choice Prevails on Internet Access," *Business Day*, (October 15, 1997).

acceptance appears to be growing that the Internet cannot really be censored successfully. Direct Internet censorship is not an imminent threat in South Africa, especially as the government is committed to respecting the country's constitutionally-entrenched right to freedom of expression.

On one level, globalization has re-shaped the essentially national character of censorship, and opposition to it. This is particularly so for South Africa, given that it re-entered the global community only in 1994. The country is attempting to recover from a terrible legacy of censorship under apartheid. Many of the institutional structures of the old order remain largely intact. The legislative framework of the country is one such structure, with attempts being made to bring the statute books and the common law into line with the constitution. Consequently, old laws are being repealed and/ or amended and new laws are being brought onto the books.

However a great deal of work still needs to be done to repeal or amend existing pieces of censorship legislation to bring the statute books into line with the constitution's freedom of expression clause.[36] The government has yet to effect these changes in spite of repeated demands by organizations such as the Freedom of Expression Institute (FXI). There are fears that it may prefer to keep these laws on the books for later use. Certainly the government has demonstrated that it is not adverse to using them to restrict the free flow of information.[37] At the same time, the effectiveness of such national censorship legislation is being eroded in the face of the global nature of technologies such as the Internet.

For example, in June 1997, the parastate arms manufacturer Denel sought an interdict against several South African newspapers to prevent them from publishing details of a R7 billion arms deal with Saudi Arabia. In addition, Denel laid criminal charges against three newspapers for details they had already published. The charges were laid under a piece of apartheid censorship legislation

---

35 See the chapter entitled "Convergence and New Media" in *Broadcasting Policy: A Green Paper for Public Discussion* (Ministry for Posts, Telecommunications and Broadcasting: Government Printers, November 1997).

36 For an audit of the most important pieces of censorship legislation still on the statute books, see the document entitled *Legislation Infringing Freedom of Expression: A Call for Amendment* (Johannesburg: Centre for Applied Legal Studies, University of the Witwatersrand, 1996).

37 For example, in June 1994, Defense Minister Joe Modise sought an interdict against the *Mail and Guardian* newspaper under the Protection of Information Act to stop it from publishing further information about attempts by former South African soldiers to secure an amnesty The attempt was later halted. See the South African entry in *So This Is Democracy? State of the Media in Southern Africa, 1995* (Windhoek: MISA, 1995) pp. 41-43. In February 1996, the Ministry of Health asked all employees to sign declarations of secrecy to prevent them from leaking MISA "sensitive information" in the wake of a scandal involving the R14-million tender for an AIDS-awareness play. The move was justified in terms of the Protection of Information Act. See the South African entry in *So This Is Democracy?* p. 33.

called the Armaments Production and Development Act of 1968.[38] Denel was particularly concerned about protecting the name of its client, arguing that the deal required a guarantee of confidentiality, and that it might fall through if it was revealed in public that the client in question was Saudi Arabia. The company further argued that if this happened, the economic consequences for the arms industry specifically, and for the country generally, would be great.[39] On the other hand, the affected newspapers and press freedom advocates argued that the country has a right to know to whom it is selling arms, especially given South Africa's none-too-commendable history in this respect.[40]

In August, the *Sunday Independent* newspaper, which broke the story, published the name of the country involved, stating that "the name has already been published abroad and is in the public domain in South Africa".[41] In fact, the information had been circulating freely on the Internet and a flurry of e-mails circulated through the country and internationally spread word of this.[42] In response, Denel dropped the interdicts, and vowed to adopt a more transparent approach towards arms deals.[43]

Another example of the Internet defeating attempts at national censorship concerned the divorce of Lady Diana's brother, the Earl of Spenser, which took place in Cape Town in late 1997. The Earl attempted to interdict two Cape Town newspapers to prevent them from publishing potentially embarrassing details about the marriage. As with the Denel case, details of the divorce the Earl was attempting to suppress were freely available on the Internet.[44]

These examples point to some of the challenges to traditional notions of censorship, especially those involving the application of statutes and court proceeding to prevent the free flow of information. Such national methods of censorship are confounded by information technologies that defy the confines of national jurisdictions.

South Africa has also become increasingly involved in the globalization of resistance to censorship. The Internet in particular is continuing to have a significant

38 "Denel Issues Leaves Many Issues Unresolved," *FXI Update* (August/September 1997), pp. 1–2.
39 "'Grossly Unreasonable' to Publish Arms Details," *The Star* (July 29, 1997).
40 See for example, "Denel, Arms and the Law," *Mail and Guardian*, (July 25, 1997); "Independent Newspapers Muzzled," *The Star* (July 26, 1997); and "The Right to Know," *Sunday Times* (July 27, 1997).
41 "We Name Denel's Secret Arms Buyer," *Sunday Independent* (August 3, 1997).
42 "Arms Industry is Not Exempt from Transparency Policy," *Business Day* (August 15, 1997).
43 M Mafata, "Denel Plans to Be More Transparent," *Sowetan* (September 12, 1997).
44 "The Cyberspace Dilemma," *Sunday Times* (November 30, 1997).

impact on the FXI's work. The FXI began to use e-mail in 1995 and launched its World Wide Web site early in 1996. Since then, both forms of Internet usage have become an integral part of the work of the organization.

The FXI uses e-mail as a means of communication with individuals and organizations around the world. It provides freedom of expression news in two weekly bulletins, and issues action alerts when freedom of expression violations take place. This information is circulated on a list server of interested individuals and organizations, as well as on the list server of the Media Institute of Southern Africa (MISA) and to the membership of the International Freedom of Expression Exchange (IFEX). MISA was formed in 1992 in response to the 1991 Windhoek Declaration on Promoting an Independent and Pluralistic Press, and is an organization promoting media freedom and diversity in the SADC region. MISA's headquarters are based in Windhoek, Namibia, and serves national chapters throughout the region.[45]

Information the FXI has circulated on the Internet has been used in various ways by international organizations such as in publications produced by MISA and Index on Censorship. Also, the FXI has become more active in the African region, intervening in the situation in Nigeria and providing support for South African-based exiles. The FXI has also contributed to countering ongoing actions against the press in Zambia and Swaziland, and has used e-mail to coordinate such activities. The ease of e-mail communications has therefore allowed the FXI to integrate into the SADC freedom of expression community, bolstering its regional activities, and has also opened it up to the global freedom of expression community.

The FXI's web site has also acted as an important repository for documents produced in the course of its work. It is a historical archive, tracing the genesis of campaigns since its launch in 1994, and contains many of the organization's publications, research documents, and press statements. It is without doubt the most well used of the FXI's media, recording as many as 35 "hits" per day. Its main users are lecturers and students in tertiary institutions, journalists, researchers, nongovernment organizations (NGOs), and government officials.

---

45 Media Institute of Southern Africa (MISA), International Freedom of Expression Exchange Clearing House; < http://wwwifex.org/org/misa/ >.

However, the underlying conception of freedom of expression attached to much on-line work is in need of examination, especially the tendency to measure the extent of freedom of expression in terms of the absence of censorship. Such a calculation is often made by examining the pervasiveness of specific acts defined as "censorship," such as attacks on journalists, or the existence of specific forms of restrictive legislation. This approach tends to involve, in the words of Anthony Smith, "measuring freedom of expression through oppression,"[46] where the social and economic conditions for the successful realization of a culture of freedom of expression do not necessarily exist.

Developing a more well-rounded conception of freedom of expression should involve an examination of the socioeconomic underpinnings of freedom of expression and access to information, while continuing to respond to discrete acts violating these rights as these factors are all too often linked. South-North relations need to be examined in the process, and the impact that some of these relationships have on widening information gaps between these two regions, and within these regions. Specifically, the efficacy of the overwhelmingly Northern "solutions" proposed for developing African communications infrastructures need to be evaluated, particularly those that advocate the reorientation of communications industries towards profit-maximization, and away from non-commercial social objectives. The frameworks laid down by GATS and the WTO need particular attention in this regard.

In relation to the Southern agenda, South Africa in particular needs to be watched, as it is balanced precariously between the realities of the South and the priorities of the North. Many have warned about the potential of South Africa to become a regional sub-imperialist, that it could use its economic primacy to re-orient the region to serve its own economic purposes. These tendencies need to be monitored to ensure that the country acts in the interests of the region as a whole with regards to freedom of expression and access to information, as its position makes it particularly susceptible to playing a piper-calls-the-tune role. Freedom-of-expression groups need to monitor their respective governments with regards to commitments to transparent policy-making: the tendency for governments to close up to achieve global competitiveness objectives has been noted and should be opposed.[47]

46 A. Smith, *The Age of the Behemoths: The Globalisation of Mass Media Firms* (New York: Priority Press Publications), p. 74.

47 L. Panitch, "Rethinking the Role of the State," in J. Mittleman, ed., *Globalisation...*, p. 86.

As information gaps between Africa and the North widen, the challenge we face is to analyze why this is happening. In researching the centers of power and the dynamics of underdevelopment, and developing strategies to reverse these trends, we will all need to critique our own countries' agendas, and those of multinational bodies that claim to operate in the global interest. Such activities may also involve critiques of our own agendas as advocates of freedom of expression, including what we choose to prioritize and why. Only once this has happened can we say that we are beginning to achieve global freedom of expression.

NEW COMMUNICATION TECHNOLOGIES AND FREEDOM OF EXPRESSION: RADIO AND TELEVISION

Alfonso Ruiz de Assín

Any analysis of the effects and contribution of new information and communication technologies must take into account the level of economic and cultural development. Development has a bearing on the freedom of expression and the effect of new technologies. Innovations in radio and television do not have the same connotation in Ethiopia as in Germany, in Bolivia as in the United States, or in Indonesia as in Japan. Industrialized countries have a tendency to focus such analyses on themselves. This often leads them to reject options they find obsolete, but which might well suit less economically and culturally developed societies, or societies that are either non-democratic or less advanced democratically. Thus, analog systems, now superseded by digital technologies in the first world, are envied by countries with more primitive communication means.

We will focus our attention on moderately or ill-developed societies, the second and third worlds, where the problems and advantages ensuing from the emergence of new technologies for the freedom of expression are more acute.

A BROADENING OF FREEDOM

First, it is clear that the new information and communication technologies will allow enormous advances in the expression and communication of thought.

On the one hand, digital radio and television broadcasting by satellite and Hertzian waves will greatly increase the number of channels and programs. Already, there has been a substantial increase. On the other hand, spectrum availability will make room for more narrowcasting. Finally, with interactivity, viewers and listeners will be able to make their opinions and ideas heard as never before. Thus, new technologies will allow unprecedented freedom of expression.

However, the reservations of some political, cultural, and social sectors cannot be ignored. New technologies, they claim, will require such large investments that only economically powerful groups will be able to take advantage of them. They are not entirely wrong. But the opposite assumption would also tend to reduce the citizens' freedom of expression. Indeed, let us imagine a country where every village has its own radio or television transmitter, or requires that such transmitters be owned by different citizens, social groups, or entrepreneurs to ensure the widest possible range of opinions. Since these broadcasters would be restricted to very small markets, they would not have the resources to invest in new technologies, or to improve their installations, at the expense of program quality, audiences, and the effective exercise of the freedom of expression.

As in most countries where radio and television started out in such conditions, stations would soon merge to build up larger audiences for economic and cultural reasons. We would end up in the same situation as today, where the trend to form conglomerates to face market realities is strengthened by the winds of liberalization blowing from the more powerful countries, on the assumption that only large communication enterprises can meet competition.

I would not want this corporate argument to be construed as an affirmation of "the bigger, the better" principle. If the Hertzian-wave environment is a public domain, citizens and social groups should be able to use the spectrum to fulfill their need to communicate and express themselves. Municipal, regional, and national governments also have a perfect right to address their constituents through their own radio and television stations.

Thus a model of coexistence of the public and private sectors would take shape, with different missions based on different resources. Public radio and television, fully warranted everywhere, would complement the private sector. It would also seem socially warranted to have regional networks in regions of a different language and culture. Finally, underserved communities should have a local radio. This public system should be financed by public funds, at a rate determined by citizens, political parties, or whatever political structure is in place. The only programming compatible with the source of funds would be public-service programming, altogether distinct from that of private radio and television, which would be financed by advertising.

Private operators would be free to expand through the creation of multimedia groups that could benefit from synergy to meet competition in a free market. However, concentration should not prevent the parallel existence of small and mid-size radio and television organizations allowing cultural, economic, ethnic, or religious groups to express themselves.

The range of private offerings would be completed by collectively-owned communal, cultural, educational, or neighborhood radio and television stations, without advertising or networking possibility, but able to play a smaller communication role.

This system, perfectly feasible with the new technologies, seems to give all citizens a guarantee that their voices will be heard.

MEDIA INDEPENDENCE

These remarks deal only with the quantitative aspects of radio and television, given the limit of available frequencies. The conditions required to guarantee freedom of expression in the media do not stop there. The qualitative aspects can't be ignored. I speak here of the principles of independence and pluralism which must guide public and private media, and the new media. The bigger and more powerful public and private communication conglomerates are, the more these principles should be strengthened. Hence the importance of media independence.

When we talk of media independence or pluralism, we are referring to relative concepts, not absolute realities. We should then talk of the degree of independence or pluralism. Realistically, we have to look for a balance between principles and market requirements, independence and pluralism, reality and economic needs, public and private broadcasters.

First, a general observation is in order. For private enterprise, communication is an economic activity like any other in the tertiary sector, subject to the rules of competition. Public broadcasters have a duty to manage public funds in a responsible manner, and private broadcasters that of obtaining for their shareholders a legitimate return on their investment. In the search for balance, the communication sector is not and should not be considered like any other profit-seeking economic sector, because it has an important added cultural value, and exercises a strong influence on the attitudes, opinions, and habits of citizens. This principle, this sense of responsibility conditions and limits independent decision-making. Hence, the question: Independence from whom, for what, and about what?

The answer is simpler for public services. They exercise their independence from governments through boards of directors representing the whole society. They are at the service of the public, not government. Governments do not own the public media, they only manage them. The owners are the citizens, the taxpayers, the whole society.

The second element of independence of public-service media is their source of financing. The current financing of public service media by both public funds and advertising revenue is unsatisfactory. Advertising revenue, because of its importance and its character, influences programming. So much so that it is now very difficult to distinguish between private and public stations when we turn on a television set.

Public broadcasters should not be inhibited by ratings. They should withdraw from all commercial activities and finance themselves only through public funds, on a basis determined by the citizens of each country. They should feature true public-service programs, which might not reach the largest audience, but set quality standards for viewers and listeners. Some European public broadcasters provide an example of this today.

There is no cause to rejoice at the European Union's approval in Amsterdam of an exceptional protocol allowing double financing. It breaks with the rules of the Rome Treaty and encourages unfair competition from the public sector, even though some restrictions were introduced at the last minute making it mandatory to justify the use of public funds.

For private broadcasters, independence cannot be guaranteed so easily because the owners are the shareholders. It is legitimate for them to expect a reasonable return on their investment, to want to expand their business and influence editorial policy. Nonetheless, the private media need also be independent to justify their existence and their social role. The fact that they draw the bulk of their income from advertising already gives private media a measure of independence. The more advertisers there are, the more independent are the media. Advertising has a neutralizing effect. But this is not enough. The private media, like the public media, must serve the public interest. To ensure an independent editorial policy, it is essential to reinforce the role of the information professionals, the journalists, through editorial councils that will block any attempt to subject information to the shareholders' viewpoints and interests.

GENUINE PLURALISM

The second basic element of true freedom of expression in radio and television is genuine pluralism, strengthened by the potential derived from the application of new communication technologies. This pluralism in information varies for private and public broadcasters.

Public broadcasters should be forced by regulations to let minorities and social-interest groups have access to public-service programming. In many European countries, national networks coexist with regional or municipal, communal, cultural, educational, or neighborhood radio and television stations, which meet the needs of their communities.

Once again, pluralism is more difficult to achieve in the private sector because of the nature of private enterprise. Often the criteria and personality of the owners are an obstacle to the participation of social-interest groups in programming. For me—but I know that not everybody agrees—the key to ensuring a degree of pluralism in private radio and television lies in the coexistence of major commercial networks with mid-size networks and small stations. This combination makes it easier for social and cultural groups to gain access to radio and television. Personally, I do not believe in strict legislation to curb media concentration in an increasingly competitive world market dominated by increasingly powerful groups. Market reality demands a sufficient size to be able to explore and implement new technologies like digital radio and television, which require investments beyond the resources of a fragmented market and small enterprises. In many cases, large communication groups offer higher and more satisfactory levels of pluralism through their multimedia operations than do their smaller competitors, whose resources are too limited. A balanced combination of large, mid-size, and small private enterprises offers a fair level of pluralism in all European countries. However, I should warn against the potential consequences for radio and television of a liberalization policy carried to the extreme, that is, the takeover of radio and television networks by telecommunication firms.

The measures against concentration stem from a desire of European social-interest groups and institutions to restrict the empires of traditional publishers. People like Berlusconi, Hersant, Polanco, Murdoch, Kirch, Bertelsmann, and others are accused of limiting pluralism with the national and cross-border expansion of their operations.

We would do well to pay attention to the ambitions of US, Japanese, and European telecommunication giants, however. If they cannot resist the temptation of supplying not only the information highways but also the cars that circulate on it through the invasion of content, particularly information content, we could end up with such homogeneity that we would regret the disappearance of traditional publishers, their commercial rivalries, their competitiveness and the pluralism they created for the benefit of society.

ADDED CULTURAL VALUE

It seems to me, therefore, that a satisfactory level of independence and pluralism can and must be achieved in two ways.

■ First, through fair and consistent competition rules that provide sufficient resources to all types of broadcasters, public and private. That is, public financing for public-service broadcasters, who must feature a distinct style and type of programming, in keeping with their mission, and aimed at setting prestige standards for the audience; and the financing of commercial enterprises through private capital and advertising revenue. Competition, if real, should guarantee that every voice that wishes to be heard will be heard.

■ Secondly, by strengthening the role of journalists to guarantee the independence and pluralism of the media. Editorial boards should be vested with enough power to ensure that publishers respect objectivity principles, the professional confidentiality, and the conscience clause.

In conclusion, I would like to make a few remarks on the added cultural value provided by broadcasters, the current added value, and the even bigger one it would be desirable to achieve. Public broadcasters in Europe must give priority to education and culture. They have to increase their educational and information content, and put entertainment in the background. Private broadcasters already give precedence to entertainment and information. But they have to be reminded that they are also part of a country's cultural structure. Music, theater, films, authors, and artists are always present in the programming of private radio and television. Private broadcasters make up, both through their direct investments and the payment of original and reproduction rights, an essential link in the economic structure on which our societies' cultural life rests. They can and must expand their role by developing new ideas and exploiting the enormous potential offered by new technologies.

ORBICOM:
International Network of UNESCO Chairs in Communications and its associates

The mandate of ORBICOM is to work on developing all communications disciplines throughout the world. Through a great many programs of activities set up by the network of UNESCO Chairs in Communications, and thanks to the work of its associates in 60 countries, ORBICOM is one of the main groups of communications specialists based on multinational partnership.

Exchanges and training periods for professor-researchers and communications professionals in the private sector, applied research and publications, colloquia and conferences, and Web site discussion groups are among the activities it undertakes to further multilateral and multidisciplinary action in information and communications.

This flexible, diversified approach makes possible public debate on the future of a society of knowledge, based increasingly on the uses and effects of technologies on intercultural relations, and on the development of content industries.

This vision presupposes the democratization of social relations as well as freedom of expression and the circulation of information which alone can guarantee both the reinforcement of civil societies and appropriate matching of training programs and the job market in this key sector.

Founded in 1994 on an initiative by UNESCO and in conjunction with the Université du Québec à Montréal, ORBICOM today boasts 17 university chairs specializing in communications in the world and 200 associates representing media, information technology, cultural, journalistic and public relations firms, as well as the university community with its researchers and contributors in the field. Five new chairs should appear shortly, completing the ORBICOM Network. Since 1997, ORBICOM has been accredited with the Economic and Social Council of the United Nations, and publishes four news bulletins annually, as well as regularly updating its Web site.

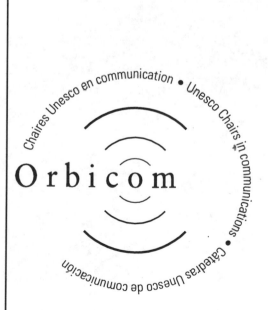

International Secretariat:

Université du Québec à Montréal

P.O. Box 8888, Downtown Branch

Montreal, Quebec H3C 3P8

Tel. (514) 7-8743

Fax: (514) 987-0249

E-mail: orbicom@er.uqam.ca

Internet: www.orbicom.uqam.ca

PRINTED AND BOUND
IN BOUCHERVILLE, QUÉBEC, CANADA
BY MARC VEILLEUX IMPRIMEUR INC.
IN OCTOBER, 1998